W9-CEG-033

KIPLING'S MIND AND ART

KIPLING'S MIND AND ART

Selected Critical Essays

Edited by
ANDREW RUTHERFORD

STANFORD UNIVERSITY PRESS
STANFORD, CALIFORNIA
1964

ABIGAIL E. WEEKS MEMORIAL LIBRARY
UNION COLLEGE
BARBOURVILLE, KENTUCKY

823.91
K57Yn

Stanford University Press
Stanford, California

First published in the United Kingdom by Oliver & Boyd Ltd.

"Re-reading Kipling": © W. L. Renwick 1940.
"The Kipling that Nobody Read": © Edmund Wilson 1941.
"Kipling": © Lionel Trilling 1943.
"Rudyard Kipling": © George Orwell 1946.
"Kipling's Place in the History of Ideas": © Noel Annan 1960.

George Shepperson, "The World of Rudyard Kipling"; Alan
Sandison, "Kipling: the Artist and the Empire"; Andrew
Rutherford "Officers and Gentlemen"; Mark Kinkead-Weekes,
"Vision in Kipling's Novels"; J. H. Fenwick, "Soldiers Three";
and W. W. Robson, "Kipling's Later Novels":
© Oliver & Boyd Ltd 1964.

All rights reserved
Library of Congress Catalog Card Number: 64-15164

Printed in Great Britain

ACKNOWLEDGMENTS

FOR PERMISSION to quote from the works of Rudyard Kipling acknowledgments are due to the following: Mrs George Bambridge; Macmillan & Co., Ltd; Methuen & Co. Ltd; Doubleday & Co., Inc.; and Macmillan Company of Canada, Limited.

Several of the essays in this collection have already been published elsewhere and for permission to reprint them here the following acknowledgments are also due: Noel Annan, "Kipling's Place in the History of Ideas," reprinted from *Victorian Studies* (1960), by permission of the author, and the editors of *Victorian Studies*; George Orwell, "Rudyard Kipling," reprinted from *Critical Essays* (1946), by permission of Martin Secker & Warburg Limited and Harcourt, Brace & World, Inc.; W. L. Renwick, "Re-reading Kipling," reprinted from *Durham University Journal* (1940), by permission of the author, and the Registrar of the University of Durham; Lionel Trilling, "Kipling," reprinted from *The Liberal Imagination* (1951), by permission of the author, Martin Secker & Warburg Limited, and Viking Press Inc.; Edmund Wilson, "The Kipling that Nobody Read," reprinted from *The Wound and the Bow* (1952), by permission of the author.

CONTENTS

INTRODUCTION

IF CRITICISM "has not yet come to terms with Kipling,"[1] the main reason is not far to seek. From their first appearance his works have seemed to raise moral and political issues with such immediacy that most readers have proceeded directly to moral and political judgments (adverse or favourable), by-passing the exploratory and testing processes of literary criticism. Even to-day, in spite of some penetrating modern commentaries, he is generally regarded simply as the representative of British Imperialism at its worst; hence discussion of his works consists too often of a mere documenting of existing prejudices, rather than an attempt to see the objects as in themselves they really are; while in the popular mind some of his most objectionable poems and stories are still seen as typical of his entire achievement.

With the passing of Kipling's Empire, however, the time has surely come for his works to be considered more historically, less hysterically, and subjected to a more impartial analysis as a prelude to evaluation. Such an analysis will be bound to stress the range and variety of his writings, the different levels of accomplishment which they display, the positive achievements as well as the vulgarities and ugliness, the manifestations of individual genius as well as those of a merely representative consciousness.

This process of reconsideration has in fact been going on – sporadically and without adequate public acknowledgment – at least since Kipling's death. This volume opens, therefore, with an obituary address delivered in 1936, and includes four other essays already in print, of which account must be taken in any present-day discussion of his writings.[2] In addition to their own

[1] Noel Annan, "Kipling's Place in the History of Ideas," see below, p. 97.

[2] These are not, of course, the only works with such a claim; but considerations of space made it impossible to represent here the very influential studies by Professor Bonamy Dobrée and Miss J. M. S. Tompkins, while the emphasis which I wished to place on Kipling's prose fiction ruled out Mr Eliot's well-known introduction to his anthology of Kipling's verse. To my regret, Professor C. S. Lewis and his publishers would not agree to the inclusion of his essay "Kipling's World."

intrinsic merits, these pieces exemplify some changing trends in Kipling criticism, and provide an essential background to the new essays which make up the remainder of this volume. The collection as a whole does not pretend to homogeneity: the contributors are of different generations, different nationalities, different disciplines, and different critical persuasions. What they have in common is no single policy (of whitewashing or denigration), but a conviction that in recent decades Kipling has been too readily, too easily dismissed – that even though adverse judgments must be passed on aspects of his work, his is a more interesting and complex case than has generally been allowed.

To demonstrate that interest and complexity, to diagnose his weaknesses with greater precision, and to reconsider his achievement as a creative artist, are the main objects of this book.

Edinburgh   A.R.
August 1963

I. GENERAL ASSESSMENTS

W. L. Renwick

RE-READING KIPLING*

NO REVIEW of the last fifty years of English literature could afford to ignore one who was so conspicuous and so successful as Rudyard Kipling. Popular success is never a safe criterion of value; but when a writer has attracted the attention, the admiration, the criticism, of men of all kinds, it is always safe to assume that there were reasons for it, reasons to be sought either in the man or in his time.

Kipling's very success is, of course, a reproach to him: so be it: that is human nature: he can afford it. Nor is the time come when the days of his greatest activity – call it 1886 to 1910, a longish time – have been unified into the dignity of a Period. No text-books, either those of the class-room or those, more pretentious and often less original, which disguise themselves as Studies in Psychology, have yet related him to the movement of thought, or grouped him with such contemporaries as W. E. Henley and G. W. Steevens, Cunninghame Graham and Mr Nevinson. He has not been "placed," and is still in the critical no-man's-land of yesterday. I do not propose to attempt such a survey as that would demand, any more than to attack Kipling or defend him; nor do I propose to attempt a valuation. I only attempt to point out a few characteristics of which, it seems to me, critics will have to take account.

There is enough to criticise in Kipling – enough and to spare. He inherited the philistinism which is part of the unintentional legacy of English Romanticism; or, if you prefer it, he inherited the somewhat degenerate Stoicism which might be regarded as

* [An obituary lecture on Kipling, delivered at King's College, Newcastle, in 1936. Reprinted from *The Durham University Journal*, VOL. XXXII (1939-40).]

a reaction from Romanticism or as a parallel growth which replaced some of the social values which Romanticism lost for us. He may be blamed for his part in the further degeneration of that Stoicism into that recent version of it called the old Public School Tradition – a phenomenon whose constituents, whether you like it or not, might be worth tracing to their varied origins in the Regency. Any notice of Kipling must observe his limitations.

These limitations may have originated in, and were certainly emphasised by, the circumstances of a childhood in exile from the family, such as is too often a part of the uncounted price of Indian dominion. You will find the record of that bitter experience in "Baa Baa Black Sheep" and the direct statement in *Something of Myself*. He emerged from it physically damaged, and with an inward-driven sensitiveness and a defensive habit that are perhaps prime causes of his philistinism. That over-worked explanation the inferiority complex might even be invoked, for he was henceforth incapacitated, physically and temperamentally, for the life and the work he most admired. I fancy that much of his bluster and show of violence was self-protective, the mark of weakness rather than of strength – a protection against critics, against the world, and, deeper and more dangerous, a protection of the self he had made for himself against the self he was born with. To some such origins – without indulging unnecessarily in speculative analysis – one may ascribe much in Kipling that we dislike – much (I may go further) that we detest.

He seems to lack entirely the artistic and scholarly curiosity he ought to have inherited from both his parents. We must remember that during the early years when the inheritance should have been passed on to him, he was suffering in exile. Artistic and scholarly curiosity, one may imagine, had a stony soil to grow in at the school described in *Stalky & Co.*; and since that school was the first society he knew – since he was denied the society of the family – its influence remained with him all his life. He learned his trade alone, on a provincial Indian paper between the ages of seventeen and twenty-four – the second formative period of a man's life. Like a proper young man, he admired the admirable people whom fortune set before his eyes: and their admirable qualities, which they had in plenty, were not often those which are frequent or at least conspicuous in the literary and artistic coteries of London.

He was indeed a strange phenomenon, this young man who first attempted to bring to the notice of the English the strange phenomena which they themselves produced under other skies. For documentation I may refer you to the story called "A Conference of the Powers," in *Many Inventions*, and to his attitude to the novelist he calls "Eustace Cleever," who is possibly Thomas Hardy. That attitude is a little critical, somewhat distant, but not unhappy. But Kipling came to London as ignorant of the literary and artistic circles, their ways, their manners, their intellectual habits and intentions, as they were of his. His suspicion of them developed into dislike – not by any means unreciprocated – and then, unfortunately, came to include suspicion, and even something like contempt, of the arts and scholarship in general. You will find among the verses in *The Seven Seas* many traces of early conflicts – and some of the reasons for them – and in the story called "My Son's Wife," in *A Diversity of Creatures*, a later and much less happy attitude to his fellow artists. We can recognise something in his caricature of the circle from which his "Frankwell Midmore" broke away in that story. But we must regret that such caricatures are Kipling's only pictures of his brother artists. It betrays a certain lack of generosity in his character, but the reason for it, I suggest, was sheer lack of opportunity, and the defensive habit. It was something more than his reputation he was defending, something more than his own moral integrity he was preserving against these weaklings he describes; it was also the Rudyard Kipling he had made. Yet there were not many young men in 1893 drawing on John Donne for mottoes to their short stories. Kipling's schoolboy philistinism was forced upon him by circumstance; instead of growing out of it, he made it a habit – a bad habit.

It is unnecessary to expose his offences against taste whether expressed or inherent in his work, or to excuse or apologise for them. Only, let us remind ourselves of some of his contemporaries, some of the pools into which his stones were thrown. When we remember that *Plain Tales from the Hills* was published in the same year as George Moore's *Confessions of a Young Man*; *Life's Handicap* in the same year as *The Picture of Dorian Gray* and

Villiers de l'Isle Adam's *Axel*; *The Jungle Book* in the year in which Aubrey Beardsley became art editor of *The Yellow Book*; *The Day's Work* the same year as Huysman's *La Cathédrale*; *Kim* the year after D'Annunzio's *Il Fuoco*; *Traffics and Discoveries* the same year as *Hadrian the Seventh*: I think we can appreciate better how Kipling appeared to some of his contemporaries and how some of them appeared to him. His "period" stretches from "*fin de siècle*" to "Bloomsbury" as well as from *Diana of the Crossways* and *The Woodlanders* to *The Testament of Beauty* and *The Seven Pillars of Wisdom*. As for his political creed and the political excursions which stimulated some people and infuriated others, we need neither praise nor denounce them, nor enlarge upon the over-emphasis that helped to make them offensive to many even of his admirers. Of all human activities, political controversy is the most mingled of truth and error; and it is the most ephemeral. Let those things die. There is enough left to justify his reputation.

For one thing, as I have said, the young Kipling was a new phenomenon. He brought new subjects, new sensations, new images, into a literature that needed such refreshment. He discovered new prose rhythms which followed closely the rhythms of colloquial speech, and new measures of verse – crude enough, often, and fatally easy to parody, but lively and resonant – in a time that was dallying with dilettante elegancies of "style," languishing in Tennysonian echoes, or, with Thomas Hardy and A. E. Housman, meditating grimly among the tombs. His banjo obbligato to brass band was – and is – distressing: so were the armies of William Booth to the orthodox churchmen. In both cases the originality lay in this, that they derived, not from established and respectable institutions, but from the primitive movements of the uninstructed people. Kipling's metres and rhythms were drawn straight from what remains to us of folk-song – the tunes of music-hall and street that are directed to the least sophisticated audience – or, further back yet, from the sources of all lyrical measures, from the rhythms of work – marching, rowing, rope-hauling, drill – and from the movement of horses, ships, machinery. They are often too obvious and too insistent – though he did learn to use them with some subtlety, he did not always study their possibilities very closely – but they are in consonance with the thought and emotion – itself usually obvious and far from subtle – which they are designed to convey. Whether it be more virtuous to observe and reproduce the cantering of horses, the beat of engines and the dip and sway of ships, or to ponder the intricacies of sprung rhythm and compensated intervals, I will not discuss. Only I must confess that, without preferring Kipling, when I find some young men hymning the glories of the modern machine in rhythms which, if I heard them in my car-engine, would make me head for the nearest garage, I suspect a discrepancy somewhere.

In any case, whether we like Kipling's verse or not, there is half a world of Dominions for which he found a voice. The only voices they have found for themselves are, with faint and few exceptions, echoes of his: a fact that proves at once his authenticity and his power. This is – or may become – a matter of some importance. The Dominions may some day produce arts of their own, though they seem slow about it; whatever they do in time produce, Kipling gave them a lead, at least, and told them, as well as us, of some of the things they might write poetry about. It is right to note also in passing that he was not without influence in France. His prose translates very directly into French, and I fancy any historian of modern French literature will record his influence, not only in providing a model and preparing an audience for "colonial" writers like Emile Nolly, but in widening the outlook of men of letters beyond the village spire that sufficed for Michelet and his generation.

In these things, then, Kipling was new. He was new also in his claims. He was a journalist, a newspaper man who graduated in the sub-editors' room, and he claimed a place with the men of letters. There were those who were very ready to deny it to him: there are those who forget exactly what he claimed and judge him as wrongly – his attitude did not help, perhaps. He was a journalist: one, that is, whose trade is to convey in writing, as directly as possible, to all sorts of people, the appearance of the world before him, and to do it quickly. The ultimate values in the facts he publishes, the complexities and subtleties of their relations, the intricate and secret recesses of human thought and feeling from which they may arise or into which they may intrude, are not his business; and in any case he has not time to pursue them. He records phenomena as they pass before his eyes, broadly, with just so much research as is required to make them immediately intelligible. In that sense, it might be said, Kipling was a journalist all his life; no artist or seer, but a tradesman.

He would, I think, accept the appellation, and with pride. It is an honourable title. No one brought up as I was, on Clydeside, in our local tradition of shipwrights and painters, can be easily misled into the cloudy romantic aestheticism that fails – or refuses – to understand that the fine work of art is also a good job of work. It was a fatal error of nineteenth-century criticism to obscure this, to regard the discussion of technique as something crude and intrusive, almost indecent. The Artist was a miracle – which he is – to be gaped at and hedged round with awe. Hence the ridiculously inflated prices which Rossetti and his friends contrived to extract from their manufacturing clients, while at the same time the tradesman was regarded as an inferior creature to be kept in his place. The nineteenth century made an opposition of what is only a gradation; whence not only political difficulties, but the degeneracy of industrial design and of the household things of daily life. Fortunately, human virtues being what they are, the tradesman had his own pride, his own strict standards, his own professional morality – perhaps more than the artists.

Kipling's understanding and appreciation of the tradesman, the mechanic, and technician, is one of the most notable and most significant of his new contributions to society's self-consciousness. He knew and made plain the important fact which the scientific and the dogmatic psychologists are alike apt to forget, that a man's personality is made and moulded by his trade as well as by his religion and his sexual history. We watch our college friends take even the physical mould of their professions, the lawyers becoming more lawyer-like, the parsons more parsonical, the schoolmasters more scholastic, the professors more professorial, year by year. And the personality, the *Self*, the total of qualities which a man brings to bear on his work – whether that work be poetry or engine-fitting – is what he was born with *plus* all his experience: all he has seen and done and wanted to do and been made to do, all he has dreamed of and all he has investigated and practised and studied, up to the moment at which he applies that totality to that particular job. Which elements in the complex are the most important varies from man to man, from job to job, from time to time. Dr Freud may be right; Mr Herbert Read may be right; Karl Marx may be right: none of them is wholly, eternally, ubiquitously, and exclusively right. Kipling, I say, added to our knowledge this other truth. He did not write treatises on it: but just as Smollett made the English aware of the English seaman, Trollope of the cleric, Maria Edgeworth of the Irish and Walter Scott of the Scottish peasant, so Kipling made them aware of the soldier, the engineer, the journalist, the native Indian of many races, and the Anglo-Indian (in both meanings of the term), through the imagination, by the methods of the story-teller. He realised, in short, the value and importance of "talking shop." He understood and appreciated, thus, the morality of the tradesman, insisting that a man's job is a thing to be done for its own sake, with his strength, knowledge, and conscience; and he saw that the business of every man, soldier, engineer, administrator, or writer, is to turn out a clean, finished job. This is a morality that most men can understand, and he could preach it easily to many men to whom books mean little, but who find in Kipling an imagery they can recognise and who therefore can get into those relations of sympathy and comprehension which must exist between reader and writer if any influence is to pass from one to the other. There is no readier bond of union between men than a shop in common. That is why, for instance, professional conferences are so much more effective in promoting international understanding than any number of societies formed for the purpose. That is why the seamen have been more successful than all the politicians, and have shown what can be done in international agreement, by the formulation and acceptance of their convention for the safety of life at sea. It is a triumph of "shop."

Kipling overdid this technical interest sometimes. Occasionally his intelligent interest degenerates into an irritating knowingness, the revelation into a trick. His appreciation of "shop" as a bond of union is contaminated by that other habit of his – perhaps to be traced also to his unhappy, isolated childhood – his love of playing the initiate. Kipling was an ardent Freemason, and at times he seems to regard the world as an aggregation of secret and semi-secret societies, a pattern of circles, intersecting indeed, but closed – English Public Schools, religions, engine-rooms, messes, nationalities, clubs, services, and professions. Up to a point it is true: a man's world, his associations, attitudes, re-actions to circumstance, and slang, as well as his personality, are conditioned by his profession. But Kipling was at times – and it grew on him – too eager to prove himself initiate of many mysteries; and it is a little annoying to be winked at by an augur when one isn't an augur oneself – or when one serves in a different temple, for, like a true religionist, Kipling was apt to despise the lodges which chance or temperament or personal antagonism tyled against him. It was unfortunate that he was tempted to despise the cults of literature and art that were nearly his – though perhaps that is human nature – it was more unfortunate that he should so often betray not merely contempt of the outsider, but a certain enjoyment in the contemplation of their relative positions.

Yet this way of approach to men through their business brought its reward. Of all talk, shop is the most interesting and the freest. We all know men who on the subject of golf, bridge, books, or pictures, are the most calamitous bores, but who are quite human and quite fascinating when they get on to steam turbines or the sugar market. Shop, sedulously collected and sedulously exploited, gave Kipling a wealth of images that were not only fresh, but precise, vivid, and evocative. It would have annoyed him excessively – or, who knows? pleased him mightily – to be told that this technical imagery is authorised by no less a poet than Ronsard. But he needed no authority: it was his own discovery. It was the natural outcome of his perennial delight in the spectacle of a world full of men working and things happening. Not only did it give him a wealth of imagery; it gave him understanding. He made the English conscious of the Dominions and their scenes and peoples, because he was an Englishman and a journalist, free of the Seven Seas. He made them conscious of the skill, resource, and courage of their own workers at many trades, because he was a tradesman himself. He made them conscious even of their games. It is a striking fact, when one considers the time and energy devoted to games in this country, that they make such a poor shape in literature. It is partly a matter of time, perhaps; our games in their present form are very recent things; but while the ancient field-sports have

their many admirable writers, I know only one imaginary game
that carries, to one who does not know the game – and that is
the true test – anything of strenuousness and excitement in it;
and that is Kipling's story "The Maltese Cat," in *The Day's Work.*

He describes that polo-match from the point of view of the
ponies, the professionals for whom it was more than a recreation;
indeed, the winning team win just because their ponies are single-
minded professionals. That is characteristic. It is characteristic,
too, that his imagination carried "shop" – the technical interest –
out of the human world into that of the animals. That trick of
the imagination carried his interest further – out of the world of
men into the world of machines. Its limitations may be studied
by a comparison of the successful story "The Ship that Found
Herself" in *The Day's Work,* with the unsuccessful story ".007"
in the same volume, a story in which some brilliant description,
and a good deal of knowledge and observation, are wasted on an
over-strained piece of anthropomorphism. In one case it is an
effort of the imagination, in the other a deliberate trick of the
pen. Kipling's animal world, of course, as exhibited in *The Jungle
Books* and elsewhere, is not an animal world at all: but this way of
regarding the animals also as sentient and intelligent beings who
have their own needs and therefore require their own technique
to satisfy those needs, provided him – and provides us – with yet
another source of bright and striking imagery. And it is perhaps
a step, if a small one, to the completer appreciation of the relations
of man and the animals as fellow-citizens of the same universe,
and so, again, a real widening of our consciousness. Meanwhile
it is good reading.

When Kipling's youthful restlessness left him and he settled
down in England – and made the English county, characteristically, into an exclusive cult – that same way of approach
helped him to give the English a new appreciation of their own
history. He continued thereby the work of sympathetic understanding begun by Sir Walter Scott. That technical interest runs
all through the historical tales. It is the inspiration, as the
tradesman's morality is the subject, of such stories as "The
Wrong Thing" in *Rewards and Fairies*; but it is everywhere, in
small observations such as this, that the Centurion Parnesius
"rapped on the great shield that never seemed to be in his way"

– a tiny thing, but a piece of real imagination, manifestly right and completely convincing. Of course the weapons – or the tools – a man carries daily, however clumsy they may appear, are never in his way. How did Kipling know how easily a Roman centurion would carry his shield? Because he had seen men who carried rifles. He brought to history, not the erudition of the trained worker among documents, but the journalist's gift of seizing upon significant detail, and the experienced journalist's knowledge of men and affairs. He had seen much in many quarters of the globe, and had known and talked with many men. Thus he saw the centurion on the Roman Wall through the officer on the Indian frontier, the Renaissance builder through the builders of his own house, the Viking through the Pathan raider, Talleyrand through many meetings with many politicians. It may be possible to cavil at some of his material facts, but his human facts are convincing; and it is to be observed that the human facts are his real subject. He was not trying to serve any other purpose – school of historiography, state, church, or party – but to attempt an interpretation of historical events in terms of people – men and women, the true subject of the novelist. And he saw men and women as people with work to do, and, usually, doing it well.

The process, admirable in itself, has, as I have said, its limitations: necessarily, because it depends on personal contacts. Kipling was a journalist: that means that he had acquired the art of selecting detail and using it to the utmost advantage; the kind of detail he could use best was technical detail: but there are techniques which cannot be acquired, even for journalistic purposes, by merely watching men at work. Some of them require a longish apprenticeship, and both the quality of the technical handling and the value of the results can be appreciated only after such an apprenticeship. As a journalist, Kipling had a strong sense of the value of time. Hence, in part at least, his impatience of the slow and scrupulous processes of the scholar, and his complete ignoring of pure science. Their ends were too far away for him; he could not follow up and correlate the workings of the library and the laboratory with the immediately applicable workings of the office and the workshop; and so he could not understand the habits of the queer creatures that inhabit such places. He was entranced by the sight and by the exploitation of the significant detail: he simply had not time or patience to follow up a multitude of details each of which might be insignificant in itself and therefore useless in selective isolation.

There are purely intellectual and emotional processes, again, that simply cannot be observed by his methods at all, though they may be so recorded; and here we arrive at the question of his failure as a novelist. It is a minor affair that in a story built up on detail, "Dayspring Mishandled" in *Limits and Renewals*, the central detail, the supposed quotation from Chaucer, should be so completely un-Chaucerian. It is fatal, when the same sort of limitation affects his long novel, *The Light that Failed*, for in the long novel the interest is not such as manifests itself in outward detail at all, and the subtle tracing of processes requires a different procedure, more patience, less pouncing on the swiftly seen and immediately exploited fragment, and more concentration on connexions which lead to a distant end. There is another factor, deeper and more important. "Dayspring Mishandled" is a story of carefully planned revenge; and that theme of plotted revenge and its variant, persecution, appears at intervals all through Kipling's work from first to last. This theme may be related to its rudimentary form, the schoolboy practical joke, of which also he is fond, and to a farcical sense of humour. It might also be referred back to his childhood and the bullying of his schooldays. It looks very like a symptom of weakness. The sensitiveness that guarded his own emotions, the defensive habit, may have made any psychological inquiry seem rather too like an inquisition – something painful, a search for hidden weakness, almost a persecution; so he recoiled from it instinctively. To put it another way: there was in Kipling a strain of the persecutor. The methods of persecution he describes always require intimate knowledge of the habits – let us use the jargon and say the "psychology" – of the victim. Therefore revelation is dangerous: one must never give oneself away. Where the step from actuality to invention is so short as it was in Kipling, the inhibition may be carried over into imaginative creation; since he cared for his heroes and heroines, he was incapable of giving *them* away – which is just what a novelist must do. I do not wish to dwell on this part of his work, especially as he himself realised his limitation and confined himself ever after to the short story.

To resume: the examination of Kipling's usual processes shows how he acquired and prepared the outward texture of his work, the imagery through which he expressed himself, and his way of establishing relations with his fellow-creatures. Within, there is the spirit that moved him in all his conduct, the positive spirit of the Western European. He might say with one of his heroines, "I like men who do things." His notion of the things worth doing may be limited, but the spirit is a proper spirit. He could not have stated it in philosophic terms, for his whole constitution, training and habit incapacitated him for philosophy. He could work only with what he believed in. Thus with all his experience of Oriental countries, with some knowledge of Oriental religion and philosophy as facts intellectually apprehended, he has broadened the Englishman's knowledge of the Englishman alone. Not even his love of France extended his understanding beyond his own people. There is one story which is almost a test piece: "The Miracle of Purun Bhagat" in *The Second Jungle Book*. There he begins by showing to the English a fellow-citizen whose concepts are utterly strange: a great worker for the public good who retires in the height of success to become a religious mendicant. He ends in action as heretical for his Brahmin as the Brahmin's inaction, if he had been orthodox, would be heresy to a British official. He sets out, as if it were a triumph, what is really a failure. Purun Bhagat strove in meditation and solitude to unify himself with the Universal Spirit, but humanity was too strong for him: he had not freed himself, and so he interfered in the purposes of the Universe. From our Western European point of view his action was right: from the Indian point of view it stands condemned.

The question here is not which is right or wrong, but the spirit that led Kipling to this misrepresentation. Elsewhere that spirit vindicates itself. I doubt whether Kipling ever apprehended the real existence, much less investigated the value or the validity, of any other. It is this positive spirit, moving within all his work, that gives it its real force; and all the more force because it is so un-self-conscious. And whatever beauty one may find in Indian and Chinese philosophies, this spirit exists, and is therefore a legitimate inspiration for a European artist. The White Man's Burden is not what has been called "the trusteeship of the native races," but the restless desire for action that makes him endlessly interfere in other people's religions and police and sanitation. It varies from meddlesomeness and priggishness to the most noble altruism; and we can't help it. However wistfully one may regard the peace and freedom from responsibility conferred by Buddhism or Taoism, mathematics or pure science, this spirit is our inheritance, and we may not deny it. No one has given it fuller expression than Kipling. True, we may be unmoved by his occasional violence. We may find his force where it is least obvious – was least conscious, perhaps, to himself, as in that story of "The Maltese Cat," which is only the story of a polo-match, but gives to me, at least, a stronger sense of universal vitality than D. H. Lawrence achieved in all his search for it. That is how the arts work: a polo-match described by Kipling, a brass pot painted by Chardin, a boy's love-song set by Mozart, are more potent in their operation than many dissertations.

This positivism which underlay his method made him a story-teller and not an analyst. Even his interest in psycho-therapeutics was that of a technician; and therein he was saved from the error that is vitiating fiction, criticism, and psychological science – especially the amateur psychological science which is so common and so devastating these days – the error of confusing pathology and physiology, of interpreting the normal by the abnormal. He had seen too much of the world to imagine that the key to humanity is contained in any textbook. He is in the line of Smollett and Scott; a lesser man than either, but of the same kind. And I am, frankly, convinced that theirs is the true line. The novel nowadays varies between a debate on sociological problems and the exhibition of psychological cases. In both varieties the theme, if any, is worked out in a multiplicity of details whose significance is only that of association in the writer's memory – an exaggeration of Wordsworth's weakness – and the writer is too often haunted not only by the curse of Adam, but by the "prophetic blessing" of Macflecknoe, "Be thou dull." What is more serious – or less serious? – they are apt to be confused with scientific demonstration. For the artist is a Maker. The cases he exhibits are of his own making. For myself, I can derive no intellectual conclusions from faked experiments. Emotional and aesthetic convictions are another matter. Viewed from that angle – which, I insist, is the true angle – all the sociological and psychological erudition is seen to be but imagery, the outward texture, as I have called it: perfectly legitimate imagery, but imagery. As our Father Aristotle said, art is imitation. It is not demonstration, nor is it susceptible of proof.

It is a great virtue in Kipling that his imagery remains imagery, and does not usurp the place of an end. His trade was not soldiering or engineering, but story-telling. He was interested in the making of things, because he was a maker himself, a tale-smith, a technician. It is through that unity of spirit that in spite of his masculinity he could appreciate Jane Austen. And so, though his imagery remains the vesture of his spirit, it is not a mere separable integument, but its true external form. His delight was in his own trade, and so he rejoiced in the spectacle of men working at their trades. He was free from the curse of Adam, because he accepted it.

And however differently we work, and however different our chosen material, if we have any touch of his great gift of sympathetic appreciation of other men's craftsmanship, we must recognise him as a deacon of his trade. As such it is our duty to judge him, not indiscriminately or in haste, but after due inspection as work should be judged – as he knew he should be judged – and by the criteria of his own trade, without complaining that his wrought-iron is not *famille-rose* porcelain or his new-cut ashlar jade. Of all his large output – I use the trade term deliberately – we may perhaps wish to preserve only a selection. His journalist's haste, his defensive habit of self-assertion, his positive delight in work, all helped to make him less critical of himself than he might have been. After much argument – and delightful argument it will be – we may select enough to fill, say, three volumes, to be put on the handy shelves between *Mr Soapy Sponge's Sporting Tour* and *Hajji Baba of Ispahan*. And where we find so much work well done, forgiving the spoiled pieces for the sake of the perfect ones, it is our duty to give honour to the workman.

Edmund Wilson

THE KIPLING THAT NOBODY
READ*

I

THE ECLIPSE of the reputation of Kipling, which began about
1910, twenty-five years before Kipling's death and when he was
still only forty-five, has been of a peculiar kind. Through this
period he has remained, from the point of view of sales, an
immensely popular writer. The children still read his children's
books; the college students still read his poetry; the men and
women of his own generation still re-read his early work. But he
has in a sense been dropped out of modern literature. The more
serious-minded young people do *not* read him; the critics do not
take him into account. During the later years of his life and even
at the time of his death, the logic of his artistic development
attracted no intelligent attention. At a time when W. B. Yeats
had outgrown his romantic youth and was receiving the reward
of an augmented glory for his severer and more concentrated
work, Rudyard Kipling, Yeats's coeval, who had also achieved
a new concentration through the efforts of a more exacting
discipline, saw the glory of his young manhood fade away. And
during the period when the late work of Henry James, who had
passed into a similar eclipse, was being retrieved and appreciated,
when the integrity and interest of his total achievement was
finally being understood, no attempt was made, so far as I know,
to take stock of Kipling's work as a whole.[1] The ordinary person

* [First published in *Atlantic Monthly*, CLXVII (1941), 201-14. Reprinted
from *The Wound and the Bow*, London 1952.]

[1] Since this was written, Mr Edward Shanks has published a book on
Kipling. Mr Shanks addresses himself to the task, but does not make very
much progress with it.

said simply that Kipling was "written out"; the reviewer rarely made any effort to trace the journey from the breeziness of the early short stories to the bitterness of the later ones. The thick, dark and surly little man who had dug himself into Bateman's, Burwash, Sussex, was left to his bristling privacy, and only occasionally evoked a rebuke for the intolerant and vindictive views which, emerging with the suddenness of a snapping turtle, he sometimes gave vent to in public.

But who *was* Kipling? What did he express? What was the history of that remarkable talent which gave him a place, as a craftsman of English prose, among the few genuine masters of his day? How was it that the art of his short stories became continually more skilful and intense, and yet that his career appears broken?

2

The publication of Kipling's posthumous memoirs – *Something of Myself for My Friends Known and Unknown* – has enabled us to see more clearly the causes for the anomalies of Kipling's career.

First of all, he was born in India, the son of an English artist and scholar, who had gone out to teach architectural sculpture at the Fine Arts School in Bombay and who afterwards became curator of the museum at Lahore. This fact is, of course, well known; but its importance must be specially emphasised. It appears that up to the age of six Kipling talked, thought and dreamed, as he says, in Hindustani, and could hardly speak English correctly. A drawing of him made by a schoolmate shows a swarthy boy with lank straight hair, who might almost pass for a Hindu.

The second important influence in Kipling's early life has not hitherto been generally known, though it figures in the first chapters of *The Light that Failed* and furnished the subject of "Baa, Baa, Black Sheep," one of the most powerful things he ever wrote. This story had always seemed rather unaccountably to stand apart from the rest of Kipling's work by reason of its sympathy with the victims rather than with the inflictors of a severely repressive discipline; and its animus is now explained by a chapter in Kipling's autobiography and by a memoir recently published by his sister. When Rudyard Kipling was six and his sister three and a half, they were farmed out for six years in England with a relative of Kipling's father.[2] John Lockwood Kipling was the son of a Methodist minister, and this woman was a religious domestic tyrant in the worst English tradition of Dickens and Samuel Butler. The boy, who had been petted and deferred to by the native servants in India, was now beaten, bullied with the Bible, pursued with constant suspicions and broken down by cross-examinations. If one of the children spilled a drop of gravy or wept over a letter from their parents in Bombay, they were forbidden to speak to one another for twenty-four hours. Their guardian had a violent temper and enjoyed making terrible scenes, and they had to learn to propitiate her by fawning on her when they saw that an outburst was imminent.

> Looking back, [says Mrs Fleming, Kipling's sister] I think the real tragedy of our early days, apart from Aunty's bad temper and unkindness to my brother, sprang from our inability to understand why our parents had deserted us. We had had no preparation or explanation; it was like a double death, or rather, like an avalanche that had swept away everything happy and familiar. . . . We felt that we had been deserted, "almost as much as on a doorstep", and what was the reason? Of course, Aunty used to say it was because we were so tiresome, and she had taken us in out of pity, but in a desperate moment Ruddy appealed to Uncle Harrison, and he said it was only Aunty's fun, and Papa had left us to be taken care of, because India was too hot for little people. But we knew better than that, because we had been to Nassick, so what was the real reason? Mamma was not ill, like that peepy-weepy Ellen Montgomery's mamma in *The Wide, Wide World*. Papa had not had to go to a war. They had not even lost their money; if they had, we could have swept crossings or sold flowers, and it would have been rather fun. But there was no excuse; they had gone happily back to our own lovely home, and had not taken us with them. There was no getting out of that, as we often said.

[2] [The children were taught to give her the courtesy title of "Aunty," but she was not in fact a relation. ED.]

Harry [Aunty's son], who had all a crow's quickness in finding a wound to pick at, discovered our trouble and teased us unmercifully. He assured us we had been taken in out of charity, and must do exactly as he told us. . . . We were just like workhouse brats, and none of our toys really belonged to us.[3]

Rudyard had bad eyes, which began to give out altogether, so that he was unable to do his work at school. One month he destroyed his report so that his guardians at home shouldn't see it; and for punishment was made to walk to school with a placard between his shoulders reading "Liar." He had finally a severe nervous breakdown, accompanied by partial blindness, and was punished by isolation from his sister. This breakdown, it is important to note, was made horrible by hallucinations. As a mist, which seemed to grow steadily thicker, shut him in from the rest of the world, he would imagine that blowing curtains were spectres or that a coat on a nail was an enormous back bird ready to swoop down upon him.

His mother came back at last, saw how bad things were – when she went up to kiss him good-night, he instinctively put up his hand to ward off the expected blow – and took the children away. But the effects of those years were lasting. Mrs Fleming tells us that her revulsion against Aunty's son Harry conditioned her reactions towards people who resembled him through all the rest of her life, and says that when, thirty years later, she set out in Southsea one day to see if the "House of Desolation" were still standing, her heart failed her, and she hurried back: "I dared not face it." Rudyard himself told her that he had had a similar experience: "I think we both dreaded a kind of spiritual imprisonment that would affect our dreams. Less than four years ago [she is writing in 1939], I asked him whether he knew if the house still stood. 'I don't know, but if so I should like to burn it down and plough the place with salt.' "[4]

Kipling asserts that this ordeal had "drained me of any capacity for real, personal hate for the rest of my days"[5]; and his sister

[3] ["Some Childhood Memories of Rudyard Kipling," *Chambers's Journal*, Eighth Series, VIII (1939), 171.]
[4] ["More Childhood Memories of Rudyard Kipling," *op. cit.*, 506.]
[5] [*Something of Myself*, Chapter One.]

denies that it produced in him any permanent injurious effects: "According to their gloomy theories [the theories of the psychoanalysts], my brother should have grown up morbid, misanthropic, narrow-minded, self-centred, shunning the world, and bearing it, and all men, a burning grudge; for certainly between the ages of six and eleven he was thwarted at every turn by Aunty and the odious Harry, and inhibitions were his daily bread."[6] Yet here is the conclusion of the story[7] which Kipling made out of this experience: "There! Told you so," says the boy to his sister. "It's all different now, and we are just as much Mother's as if she had never gone." But, Kipling adds: "Not altogether, O Punch, for when young lips have drunk deep of the bitter waters of Hate, Suspicion, and Despair, all the Love in the world will not wholly take away that knowledge; though it may turn darkened eyes for a while to the light, and teach Faith where no Faith was."

And actually the whole work of Kipling's life is to be shot through with hatred.

He was next sent to a public school in England. This school, the United Services College, at a place called Westward Ho!, had been founded by Army and Navy officers who could not afford to send their sons to the more expensive schools. The four and a half years that Kipling spent there gave him *Stalky & Co.*; and the relation of the experience to the book provides an interesting psychological study. The book itself, of course, presents a hair-raising picture of the sadism of the English public-school system. The older boys have fags to wait on them, and they sometimes torment these younger boys till they have reduced them almost to imbecility; the masters are constantly caning the boys in scenes that seem almost as bloody as the floggings in old English sea stories; and the boys revenge themselves on the masters with practical jokes as catastrophic as the Whams and Zows of the comic strip.

The originals of two of Kipling's characters – Major-General L. C. Dunsterville and Mr G. C. Beresford – have published in their later years (*Stalky's Reminiscences* and *Schooldays with Kipling*)

---

[6] [*Chambers's Journal*, Eighth Series, VIII (1939), 168-9.]
[7] ["Baa, Baa, Black Sheep," *Wee Willie Winkie*.]

accounts rather discrepant with one another of life at the United Services College. Mr Beresford, who is a highbrow in *Stalky & Co.* and reads Ruskin in the midst of the mêlée, turns out to be a Nationalist Irishman, who is disgusted with his old friend's later imperialism. He insists that the fagging system did not exist at Westward Ho!; that the boys were never caned on their bare shoulders; and that Kipling, so far as he remembers, was never caned at all except by a single exceptional master. Dunsterville, on the other hand, reports that the younger boys were barbarously bullied by the older: held out of high windows by their ankles and dropped down a stair-well in "hangings" which in one case broke the victim's leg; and that "in addition to the blows and the kicks that inevitably accompanied the bullying" he "suffered a good deal from the canes of the masters, or the ground-ash sticks of the prefects. I must have been perpetually black and blue. That always sounds so dreadful. . . . But the truth of the matter is, any slight blow produces a bruise. . . . And with one or two savage exceptions, I am sure that the blows I received as a result of bullying or legitimate punishment were harmless enough. . . ." "Kicks and blows," he goes on, "I minded little, but the moral effect was depressing. Like a hunted animal I had to keep all my senses perpetually on the alert to escape from the toils of the hunter – good training in a way, but likely to injure permanently a not very robust temperament. I was robust enough, I am glad to say, and possibly benefited by the treatment."[8]

Kipling was, of course, not robust; and the school evidently aggravated the injury which had been done him during his captivity at Southsea. He admits, in *Something of Myself*, that the fagging system was not compulsory; but he asserts that the discipline was brutal, that the students were wretchedly fed, and that he himself, addicted to books and too blind to participate in games, endured a good deal of baiting. The important thing is that he suffered. If we compare the three accounts of Westward Ho! – *Stalky & Co.* with the reminiscences of the two others – the emphasis of Kipling's becomes plain. It is significant that the single master whom Beresford mentions as persecuting the boys should have been inquisitorial and morbidly suspicious –

[8] [*Stalky's Reminiscences*, London 1928, pp. 30-1.]

that is, that he should have treated Kipling in the same way that he had already been treated by the "Baa, Baa, Black Sheep" people. And it is also significant that this master does not figure in *Stalky & Co.*, but only appears later in one of the more scrupulous stories which Kipling afterwards wrote about the school. The stimulus of unjust suspicion, which did not leave any lasting bitterness with Beresford, had evidently the effect upon Kipling of throwing him back into the state of mind which had been created by the earlier relationship – just as the kickings and canings that Dunsterville nonchalantly shook off sunk deep into the spirit of Kipling. For a boy who has been habitually beaten during the second six years of his life, any subsequent physical punishment, however occasional or light, may result in the re-awakening of the terror and hatred of childhood. It thrust him back into the nightmare again, and eventually made a delirium of the memory of Westward Ho! *Stalky & Co.* – from the artistic point of view, certainly the worst of Kipling's books: crude in writing, trashy in feeling, implausible in a series of contrivances which resemble moving-picture "gags" – is in the nature of an hysterical outpouring of emotions kept over from school-days, and it probably owes a part of its popularity to the fact that it provides the young with hilarious and violent fantasies on the theme of what they would do to the school bully and their masters if the laws of probability were suspended.

We shall deal presently with the social significance which Kipling, at a later period, was to read back into Westward Ho! In the meantime, we must follow his adventures when he leaves it in July 1882, not yet quite seventeen, but remarkably mature for his age and with a set of grown-up whiskers. He went back to his family in India, and there he remained for seven years. The Hindu child, who had lain dormant in England, came to life when he reached Bombay, and he found himself reacting to the old stimuli by beginning to talk Hindustani without understanding what he was saying. "Seven Years Hard" is his heading for his chapter on this phase of his life. His family – as we gather from his address on *Independence* – were by no means well-to-do; and he started right in on a newspaper in Lahore as sole assistant to the editor, and worked his head off for a chief he detested. It was one of the duties of the English journalist in India to play down the periodical epidemics. Kipling himself survived dysentery and fever, and kept on working through his severest illnesses. One hot night in 1886, when he felt, as he says, that he "had come to the edge of all endurance" and had gone home to his empty house with the sensation that there was nothing left in him but "the horror of a great darkness, that I must have been fighting for some days," he read a novel by Walter Besant about a young man who had wanted to be a writer and who had eventually succeeded in his aim. Kipling decided he would save some money and get away to London. He wrote short stories called *Plain Tales from the Hills*, which were run to fill up space in the paper, and he brought out a book of verse. His superiors disapproved of his flippancy, and when he finally succeeded in leaving India, the managing director of the paper, who had considered him overpaid, told the young man that he could take it from him that he would never be worth anything more than four hundred rupees a month.

The Kipling of these early years is a lively and sympathetic figure. A newspaper man who has access to everything, the son of a scholar who has studied the natives; he sees the community, like Asmodeus, with all the roofs removed. He is interested in the British of all classes and ranks – the bored English ladies, the vagabond adventurers, the officers and the soldiers both.

> Having no position to consider, [he writes] and my trade enforcing it, I could move at will in the fourth dimension. I came to realise the bare horrors of the private's life, and the unnecessary torments he endured. . . . Lord Roberts, at that time Commander-in-Chief in India, who knew my people, was interested in the men, and – I had by then written one or two stories about soldiers – the proudest moment of my young life was when I rode up Simla Mall beside him on his usual explosive red Arab, while he asked me what the men thought about their accommodation, entertainment-rooms, and the like. I told him, and he thanked me as gravely as though I had been a full Colonel.[9]

He is already tending to think about people in terms of social and

9 [*Something of Myself*, Chapter Three.]

racial categories; but his interest in them at this time is also personal:

> All the queer outside world would drop into our workshop sooner or later – say a Captain just cashiered for horrible drunkenness, who reported his fall with a wry, appealing face, and then – disappeared. Or a man old enough to be my father, on the edge of tears because he had been overpassed for Honours in the Gazette. . . . One met men going up and down the ladder in every shape of misery and success.[10]

And he gives us in his soldier stories, along with the triumphs of discipline and the exploits of the native wars, the hunger of Private Ortheris for London when the horror of exile seizes him; the vanities and vices of Mulvaney which prevent him from rising in the service ("The Courting of Dinah Shadd," admired by Henry James, is one of the stories of Kipling which sticks closest to unregenerate humanity); even the lunatic obsessions and the crack-up of the rotter gentleman ranker in "Love o' Women."

The natives Kipling probably understood as few Englishmen did in his time; certainly he presented them in literature as nobody had ever done. That Hindu other self of his childhood takes us through into its other world. The voices of alien traditions – in the monologues of *In Black and White* – talk an English which translates their own idiom; and we hear of great lovers and revengers who live by an alien code; young men who have been educated in England and, half-dissociated from native life, find themselves impotent between two civilisations; fierce Afghan tribesmen of the mountains, humble people who have been broken to the mines; loyal Sikhs and untamed mutineers. It is true that there is always the implication that the British are bringing to India modern improvements and sounder standards of behaviour. But Kipling is obviously enjoying for its own sake the presentation of the native point of view, and the whole Anglo-Indian situation is studied with a certain objectivity.

He is even able to handle without horror the mixture of the black and the white.

10 [*Ibid.*]

ABIGAIL E. WEEKS MEMORIAL LIBRARY
UNION COLLEGE
BARBOURVILLE, KENTUCKY

The "railway folk", [says Mr E. Kay Robinson, who worked with him on the paper in Lahore] that queer colony of white, half white and three-quarters black, which remains an uncared-for and discreditable excrescence upon British rule in India, seemed to have unburdened their souls to Kipling of all their grievances, their poor pride, and their hopes. Some of the best of Kipling's work is drawn from the lives of these people; although to the ordinary Anglo-Indian, whose social caste restrictions are almost more inexorable than those of the Hindu whom he affects to despise on that account, they are as a sealed book.[11]

And one of the most sympathetic of these early stories – the once famous "Without Benefit of Clergy" – is a picture of an Anglo-Indian union: an English official who lives with a Mahomedan girl. Though Kipling deals rarely in fortunate lovers, these lovers enjoy their happiness for a time. To their joy, the mother gives birth to a son, who turns into "a small gold-coloured little god," and they like to sit on the roof and eat almonds and watch the kites. But then the baby dies of the fever, and the young wife dies of the cholera; and the husband is called away to fight the famine and the epidemic. Even the house where they have lived is destroyed, and the husband is glad that no one else will ever be able to live there. This idyll, unhallowed and fleeting, is something that the artist in Kipling has felt, and put down for its sweetness and pathos.

Through all these years of school and of newspaper work, with their warping and thwarting influences, Kipling worked staunchly at mastering his craft. For he had been subjected to yet another influence which has not been mentioned yet. His father was a painter and sculptor, and two of his mother's sisters were married to artists – one to Edward Poynter, the Academician, and the other to the Pre-Raphaelite, Burne-Jones. Besides India and the United Services College, there had been the Pre-Raphaelite movement. In England, Kipling's vacation had always been spent in London with the Burne-Joneses. Mr Beresford says that Kipling's attitude at school had been that of the aesthete who disdains athletics and has no aptitude for mechanical

[11] ["Kipling in India," *McClure's Magazine*, VII (1896), 104.]

matters, that he was already preoccupied with writing, and that his literary proficiency and cultivation were amazingly developed for his age. He had had from his childhood the example of men who loved the arts for their own sake and who were particularly concerned about craftsmanship (it is also of interest that his father's family had distinguished themselves in the eighteenth century as founders of bronze bells). Kipling evidently owes his superiority as a craftsman to most of even the ablest English writers of fiction of the end of the century and the early nineteen hundreds, to this inspiration and training. Just as the ballad of "Danny Deever" derives directly from the ballad of "Sister Helen," so the ideal of an artistic workmanship which shall revert to earlier standards of soundness has the stamp of William Morris and his circle. In 1878, when Rudyard was twelve years old, his father had taken him to the Paris Exhibition, and insisted that he learn to read French. The boy had then conceived an admiration for the civilisation of the French which evidently contributed later to his interest in perfecting the short story in English.

With all this, his earlier experience in the "House of Desolation" had equipped him, he says, with a training not unsuitable for a writer of fiction, in that it had "demanded constant wariness, the habit of observation, and attendance on moods and tempers; the noting of discrepancies between speech and action; a certain reserve of demeanour; and automatic suspicion of sudden favours."[12]

With such a combination of elements, what might one not expect? It is not surprising to learn that the young Kipling contemplated, after his return to England, writing a colonial *Comédie Humaine*. "Bit by bit, my original notion," he writes, "grew into a vast, vague conspectus – Army and Navy Stores List, if you like – of the whole sweep and meaning of things and efforts and origins throughout the Empire."[13] Henry James, who wrote an appreciative preface for a collection of Kipling's early stories, said afterwards that he had thought at that time that it might perhaps be true that Kipling "contained the seeds of an English Balzac."[14]

[12] [*Something of Myself*, Chapter One.]
[13] [*Op. cit.*, Chapter Four.]
[14] [*The Letters of Henry James*, ed. P. Lubbock, London 1920, I, 278.]

3

What became of this English Balzac? Why did the author of the
brilliant short stories never develop into an important novelist?

Let us return to "Baa, Baa, Black Sheep" and the situation with
which it deals. Kipling says that his Burne-Jones aunt was never
able to understand why he had never told anyone in the family
about how badly he and his sister were being treated, and he
tries to explain this on the principle that "children tell little more
than animals, for what comes to them they accept as eternally
established," and says that "badly-treated children have a clear
notion of what they are likely to get if they betray the secrets of
a prison-house before they are clear of it." But *is* this inevitably
true? Even young children do sometimes run away. And, in
any case, Kipling's reaction to this experience seems an abnormally
docile one. After all, Dickens made David Copperfield bite Mr
Murdstone's hand and escape; and he makes war on Mr Murdstone through the whole of his literary career. But though the
anguish of these years had given Kipling a certain sympathy
with the neglected and persecuted, and caused him to write this
one moving short story, it left him – whether as the result of the
experience itself or because he was already so conditioned – with
a fundamental submissiveness to authority.

Let us examine the two books in which Kipling deals, respect-
ively, with his schooldays and with his youth in India: *Stalky &
Co.* and *Kim.* These works are the products of the author's
thirties, and *Kim,* at any rate, represents Kipling's most serious
attempt to allow himself to grow to the stature of a first-rate
creative artist. Each of these books begins with an antagonism
which in the work of a greater writer would have developed into
a fundamental conflict; but in neither *Stalky* nor *Kim* is the
conflict ever permitted to mount to a real crisis. Nor can it even
be said to be resolved: it simply ceases to figure as a conflict. In
Stalky, we are at first made to sympathise with the baiting of the
masters by the schoolboys as their rebellion against a system
which is an offence against human dignity; but then we are
immediately shown that all the ragging and flogging are justified
by their usefulness as a training for the military caste which is to
govern the British Empire. The boys are finally made to recognise that their headmaster not only knows how to dish it out but

is also able to take it, and the book culminates in the ridiculous scene – which may perhaps have its foundation in fact but is certainly flushed by a hectic imagination – in which the Head, in his inflexible justice, undertakes personally to cane the whole school while the boys stand by cheering him wildly.

There is a real subject in *Stalky & Co.*, but Kipling has not had the intelligence to deal with it. He cannot see around his characters and criticise them, he is not even able properly to dramatise; he simply allows the emotions of the weaker side, the side that is getting the worst of it, to go over to the side of the stronger. You can watch the process all too clearly in the episode in which Stalky and his companions turn the tables on the cads from the crammers' school. These cads have been maltreating a fag, and a clergyman who is represented by Kipling as one of the more sensible and decent of the masters suggests to Stalky & Co. that they teach the bullies a lesson. The former proceed to clean up on the latter in a scene which goes on for pages, to the reckless violation of proportion and taste. The oppressors, true enough, are taught a lesson, but the cruelty with which we have already been made disgusted has now passed over to the castigators' side, and there is a disagreeable implication that, though it is caddish for the cads to be cruel, it is all right for the sons of English gentlemen to be cruel to the cads.

Kim is more ambitious and much better. It is Kipling's only successful long story: an enchanting, almost a first-rate book, the work in which more perhaps than in any other he gave the sympathies of the imagination free rein to remember and to explore, and which has in consequence more complexity and density than any of his other works. Yet the conflict from which the interest arises, though it is very much better presented, here also comes to nothing: the two forces never really engage. Kim is the son of an Irish soldier and an Irish nursemaid, who has grown up as an orphan in India, immersed in and assimilated to the native life, so that he thinks, like the young Kipling, in Hindustani. The story deals with the gradual dawning of his consciousness that he is really a Sahib. As a child he has been in the habit of making a little money by carrying messages for a native agent of the British Secret Service, and the boy turns out to be so bright and so adept at acting the role of a native that the authorities decide to train him. He is sent to an English school but does not willingly submit to the English system. Every vacation he dresses as a native and disappears into the sea of native life. The Ideal of this side of his existence is represented by a Thibetan lama, a wandering Buddhist pilgrim, whom he accompanies in the character of a disciple.

Now what the reader tends to expect is that Kim will come eventually to realise that he is delivering into bondage to the British invaders those whom he has always considered his own people, and that a struggle between allegiances will result. Kipling has established for the reader – and established with considerable dramatic effect – the contrast between the East, with its mysticism and its sensuality, its extremes of saintliness and roguery, and the English, with their superior organisation, their confidence in modern method, their instinct to brush away like cobwebs the native myths and beliefs. We have been shown two entirely different worlds existing side by side, with neither really understanding the other, and we have watched the oscillations of Kim, as he passes to and fro between them. But the parallel lines never meet; the alternating attractions felt by Kim never give rise to a genuine struggle. And the climax itself is double: the adventures of the Lama and of Kim simply arrive at different consummations, without any final victory or synthesis ever being allowed to take place. Instead, there are a pair of victories, which occur on separate planes and do not influence one another: the Lama attains to a condition of trance which releases him from what the Buddhists call the Wheel of Things at the same moment that the young Anglo-Indian achieves promotion in the British Secret Service.

The salvation of the Lama has been earned by penitence for a moment of passion: he had been tempted to kill a man who had torn his sacred chart and struck him, a Russian agent working against the British. But the pretences of Kim to a spiritual vocation, whatever spell has been exerted over him by the Lama, are dispelled when the moment for action comes, when the Irishman is challenged to a fight: Kim knocks the Russian down and bangs his head against a boulder. "I am Kim. I am Kim. And what is Kim?" his soul repeats again and again, in his exhaustion and collapse after this episode. He feels that his soul is "out of gear with its surroundings – a cog-wheel unconnected with any machinery, just like the idle cog-wheel of a cheap Beheea sugar-crusher laid by in a corner." But he now gets this un-attached soul to find a function in the working of the crusher – note the mechanical metaphor: dissociating himself from the hierarchy represented by the Abbot-Lama, he commits himself to a role in the hierarchy of a practical organisation. (So the wolf-reared Mowgli of the *Jungle Books*, the prototype of Kim, ends up rather flatly as a ranger in the British Forestry Service.) Nor does Kipling allow himself to doubt that his hero has chosen the better part. Kim must now exploit his knowledge of native life for the purpose of preventing and putting down any native resistance to the British; but it never seems to occur to his creator that this constitutes a betrayal of the Lama. A sympathy with the weaker party in a relationship based on force has again given way without a qualm to a glorification of the stronger. As the bullying masters of *Stalky & Co.* turn into beneficent Chirons, so even the overbearing officer who figures on his first appearance in *Kim* as a symbol of British stupidity turns out to be none other than Strickland, the wily police superintendent, who has here been acting a part. (It should also be noted that the question of whether or not Kim shall allow himself to sleep with a native woman has here become very important, and that his final emergence as a Sahib is partly determined by his decision in the negative. This is no longer the Kipling of "Without Benefit of Clergy.")

The Lama's victory is not of this world: the sacred river for which he has been seeking, and which he identifies in his final revelation with a brook near which his trance has occurred, has no objective existence, it is not on the British maps. Yet the anguish of the Lama's repentance – a scene, so far as I remember, elsewhere unmatched in Kipling – is one of the most effective things in the book; and we are to meet this Lama again in strange and unexpected forms still haunting that practical world which Kipling, like Kim, has chosen. The great eulogist of the builder and the man of action was no more able to leave the Lama behind than Kim had been able to reconcile himself to playing the game of English life without him.

4

The fiction of Kipling, then, does not dramatise any fundamental conflict because Kipling would never face one. This is probably one of the causes of his lack of success with long novels. You can make an effective short story, as Kipling so often does, about somebody's scoring off somebody else; but this is not enough for a great novelist, who must show us large social forces, or uncontrollable lines of destiny, or antagonistic impulses of the human spirit, struggling with one another. With Kipling, the right and the wrong of any opposition of forces is usually quite plain at the start; and there is not even the suspense which makes possible the excitement of melodrama. There is never any doubt as to the outcome. The Wrong is made a guy from the beginning, and the high point of the story comes when the Right gives it a kick in the pants. Where both sides are sympathetically presented, the battle is not allowed to occur.

But this only drives us back on another question: how was it that the early Kipling, with his sensitive understanding of the mixed population of India, became transformed into the later Kipling, who consolidated and codified his snobberies instead of progressively eliminating them as most good artists do, and who, like Kim, elected as his lifework the defence of the British Empire? The two books we have been discussing indicate the end of a period in the course of which Kipling had arrived at a decision. *Stalky* came out in 1899, and *Kim* in 1901. The decade of the 'nineties had been critical for Kipling; and in order to understand the new phase of his work which had begun by the beginning of the century, we must follow his adventures in the United States, which he visited in 1889, where he lived from 1892 to 1896, and to which he tried to return in 1899. Kipling's relations with America are certainly the most important factor in his experience during these years of his later twenties and early thirties; yet they are the link which has been dropped out of his story in most of the accounts of his life and which even his posthumous memoirs, revelatory in respect to his earlier years, markedly fail to supply.

The young man who arrived in London in the fall of 1889 was very far from being the truculent British patriot whom we knew in the nineteen-hundreds. He had not even gone straight back to England, but had first taken a trip around the world, visiting Canada and the United States. Nor did he remain long in the mother-country when he got there. His whole attitude was that of the colonial who has sweated and suffered at the outposts of Empire, making the acquaintance of more creeds and customs than the philosophy of London dreamt of, and who feels a slight touch of scorn toward the smugness of the people at home, unaware of how big, varied, and active the world around them is. His "original notion," he says, had been to try "to tell to the English something of the world outside England – not directly but by implication": "What can they know of England who only England know?" He rounded out his knowledge of the colonies by travelling in New Zealand, Australia, South Africa, and Southern India. In the January of 1892, he married an American wife.

Kipling's experience of the United States was in certain ways like that of Dickens. Neither of them fitted very well into the English system at home, and both seem to have been seeking in the new English-speaking nation a place where they could be more at ease. Both winced at the crudeness of the West; both were contemptuously shocked by the boasting – the Pacific Coast in Kipling's day was what the Mississippi had been in Dickens'. Both, escaping from the chilliness of England, resented the familiarity of the States. Yet Kipling, on the occasion of his first visit, which he records in *From Sea to Sea*, is obviously rejoiced by the naturalness of social relations in America. He tells of "a very trim maiden" from New Hampshire, with "a delightful mother and an equally delightful father, a heavy-eyed, slow-voiced man of finance," whom he met in the Yellowstone.

Now an English maiden who had stumbled on a dust-grimed, lime-washed, sun-peeled, collarless wanderer come from and going to goodness knows where, would, her mother inciting her and her father brandishing his umbrella, have regarded him as a dissolute adventurer. Not so those delightful people from New Hampshire. They were good enough to treat me – it sounds almost incredible – as a human being, possibly respectable, probably not in immediate need of financial assistance.

Papa talked pleasantly and to the point. The little maiden strove valiantly with the accent of her birth and that of her reading, and mamma smiled benignly in the background.

Balance this with a story of a young English idiot I met knocking about inside his high collars, attended by a valet. He condescended to tell me that "you can't be too careful who you talk to in these parts", and stalked on, fearing, I suppose, every minute for his social chastity. Now that man was a barbarian (I took occasion to tell him so), for he comported himself after the manner of the head-hunters of Assam, who are at perpetual feud one with another.[15]

He declares his faith in the Americans in a conversation with an Englishman "who laughed at them."

"I admit everything," said I. "Their Government's provisional; their law's the notion of the moment; their railways are made of hair-pins and match-sticks, and most of their good luck lives in their woods and mines and rivers and not in their brains; but for all that, they be the biggest, finest, and best people on the surface of the globe! Just you wait a hundred years and see how they'll behave when they've had the screw put on them and have forgotten a few of the patriarchal teachings of the late Mr. George Washington. Wait till the Anglo-American-German-Jew – the Man of the Future – is properly equipped. He'll have just the least little kink in his hair now and again; he'll carry the English lungs above the Teuton feet that can walk for ever; and he will wave long, thin, bony Yankee hands with the big blue veins on the wrist, from one end of the earth to the other. He'll be the finest writer, poet, and dramatist, 'specially dramatist, that the world as it recollects itself has ever seen. By virtue of his Jew blood – just a little, little drop – he'll be a musician and a painter too. At present there is too much balcony and too little Romeo in the life-plays of his fellow-citizens. Later on, when the proportion is adjusted and he sees the possibilities of his land, he will produce things that will make the effete East stare. He will also be a complex and highly composite administrator. There is nothing known to man than he will

---

[15] [*From Sea to Sea*, ii, Chapter Thirty-One.]

not be, and his country will sway the world with one foot as
a man tilts a see-saw plank!"

"But this is worse than the Eagle at its worst. Do you
seriously believe all that?" said the Englishman.

"If I believe anything seriously, all this I most firmly believe.
You wait and see. Sixty million people, chiefly of English
instincts, who are trained from youth to believe that nothing
is impossible, don't slink through the centuries like Russian
peasantry. They are bound to leave their mark somewhere,
and don't you forget it."[16]

"I love this People . . ." he wrote. "My heart has gone out to
them beyond all other peoples."[17] And he reiterated his faith, in
the poem called "An American," in which "The American
spirit speaks":

> Enslaved, illogical, elate,
>   He greets th' embarrassed Gods, nor fears
> To shake the iron hand of Fate
>   Or match with Destiny for beers.
>
> Lo, imperturbable he rules,
>   Unkempt, disreputable, vast –
> And, in the teeth of all the schools,
>   I – I shall save him at the last!

Kipling took his wife to America, and they lived for a time on
the estate of her family in Brattleboro, Vermont; then Kipling
built a large house: his books were already making him rich.
They lived in the United States four years; two daughters were
born to them there. Kipling was ready to embrace America, or
those aspects of America which excited him; he began using
American subjects for his stories: the railroads in ".007," the
Gloucester fishermen in *Captains Courageous*. He enormously
admired Mark Twain, whose acquaintance he had made on his
first visit. Yet the effect of contact with the United States was
eventually to drive Kipling, as it had Dickens, back behind his
British defences. A disagreeable episode occurred, which, un-
dignified and even comic though it seems, is worth studying

[16] [*From Sea to Sea*, II, Chapter Thirty-Three.]
[17] [*Ibid.*]

because it provided the real test of Kipling's fitness to flourish in America, and not merely the test of this, but, at a critical time in his life, of the basic courage and humanity of his character.

The story has been told since Kipling's death in a book called *Rudyard Kipling's Vermont Feud* by Mr Frederick F. Van de Water. A brother of Mrs Kipling's, Kipling's friend Wolcott Balestier, had been in the publishing business with Heinemann in London, and Mrs Kipling had lived much in England and was by way of being an Anglophile. Thus the impulse on Kipling's part to assimilate himself to the Americans was neutralised in some degree by Mrs Kipling's desire to be English. Kipling, who was accustomed to India, had his own instinctive rudeness. In Vermont, he and Mrs Kipling tended to stick to the attitudes of the traditional governing-class English maintaining their caste in the colonies: they drove a tandem with a top-hatted English coachman, dressed every night for dinner, kept their New England neighbours at a distance.

But Mrs Kipling had a farmer brother who – the family were partly French – was as Americanised as possible. He was a drinker, a spendthrift and a great local card, famous alike for his ribaldry, his sleigh-racing and his gestures of generosity of a magnificence almost feudal. Mr Van de Water tells us that, at the time he knew Beatty Balestier, he had the swagger of Cyrano de Bergerac and a leathery face like "an ailing eagle." His farm and family suffered. The Kiplings lent him money, and he is said to have paid it back; but they disapproved of his disorderly existence. They seem to have persisted in treating him with some lack of consideration or tact. Beatty was, in any case, the kind of man – unbalanced in character but independent in spirit – who is embittered by obligations and furiously resents interference. Kipling went to Beatty one day and offered to support his wife and child for a year if Beatty would leave town and get a job. He was surprised at the explosion he provoked. This was followed by a dispute about some land across the road from the Kiplings' house. The land belonged to Beatty and he sold it for a dollar to the Kiplings, who were afraid that somebody would some day built on it – on the friendly understanding, as he claimed, that he could continue to use it for mowing. When the transfer had been effected, Mrs Kipling set out to landscape-garden it. The result was that Beatty stopped speaking to them and refused to receive Kipling when he came to call.

This went on for about a year, at the end of which a crisis occurred. Kipling was indiscreet enough to remark to one of the neighbours that he had had "to carry Beatty for the last year – to hold him up by the seat of his breeches." This soon reached his brother-in-law's ears. One day Beatty, driving his team and drunk, met Kipling riding his bicycle. He blocked the road, making Kipling fall off, and shouted angrily: "See here! I want to talk to you!" Kipling answered, "If you have anything to say, say it to my lawyers." "By Jesus, this is no case for lawyers!" retorted Beatty, loosing a tirade of profanity and abuse. He threatened Kipling, according to Kipling, to kill him; according to Beatty, merely to beat him up if he did not make a public retraction.[18]

Kipling had always deplored the lawlessness of America; in his account of his first trip through the West, his disgust and trepidation over the shootings of the frontier are expressed in almost every chapter. And he now became seriously alarmed. He proceeded to have Beatty arrested on charges of "assault with indecent and opprobrious names and epithets and threatening to kill." He did not realise that that kind of thing was not done in the United States, where such quarrels were settled man to man, and he could not foresee the consequences. Beatty, who loved scandal, was delighted. He allowed the case to come into court and watched Kipling, who hated publicity, make himself ridiculous in public. The Kiplings at last fled abroad – it was August 1896 – before the case could come before the Grand Jury.

"So far as I was concerned," says Kipling of his relations with Americans in general, "I felt the atmosphere was to some extent hostile."[19] It was a moment of antagonism toward England. In the summer of 1895, Venezuela had appealed to the United States for protection against the English in a dispute over the boundaries of British Guiana, and President Cleveland had invoked the Monroe Doctrine and demanded in strong language that England submit the question to arbitration. The Jameson raid on the Transvaal Republic early in 1896, an unauthorised

[18] [*Rudyard Kipling's Vermont Feud*, New York 1937, pp. 91-2, 15-16.]
[19] [*Something of Myself*, Chapter Five.]

and defeated attempt by an agent of the British South Africa
Company to provoke a rising against the Boers, had intensified
the feeling against England. Kipling was brought face to face
with the issue by an encounter with another American who
seemed almost as unrestrained as Beatty Balestier. When Kipling
met Theodore Roosevelt, then Assistant Secretary of the Navy,
the latter "thanked God in a loud voice that he had not one drop
of British blood in him," that his ancestry was pure Dutch, and
declared that American fear of the British would provide him
with funds for a new navy. John Hay had told Kipling that it
was hatred of the English that held the United States together.

But during the years that immediately followed the Kiplings'
return to England, American relations with England improved.
The United States took over the Philippines in 1898 as a result of
the Spanish War, and annexed the Hawaiian Islands; and the
imperialistic England of Joseph Chamberlain, in fear of Germany,
which had favoured the Spanish, became extremely sympathetic
with the policy of the United States. At the beginning of 1899,
then, Rudyard Kipling set forth on an attempt to retrieve his
position in America, where he had abandoned the big Brattleboro
house. He first composed the celebrated set of verses, in which he
exhorted the United States to collaborate with the British Empire
in "taking up the White Man's burden" of "your new-caught,
sullen peoples, half-devil and half-child," who were to be benefited and disciplined in spite of themselves, though at a bitter
expense to their captors; and had the poem published on both
sides of the Atlantic early in February, at the moment of his
sailing for America. But what confronted him on his landing
was an announcement in the New York papers that Beatty
Balestier was bringing a $50,000 countersuit against him for
"malicious persecution, false arrest and defamation of character":
and the report that Beatty himself either had arrived in New York
or was just about to arrive. It was simply another of Beatty's
gestures: no suit was ever brought; but it prevented the Kiplings
from returning to Vermont. Rudyard had caught cold on the
boat, and he now came down with double pneumonia and
seemed in danger of not pulling through. His two little girls had
pneumonia, too, and one of them died while he was ill. When
he recovered, he had to hear of her death. He went back to

England in June, as soon as he was able to travel, and never tried to live in the United States again.

"It will be long and long," he wrote in a letter supposed to date from 1900, "before I could bring myself to look at the land of which she [his daughter] was so much a part." And his cousin Angela Thirkell writes that, "Much of the beloved Cousin Ruddy of our childhood died with Josephine and I feel that I have never seen him as a real person since that year."[20]

The fear and hatred awakened in Kipling by those fatal six years of his childhood had been revived by the discipline of Westward Ho! The menaces of Beatty Balestier, behind which must have loomed for Kipling all that was wild, uncontrollable, brutal in the life of the United States, seem to have prodded again the old inflammation. The schoolboy, rendered helpless in a fight by his bad eyes and his small stature, was up against the bully again, and fear drove him to appeal to the authorities. How else can we account for the fact that the relations of Kipling with Beatty were ever allowed to get to this point? The truth was, as Beatty himself later confessed to Mr Van de Water, that Rudyard had become involved in a family quarrel between himself and his sister; and one's impulse is to say that Kipling ought to have been able to find some way of extricating himself and making contact with the rather childlike friendliness that seems to have lurked behind the rodomontade of Beatty. But the terrible seriousness of the issue which the incident had raised for Kipling is shown by his statement at the hearing that he "would not retract a word under threat of death from any living man."[21]

5

It was the fight he had fought at school, and he would not capitulate to Beatty Balestier. But he surrendered at last to the "Proosian Bates." He invoked the protection of the British system and at the same time prostrated himself before the power of British conquest, which was feared in the United States and which even at that moment in South Africa – the Transvaal Republic declared war on Great Britain in the October of the year of his return – was chastising truculent farmers.

[20] [*Three Houses*, London 1931, p. 86.]
[21] [*Rudyard Kipling's Vermont Feud*, p. 111.]

It is at the time of his first flight from America and during the years before his attempt to return – 1897-99 – that Kipling goes back to his school-days and depicts them in the peculiar colours that we find in *Stalky & Co.* How little inevitable these colours were we learn from Mr Beresford's memoir. The headmaster of Westward Ho!, it appears, though really known as the "Proosian Bates," was by no means the intent Spartan trainer for the bloody and risky work of the Empire into which Kipling thought it proper to transform him. The fact was that Mr Cormell Price had been literary rather than military, a friend of Edward Burne-Jones, and an earnest anti-Imperialist. He and Burne-Jones had actually organised, at the time of the Russo-Turkish War, a Workers' Neutrality Demonstration against British intervention. But Kipling must now have a headmaster who will symbolise all the authority of the British educational system, and a school that will represent all that he has heard or imagined – see his high-lighting of the fagging system – about the older and more official public schools. The colonial who has criticised the motherland now sets out systematically to glorify her; and it is the proof of his timidity and weakness that he should loudly overdo this glorification.

And now, having declared his allegiance, he is free to hate the enemies of England. His whole point of view has shifted. The bitter animus so deeply implanted by those six years of oppression of his childhood has now become almost entirely dissociated from the objects by which it was originally aroused. It has turned into a generalised hatred of those nations, groups and tendencies precisely, which stand toward the dominating authority in the relationship of challengers or victims.

The ideal of the "Anglo-American-German Jew," which at the time of Kipling's first trip to America represented for him the future of civilisation, now immediately goes by the board. His whole tone toward the Americans changes. In "An Error in the Fourth Dimension"– in *The Day's Work*, published in 1898 – he makes a rich Anglicised American, the son of a railroad king, deciding for no very good reason that he must immediately go to London, flag and stop an English express train. The railroad first brings charges against him, then decides that he must be insane. They cannot understand his temerity, and he cannot understand their consternation at having the British routine interrupted. Kipling no longer admires the boldness of Americans: this story is a hateful caricature, so one-sided that the real comedy is sacrificed. "The Captive"[22] followed in 1902. Here a man from Ohio named Laughton O. Zigler sells to the Boers, during their war with the British, a new explosive and a new machine-gun he has invented. He is captured by the English, who grin at him and ask him why he "wasn't in the Filipeens suppressing our war!" Later he runs into a man from Kentucky, who refuses to shake his hand and tells him that "he's gone back on the White Man in six places at once – two hemispheres and four continents – America, England, Canada, Australia, New Zealand, and South Africa. . . . Go on and prosper . . . and you'll fetch up by fighting for niggers, as the North did." As a result of these taunts, and of the respect which has been inspired in him by the spectacle of the splendid behaviour of the British, Mr Zigler gives them the formula for his explosive, insists upon remaining their prisoner, and resolves to settle permanently in South Africa. A still later story, "An Habitation Enforced," in a collection published in 1909,[23] tells of the victory of the English countryside over an American businessman and his wife, who have been aimlessly travelling about Europe. The American wife discovers that her own ancestors came originally from the very locality where they have settled, and they are finally – it is the climax of the story – accepted by the English: "That wretched Sangres man has twice our money. Can you see Marm Conant slapping him between the shoulders? Not by a jugful! The poor beast doesn't exist!" The Americans succumb, deeply gratified. The husband had had a breakdown from overwork, but his equanimity is quite re-established. In short, Kipling's attitude toward Americans has now been almost reversed since the day of his first visit to the States when he had written, "I love this People." He now approves of them only when they are prepared to pay their tribute to Mother England and to identify her interests with theirs.

Later still, during the first years of the World War when Americans were figuring as neutrals, his bitterness became absolutely murderous – as in "Sea Constables: A Tale of '15" –

<hr />

[22] [*Traffics and Discoveries.*]   [23] [*Actions and Reactions.*]

and so had his feeling against the Germans even before the war had begun. In "The Edge of the Evening" (1913),[24] Laughton O. Zigler of Ohio turns up again, this time in England, as occupant of a Georgian mansion inherited by one of the British officers who captured him in South Africa. "Bein' rich suits me. So does your country, sir. My own country? You heard what that Detroit man said at dinner. 'A Government of the alien, by the alien, for the alien.' Mother's right, too. Lincoln killed us. From the highest motives – but he killed us." What his mother had said was that Lincoln had "wasted the heritage of his land by blood and fire, and had surrendered the remnant to aliens": " 'My brother, suh,' she said, 'fell at Gettysburg in order that Armenians should colonise New England to-day.' " (*Something of Myself* confirms the assumption that these were Kipling's own views.) One night a foreign plane makes a forced landing on the estate. Two men get out of the plane, and one of them shoots at his lordship. Zigler lays him out with a golf-club while another of the Englishmen present collars the other man and breaks his neck (it is all right for an American to be lawless, or even for the right sort of Englishman, if he is merely laying low the alien who is the natural enemy of both). They put the dead German spies in the plane and send it up and out over the Channel.

Kipling is now, in fact, implacably opposed to every race and nation which has rebelled against or competed with the Empire, and to every movement and individual – such as the Liberals and Fabians – in England who has criticised the imperial policies. His attitude toward the Irish, for example, illustrates the same simple-minded principle as his attitude toward the Americans. So long as the Irish are loyal to England, Kipling shows the liveliest appreciation of Irish recklessness and the Irish sense of mischief: Mulvaney is Irish, M'Turk is Irish, Kim is Irish. But the moment they display these same qualities in agitation against the English, they become infamous assassins and traitors. Those peoples who have never given trouble – the Canadians, the New Zealanders, the Australians – though Kipling has never found them interesting enough to write about on any considerable scale, he credits with the most admirable virtues.

And as a basis for all these exclusions, he has laid down a

[24] [*A Diversity of Creatures.*]

more fundamental principle for the hatred and fear of his fellows: the anti-democratic principle. We are familiar with the case of the gifted man who has found himself at a disadvantage in relation to his social superiors and who makes himself the champion of all who have suffered in a similar way. What is not so familiar is the inverse of this: the case of the individual who at the period when he has most needed freedom to develop superior abilities has found himself cramped and tormented by the stupidity of social inferiors, and who has in consequence acquired a distrust of the whole idea of popular government. Rudyard Kipling was probably an example of this. The ferocious antagonism to democracy which finally overtakes him must have been fed by the fear of that household at Southsea which tried to choke his genius at its birth. His sister says that through all this period he was in the habit of keeping up their spirit by reminding himself and her that their guardian was "of such low caste as not to matter . . . She was a *Kuch-nay*, a Nothing-at-all, and that secret name was a great comfort to us, and useful, too, when Harry practised his talent for eavesdropping."[25] Some very unyielding resistance was evidently built up at this time against the standards and opinions of people whom he regarded as lower-class.

The volume called *Traffics and Discoveries*, published in 1904, marks the complete metamorphosis of Kipling. The collection that preceded, *The Day's Work*, though these tendencies had already begun to appear in it, still preserves certain human values: the English officials in the Indian stories – "The Tomb of His Ancestors" and "William the Conqueror" – still display some sympathetic interest in the natives. But the Kipling of the South African stories is venomous, morbid, distorted.

When the Boer War finally breaks, Kipling is at once on the spot, with almost all the correct reactions. He is now at the zenith of his reputation, and he receives every official courtesy. And though he may criticise the handling of a campaign, he never questions the rightness of its object. He has the impulse to get close to the troops, edits a paper for the soldiers; but his attitude toward the Tommy has changed. He had already been entertained and enlightened by Lord Dufferin, the British Viceroy

[25] [*Chambers's Journal*, Eighth Series, VIII, 169.]

in India. Hitherto, he tells us in his memoirs, he "had seen administrative machinery from beneath, all stripped and overheated. This was the first time I had listened to one who had handled it from above."[26] Another passage from *Something of Myself* shows how his emphasis has altered:

> I happened to fall unreservedly, in darkness, over a man near the train, and filled my palms with gravel. He explained in an even voice that he was "fractured 'ip, sir. 'Ope you ain't 'urt yourself, sir?" I never got at this unknown Philip Sidney's name. They were wonderful even in the hour of death – these men and boys – lodge-keepers and ex-butlers of the Reserve and raw town-lads of twenty.[27]

Here he is trying to pay a tribute; yet it is obvious that the Kipling who was proud to be questioned in India by Lord Roberts as if he were a colonel has triumphed over the Kipling who answered him as a spokesman for the unfortunate soldiers. Today he is becoming primarily a man whom a soldier addresses as "sir," as a soldier is becoming for Kipling a man whose capacity for heroism is indicated by remaining respectful with a fractured hip. The cockney Ortheris of *Soldiers Three* and the officer who had insulted him at drill had waived the Courts-martial manual and fought it out man to man; but by the time of the Boer War the virtue of Kipling's officers and soldiers consists primarily in knowing their stations.

Kipling had written at the beginning of the war a poem called "The Absent-minded Beggar," which was an appeal for contributions to a fund for the families of the troops in South Africa; but this poem is essentially a money-raising poem: it had nothing like the spontaneous feeling of

> I went into a public-'ouse to get a pint o' beer,
> The publican 'e up an' sez, "We serve no red-coats 'ere."

The Barrack-Room Ballads were good in their kind: they gave the Tommy a voice, to which people stopped and listened. Kipling was interested in the soldier for his own sake, and made some effort to present his life as it seemed to the soldier himself. The

[26] [*Something of Myself*, Chapter Four. This visit to Lord Dufferin was made in October 1890. ED.]   [27] [*Op. cit.*, Chapter Six.]

poem called "Loot," for example, which worries Mr Edward
Shanks because it appears to celebrate a reprehensible practice,
is in reality perfectly legitimate because it simply describes one
of the features of the soldier's experience in India. There is no
moral one way or the other. The ballads of *The Five Nations*, on
the other hand, the fruits of Kipling's experience in South Africa,
are about 90 per cent. mere rhymed journalism decorating the
readymade morality of a patriotic partisan. Compare one of the
most successful of the earlier series with one of the most ambitious
of the later.

> The Injian Ocean sets an' smiles
>   So sof', so bright, so bloomin' blue;
> There aren't a wave for miles an' miles
>   Excep' the jiggle from the screw.
> The ship is swep', the day is done,
>   The bugle's gone for smoke and play;
> An' black agin' the settin' sun
>   The Lascar sings, '*Hum deckty hai!*'
>
> *For to admire an' for to see,*
>   *For to be'old this world so wide –*
> *It never done no good to me,*
>   *But I can't drop it if I tried!*

Contrast this with "The Return" (from South Africa):

> Peace is declared, an' I return
>   To 'Ackneystadt, but not the same;
> Things 'ave transpired which made me learn
>   The size an' meanin' of the game.
> I did no more than others did,
>   I don't know where the change began.
> I started as an average kid,
>   I finished as a thinkin' man.
>
> *If England was what England seems*
>   *An' not the England of our dreams,*
> *But only putty, brass an' paint,*
>   *'Ow quick we'd drop 'er! But she ain't!*
>
> Before my gappin' mouth could speak
>   I 'eard it in my comrade's tone.
> I saw it on my neighbour's cheek
>   Before I felt it flush my own.

An' last it come to me – not pride,
Nor yet conceit, but on the 'ole
(If such a term may be applied),
The makin's of a bloomin' soul.

This is hollow, synthetic, sickening. *"Having no position to consider and my trade enforcing it, I could move at will in the fourth dimension."* He *has* a position to consider to-day, he eats at the captain's table, travels in special trains; and he is losing the freedom of that fourth dimension. There is a significant glimpse of the Kipling of the South African imperialist period in the diary of Arnold Bennett:

> I was responding to Pauline Smith's curiosity about the personalities of authors when Mrs Smith began to talk about Kipling. She said he was greatly disliked in South Africa. Regarded as conceited and unapproachable. The officers of the Union Castle ships dreaded him, and prayed not to find themselves on the same ship as him. It seems that on one ship he had got all the information possible out of the officers, and had then, at the end of the voyage, reported them at headquarters for flirting with passengers – all except the chief engineer, an old Scotchman with whom he had been friendly. With this exception they were all called up to headquarters and reprimanded, and now they would have nothing to do with passengers.[28]

As for the Indians, they are now to be judged rigorously on the basis of their loyalty to the English in Africa. There are included in *Traffics and Discoveries* two jingoistic Sunday School stories which are certainly among the falsest and most foolish of Kipling's mature productions. In "The Comprehension of Private Copper," he vents his contempt on an Anglicised Indian, the son of a settler in the Transvaal, who has sided with the Boers against the English; "A Sahibs' War," on the other hand, presents an exemplary Sikh, who accompanies a British officer to South Africa, serves him with the devotion of a dog, and continues to practise after his leader's death the public-school principle of sportsmanship he has learned from him, in the face of the temptation to a cruel revenge against the treachery of the

[28] [*The Journal of Arnold Bennett*, New York 1933, p. 319.]

Boers. As for the Boers themselves, Kipling adopts towards them a systematic sneer. The assumption appears to be that to ambush the British is not cricket. Though the Dutch are unquestionably white men, Kipling manages somehow to imply that they have proved renegades to white solidarity by allying themselves with the black natives.

One is surprised to learn from *Something of Myself* that over a period of seven years after the war (1900-07), Kipling spent almost half his time in South Africa, going there for five or six months every year. He seems to have so little to show for it: a few short stories, and most of these far from his best. He had made the acquaintance of Cecil Rhodes, and must simply have sat at his feet. The Kiplings lived in a house just off the Rhodes estate; and Kipling devotes long pages to the animals in Rhodes's private zoo and to architectural details of Rhodes's houses. Even writing in 1935, he sounds like nothing so much as a high-paid publicity agent. It turns out that the Polonius-precepts in the celebrated verses called "If—" were inspired by Kipling's conception of the character of Dr Jameson, the leader of the Jameson raid.

It may be worth mentioning here in connexion with Kipling's submission to official authority that he has been described by a close friend, Viscount Castlerosse, as having abdicated his authority also in other important relations. "They [the Kiplings]," he says,

> were among the few happy pairs I have ever met; but as far as Kipling was concerned, his married life was one of complete surrender. To him Carrie, as he called her, was more than a wife. She was a mistress in the literal sense, a governess and a matron. In a lesser woman I should have used the term "nurse". Kipling handed himself over bodily, financially and spiritually to his spouse. He had no banking account. All the money which he earned was handed over to her, and she, in turn, would dole him out so much pocket money. He could not call his time or even his stomach his own. . . .
> Sometimes in the evening, enlivened by wine and company, he would take a glass more than he was accustomed to, and then those great big eyes of his would shine brightly behind

his strong spectacles, and Rud would take to talking faster and his views would become even more emphatic. If Mrs Kipling was with him, she would quickly note the change and, sure enough, in a decisive voice she would issue the word of command: "Rud, it is time you went to bed", and Rud always discovered that it was about time he went to bed.

I myself during the long years never once saw any signs of murmuring or of even incipient mutiny.[29]

In any case, Kipling has committed one of the most serious sins against his calling which are possible for an imaginative writer. He has resisted his own sense of life and discarded his own moral intelligence in favour of the point of view of a dominant political party. To Lord Roberts and Joseph Chamberlain he has sacrificed the living world of his own earlier artistic creations and of the heterogeneous human beings for whom they were offered as symbols. Here the constraint of making the correct pro-imperialist point is squeezing out all the kind of interest which is proper to a work of fiction. Compare a story of the middle Kipling with a story by Stephen Crane or Joseph Conrad, who were dealing with somewhat similar subjects. Both Conrad and Crane are pursuing their independent researches into the moral life of man. Where the spy who is the hero of *Under Western Eyes* is a tormented and touching figure, confused in his allegiances by the circumstances of his birth, a secret agent in Kipling must invariably be either a stout fellow, because his ruses are to the advantage of the British, or a sinister lying dog, because he is serving the enemy. Where the killing of "The Blue Hotel" is made to implicate everybody connected with it in a common human guilt, a killing in a story by Kipling must absolutely be shown to be either a dastardly or a virtuous act.

To contrast Kipling with Conrad or Crane is to enable us to get down at last to what is probably the basic explanation of the failure of Kipling's nerve. He lacked faith in the artist's vocation. We have heard a good deal in modern literature about the artist in conflict with the *bourgeois* world. Flaubert made war on the *bourgeois*; Rimbaud abandoned poetry as piffling in order to realise the adventure of commerce; Thomas Mann took as his

---

[29] [Cp. Charles Carrington, *Rudyard Kipling*, London 1955, pp. 451-2, 516.]

theme the emotions of weakness and defeat of the artist over-
shadowed by the businessman. But Kipling neither faced the
fight like Flaubert, nor faced the problem in his life like Rimbaud,
nor faced the problem in his art like Mann. Something in him,
something vulgar in the middle-class British way, something
perhaps connected with the Methodist ministers who were his
grandfathers on both sides, a tradition which understood preaching and could understand craftsmanship, but had a good deal of
respect for the powers that governed the material world and
never thought of putting the artist on a par with them – something of this sort at a given point prevented Kipling from playing
through his part, and betrayed him into dedicating his talents to
the praise of the practical man. Instead of *becoming* a man of
action like Rimbaud, a course which shows a boldness of logic,
he fell into the ignominious role of the artist who prostrates his
art before the achievements of soldiers and merchants, and who
is always declaring the supremacy of the "doer" over the man of
ideas.

The results of this are very curious and well worth studying
from the artistic point of view – because Kipling it must always
be remembered, was a man of really remarkable abilities. Certain
of the symptoms of his case have been indicated by George
Moore and Dixon Scott, whose discussions of him in *Avowals* and
Men of Letters are among the few first-rate pieces of criticism that
I remember to have seen on the subject. George Moore quotes
a passage from *Kim*, a description of evening in India, and
praises it for "the perfection of the writing, of the strong masculine rhythm of every sentence, and of the accuracy of every
observation"; but then goes on to point out that "Mr Kipling
has seen much more than he has felt," that "when we come to
analyse the lines we find a touch of local colour not only in every
sentence, but in each part between each semicolon."[30] So Scott
diagnoses admirably the mechanical ingenuity of plot that dis-
tinguishes the middle Kipling.

Switch, [he says,] this imperatively map-making, pattern-
making method upon . . . the element of human nature, and
what is the inevitable result? Inevitably, there is the same

[30] [*Avowals*, London 1919, p. 170.]

sudden stiffening and formulation. The characters spring to attention like soldiers on parade; they respond briskly to a sudden description; they wear a fixed set of idiosyncrasies like a uniform. A mind like this *must* use types and set counters; it feels dissatisfied, ineffective, unsafe, unless it can reduce the fluid waverings of character, its flitting caprices and twilit desires, to some tangible system. The characters of such a man will not only be definite, they will be definitions.[31]

And he goes on to show how Kipling's use of dialect makes a screen for his relinquishment of his grip on the real organism of human personality:

For dialect, in spite of all its air of ragged lawlessness, is wholly impersonal, typical, fixed, the code of a caste, not the voice of an individual. It is when the novelist sets his characters talking King's English that he really puts his capacity for reproducing the unconventional and capricious on its trial. Mr Kipling's plain conversations are markedly unreal. But honest craftsmanship and an ear for strong rhythms have provided him with many suits of dialects. And with these he dresses the talk till it seems to surge with character.[32]

The packed detail, the automatic plot, the surfaces lacquered with dialect, the ever-tightening tension of form, are all a part of Kipling's effort to impose his scheme by main force. The strangest result of this effort is to be seen in a change in the subject matter itself. Kipling actually tends at this time to abandon human beings altogether. In that letter of Henry James in which he speaks of his former hope that Kipling might grow into an English Balzac, he goes on: "But I have quite given that up in proportion as he has come steadily from the less simple in subject to the more simple – from the Anglo-Indians to the natives, from the natives to the Tommies, from the Tommies to the quadrupeds, from the quadrupeds to the fish, and from the fish to the engines and screws."[33] This increasing addiction of Kipling to animals, insects and machines is evidently to be explained by his need to

---

[31] [*Men of Letters*, London 1923, pp. 57-8.]
[32] [*Op. cit.*, pp. 59-60.]
[33] [*The Letters of Henry James*, ed. Lubbock, 1, 278.]

find characters which will yield themselves unresistingly to being presented as parts of a system. In the *Jungle Books*, the animal characters are each one all of a piece, though in their ensemble they still provide a variety, and they are dominated by a "Law of the Jungle," which lays down their duties and rights. The animals have organised the Jungle, and the Jungle is presided over by Mowgli in his function of forest ranger, so that it falls into its subsidiary place in the larger organisation of the Empire.

Yet the *Jungle Books* (written in Vermont) are not artistically off the track; the element of obvious allegory is not out of place in such fairy tales. It is when Kipling takes to contriving these animal allegories for grown-ups that he brings up the reader's gorge. What is proved in regard to human beings by the fable called "A Walking Delegate," in which a pastureful of self-respecting horses turn and rend a yellow loafer from Kansas, who is attempting to incite them to rebellion against their master, Man? A labour leader and the men he is trying to organise are, after all, not horses but men. Does Kipling mean to imply that the ordinary working man stands in the same relation to the employing and governing classes as that in which the horse stands to its owner? And what is proved by "The Mother Hive," in which an invasion of wax-moths that ruin the stock of the swarm represents the infiltration of socialism? (Compare these with that more humane fable of 1893, "The Children of the Zodiac," which deals with gods become men.) And, though the discipline of a military unit or of the crew of a ship or a plane may provide a certain human interest, it makes us a little uncomfortable to find Kipling taking up locomotives and representing ".007" instead of the engineer who drives it as the hero of the American railroad; and descending even to the mechanical parts, the rivets and planks of a ship, whose drama consists solely of being knocked into place by the elements so that it may function as a co-ordinated whole.

We may lose interest, like Henry James, in the animal or mechanical characters of Kipling's middle period; but we must admit that these novel productions have their own peculiar merit. It is the paradox of Kipling's career that he should have extended the conquests of his craftsmanship in proportion to the shrinking of the range of his dramatic imagination. As his responses to human beings became duller, his sensitivity to his medium increased.

In both tendencies he was, of course, quite faithful to certain aspects of the life of his age. It was a period, those early nineteen-hundreds, of brilliant technological improvement and of generally stunted intelligence. And Kipling now appeared as the poet both of the new mechanical methods and of the ideals of the people who spread them. To re-read these stories to-day is to feel again a little of the thrill of the plushy transcontinental Pullmans and the spick-and-span transatlantic liners that carried us around in our youth, and to meet again the bright and bustling people, talking about the polo field and the stock market, smart Paris and lovely California, the latest musical comedy and Kipling, in the smoking-rooms or among the steamer-chairs.

Kipling reflected this mechanical progress by evolving a new prose technique. We have often since Kipling's day been harangued by the Futurists and others about the need for artistic innovations appropriate to the life of the machine age; but it is doubtful whether any rhapsodist of motor-cars or photographer of dynamos and valves has been so successful at this as Kipling was at the time he wrote *The Day's Work*. These stories of his get their effects with the energy and accuracy of engines, by means of words that, hard, short and close-fitting, give the impression of ball-bearings and cogs. Beside them, the spoutings of the machine fans look like the old-fashioned rhetoric they are. For these latter could merely whoop and roar in a manner essentially romantic over the bigness, the power, the speed of the machines, whereas Kipling exemplified in his form itself the mechanical efficiency and discipline, and he managed to convey with precision both the grimness and the exhilaration which characterised the triumph of the machine.

He also brought to perfection the literary use of the language of the specialised industrial world. He must have been the principal artisan in the creation of that peculiar modern *genre* in which we are made to see some comedy or tragedy through the cheapening or obscuring medium of technical vocabulary or professional slang. He did not, of course, invent the dialect monologue; but it is improbable that we should have had, for example, either the baseball stories of Ring Lardner or the Cyclops episode in *Ulysses* if Kipling had never written.

This is partly no doubt pure virtuosity. Mr Beresford says that Kipling was by nature as unmechanical as possible, could do nothing with his hands except write; and I have heard an amusing story of his astonishment and admiration at the mechanical proficiency of an American friend who had simply put a castor back on a chair. He had never worked at any of the processes he described, had had to get them all up through the methods of the attentive reporter. But it is virtuosity on a much higher level than that of the imitation literature so often admired in that era. Where Stevenson turns out paler *pastiches* of veins which have already been exploited, Kipling really finds new rhythms, new colours and textures of words, for things that have not yet been brought into literature. For the most part a second-rate writer of verse, because though he can imitate the language of poetry as he can imitate all the other languages, he cannot compensate for the falsity of his feeling by his sharp observation and his expert technique, he is extraordinary as a worker in prose. It is impossible still for a prose writer to read, for example, the first part of "The Bridge-Builders" without marvelling at the author's mastery. How he has caught the very look and feel of the materials that go to make bridges and of the various aspects of the waters they have to dominate! And the manoeuvres of modern armies against the dusty South African landscapes, and the tempo of American trains, and the relation of the Scotch engineer to the patched-up machines of his ship. The Kipling who put on record all these things was an original and accomplished artist.

For the rest, he writes stories for children. One is surprised in going back over Kipling's work to find that, dating from the time of his settling with his family in Vermont, he published no less than nine children's books: the two *Jungle Books, Captains Courageous, Just So Stories, Stalky & Co., Puck of Pook's Hill, Rewards and Fairies, A History of England, Land and Sea Tales for Scouts and Scout Masters.* It is as if the natural human feelings progressively forced out of his work by the rigours of organisation for its own sake were seeking relief in a reversion to childhood, when one has not yet become responsible for the way that the world is run, where it is enough to enjoy and to wonder at what we do not yet understand. And, on the other hand, the simplified morality to which Kipling has now committed himself is easier to make acceptable to one's readers and oneself if one approaches it from the point of view of the child. (The truth is that much of his work of this period which aims at the intelligence of grown people might almost equally well be subtitled *For Scouts and Scout Masters*.) These stories, excellent at their best, are most successful when they are *most* irresponsible – as in the *Just So Stories*; least so, as in *Captains Courageous*, when they lean most heavily on the schoolboy morality.

The most ambitious of them – the two series about Puck of Pook's Hill (1906 and 1910) – have, I know, been much admired by certain critics, including the sensitive Dixon Scott; but my own taste rejects them on re-reading them as it did when I read them first at the age for which they were presumably intended. Kipling tells us that the stories in *Rewards and Fairies* were designed to carry a meaning for adults as well as to interest children. But their technical sophistication puts them slightly above the heads of children at the same time that their sugared exploitation of Kipling's Anglo-Spartan code of conduct makes them slightly repugnant to grown-ups.

They are, to be sure, the most embroidered productions of Kipling's most elaborate period. The recovery of obsolete arts and crafts, the re-creation of obsolete idioms, are new pretexts for virtuosity. Kipling's genius for words has been stimulated by the discovery of the English earth and sea; he spreads on the rich grassiness of the English country, the dense fogginess of the English coast, the layers upon layers of tradition that cause the English character to seem to him deep-rooted, deep-coloured, deep-meaning. He has applied all his delicacy and strength to this effort to get the mother-country into prose; but his England is never so real as was his India; and the effect, for all the sinewy writing, is somehow fundamentally decadent. The Normans and the Saxons and the Elizabethans, the great cathedral-builders and sailors and divines, perpetrating impossible "gags," striking postures that verge on the "ham," seem almost to anticipate Hollywood. The theme of the role and the ordeal of the artist which figures in *Rewards and Fairies* suffers from being treated in the vein of *Stalky & Co.* In the story called "The Wrong Thing," he embarks on a promising subject: the discrepancy between the aim of the artist who is straining to top the standards of his craft, and the quite irrelevant kinds of interest that the powers that employ him may take in him; but he turns it into a farce and ruins it.

Kipling's England is perhaps the most synthetic of all his creations of this period, when he depends so much on tools and materials as distinguished from sympathy and insight. Scott says that these stories are opalescent; and this is true, but they show the defects of opals that have been artificially made and whose variegated glimmerings and shiftings do not seem to convey anything mysterious.

6

Yet, in locating the Ideal in the Empire, Kipling was not without his moments of uneasiness. *If* the Empire is really founded on self-discipline, the fear of God, the code of *noblesse oblige*, if it really involves a moral system, then we are justified in identifying it with "the Law"; but suppose that it is not really so dedicated.

> If England was what England seems,
> An' not the England of our dreams,
> But only putty, brass an' paint,
> 'Ow quick we'd drop 'er! *But she ain't!*

Yet "Recessional," perhaps the best set of verses that Kipling ever wrote, is a warning that springs from a doubt; and the story called "The Man Who Would Be King" is surely a parable of what might happen to the English if they should forfeit their moral authority. Two low-class English adventurers put themselves over on the natives of a remote region beyond Afghanistan, organise under a single rule a whole set of mountain tribes; but the man who has made himself king is destroyed by the natives that have adored him the instant they come to realise that he is not a god, as they had supposed, but a man. The Wesleyan preacher in Kipling knows that the valiant dust of man can build only on dust if it builds not in the name of God; and he is prepared to pound the pulpit and call down the Almighty's anger when parliamentarians or ministers or generals debauch their office or hold it light. Kipling always refused official honours in

KMA E

order to keep himself free; and his truculence had its valuable aspect in that it aided him to resist the briberies of his period of glory and fortune. In the volume of his collected addresses, which he calls *A Book of Words*, there are some sincere and inspiriting sermons. "Now I do not ask you not to be carried away by the first rush of the great game of life. That is expecting you to be more than human," he told the students at McGill University in the fall of 1907, when the height of his popularity was past.

But I *do* ask you, after the first heat of the game, that you draw breath and watch your fellows for a while. Sooner or later, you will see some man to whom the idea of wealth as mere wealth does not appeal, whom the methods of amassing that wealth do not interest, and who will not accept money if you offer it to him at a certain price. At first you will be inclined to laugh at this man and to think that he is not "smart" in his ideas. I suggest that you watch him closely, for he will presently demonstrate to you that money dominates everybody except the man who does not want money. You may meet that man on your farm, in your village, or in your legislature. But be sure that, whenever or wherever you meet him, as soon as it comes to a direct issue between you, his little finger will be thicker than your loins. You will go in fear of him: he will not go in fear of you. You will do what he wants: he will not do what you want. You will find that you have no weapon in your armoury with which you can attack him; no argument with which you can appeal to him. Whatever you gain, he will gain more.

If Kipling had taken a bribe, it was not that of reputation or cash; it was rather the big moral bribe that a political system can offer: the promise of mental security. And even here a peculiar integrity – as it were, an integrity of *temperament* that came to exist in dissociation from the intellect – survived the collapse of the system and saved Kipling in the end from his pretences. How this happened is the last chapter of his story.

There was, as I say, a Wesleyan preacher in Kipling. The Old Testament served him as an armoury of grim instances and menacing visions to drive home the imperial code; or, on occasions when the imperial masters failed to live up to this code, of scorching rhetorical language (though with more of malignancy than of grandeur) for the chastisement of a generation of vipers. But Kipling had no real religion. He exploited, in his poems and his fiction, the mythology of a number of religions.

We may be inclined to feel, in reading Kipling – and to some extent we shall be right – that the various symbols and gods which figure in his stories and poems are mere properties which the writer finds useful for his purposes of rhetoric or romance. Yet we cannot but suspect in *Kim* and in the stories of metempsychosis that Kipling has been seriously influenced by the Buddhism which he had imbibed with his first language in his boyhood. Mr Beresford corroborates this: he says that the Kipling of Westward Ho! talked Buddhism and reincarnation. And it is certainly with Buddhism that we first find associated a mystical side of Kipling's mind which, in this last phase, is to emerge into the foreground.

We left the Lama of *Kim* attaining the Buddhist ecstasy and escaping from the Wheel of Things at the same moment that Kim gets promotion and finally becomes a spoke in the wheel of British administration. But the world-beyond of the Lama is to seep back into Kipling's work in queer and incongruous forms. Among the strained political fables of the collection called *Traffics and Discoveries*, which is the beginning of the more sombre later Kipling, there is a story of a wireless operator who is possessed by the soul of Keats. It may be that Kipling's Southsea experience in driving him back into his imagination for defence against the horror of reality, had had the effect both of intensifying his fancies and of dissociating them from ordinary life – so that the ascent out of the Wheel of Things and the visitations of an alien soul became ways of representing this. The effort of the grown-up Kipling to embrace by the imagination, to master by a disciplined art, what he regarded as the practical realities is to be subject to sudden recoils. In the Kipling of the middle period, there is a suppressed but vital element which thrusts periodically a lunatic head out of a window of the well-bricked façade.

This element is connected with the Lama, but it is also connected with something else more familiar to the Western world: the visitations and alienations of what is now known as neurotic

personality. Here again Kipling was true to his age. While the
locomotives and airplanes and steamers were beating records
and binding continents, the human engine was going wrong. The
age of mechanical technique was also the age of the nerve sana-
torium. In the stories of the early Kipling, the intervention of
the supernatural has, as a rule, within the frame of the story
itself, very little psychological interest; but already in "They"
and "The Brushwood Boy" the dream and the hallucination are
taking on a more emphatic significance. With "The House
Surgeon" and "In The Same Boat," they are in process of emerging from the fairy tale: they become recognisable as psychiatric
symptoms. The depression described in "The House Surgeon"[34]
has been transferred, by the artifice of the story, to persons un-
concerned in the tragedy through the influence from a distance
of someone else; but the woman with whom the terror originates
is suffering morbidly from feelings of guilt, and the sensations
are evidently based on the first-hand experience of the author.

And it was just then that I was aware of a little grey shadow,
as it might have been a snowflake seen against the light,
floating at an immense distance in the background of my
brain. It annoyed me, and I shook my head to get rid of it.
Then my brain telegraphed that it was the forerunner of a
swift-striding gloom which there was yet time to escape if I
would force my thoughts away from it, as a man leaping for
life forces his body forward and away from the fall of a wall.
But the gloom overtook me before I could take in the meaning
of the message. I moved toward the bed, every nerve already
aching with the foreknowledge of the pain that was to be dealt
it, and sat down, while my amazed and angry soul dropped,
gulf by gulf, into that Horror of great darkness which is
spoken of in the Bible, and which, as auctioneers say, must be
experienced to be appreciated.

Despair upon despair, misery upon misery, fear after fear,
each causing their distinct and separate woe, packed in upon
me for an unrecorded length of time, until at last they blurred
together, and I heard a click in my brain like the click in the
ear when one descends in a diving-bell, and I knew that the

[34] [*Actions and Reactions.*]

pressures were equalized within and without, and that, for the moment, the worst was at an end. But I knew also that at any moment the darkness might come down anew; and while I dwelt on this speculation precisely as a man torments a raging tooth with his tongue, it ebbed away into the little grey shadow on the brain of its first coming, and once more I heard my brain, which knew what would recur, telegraph to every quarter for help, release or diversion.

And although the periodical irrational panics of the couple of "In the Same Boat" are explained as the result of pre-natal shocks, the description of the man and woman themselves, with their "nerve doctors," their desperate drug-taking, their shaky and futile journeys in flight from their neurotic fears, their peculiar neurotic relationship, constitutes an accurate account of a phenomenon of contemporary life which, at the time that Kipling was writing, had hardly been described in fiction.

Observe that in both these stories, as in the stories of war neurosis that will follow, the people who suffer thus are quite innocent, their agony is entirely unearned. I believe that the only cases in which the obsessive horror is connected with any kind of guilt are those in which a man is hounded to death by the vision of a woman he has wronged. This theme recurs regularly with Kipling from the time of "The Phantom Rickshaw," one of the very first of his short stories, through the remarkable "Mrs Bathurst" of his middle period, and up to the strange and poisoned "Dayspring Mishandled," which was one of the last things he wrote. We cannot speculate with very much assurance on the relation of this theme of betrayal to the other recurring themes of Kipling's work. We do not know enough about his life to be able to assign it to an assumption on the part of the six-year-old Kipling that he must somehow have sinned against the mother who had abandoned him so inexplicably at Southsea; or to relate it to the strange situation of Dick Heldar in *The Light that Failed*, who vainly adores, and goes blind in adoring, the inexplicably obdurate Maisie. All we can say is that the theme of the anguish which is suffered without being deserved has the appearance of having been derived from a morbid permanent feeling of injury inflicted by his experience at Southsea.

Certainly the fear of darkness passing into the fear of blindness which runs all through his work from *The Light that Failed* to "They" is traceable directly to his breakdown and to the frightening failure of his eyes. This was a pattern he seems to have repeated. Illnesses were critical for Kipling. It was after his illness in India that he set out to contend with a society which must have seemed to him indifferent and brutal by making himself a writer; and it was after his illness in New York that he decided to turn his back on America and to accept all the values that that retreat implied. It was after the breakdown in which Kim had brooded on his true identity that he emerged as a fullblown British agent. From the darkness and the physical weakness, the Kipling of the middle period has come forth with tightened nerves, resolved to meet a state of things in which horses are always being whipped or having their heads blown off, in which schoolboys are bullied and flogged, in which soldiers are imprisoned in barracks and fed to the bayonets and guns. By identifying himself with horses (as in the story called "A Walking Delegate") that gang together to kick and maul another horse, with schoolboys (as in "The Moral Reformers" of *Stalky*) that gloat in torturing other schoolboys, with soldiers that get the sharpest satisfaction from stabbing and pot-shotting other soldiers, he has set himself with all the stiff ribs of a metal-armatured art to stand up to this world outside that gets its authority from its power to crush and kill: the world of the Southsea house that has turned into the world of the Empire; to compete with it on its own terms. And yet the darkness and the illness return. It is a key to the whole work of Kipling that the great celebrant of physical courage should prove in the long run to convey his most moving and convincing effects in describing moral panic. Kipling's bullyings and killings are contemptible: they are the fantasies of the physically helpless. The only authentic heroism to be found in the fiction of Kipling is the heroism of moral fortitude on the edge of a nervous collapse.

And in the later decades of Kipling's life the blackness and the panic close down; the abyss becomes more menacing. It is the Crab, both devil and destiny, which in the story called "The Children of the Zodiac" lies always in wait for the poet and finally comes to devour him. The nurse-like watchfulness of

Mrs Kipling and Kipling's fear of stepping out of her regime, which appeared to his friend an impediment to the development of his genius, were no doubt, on the contrary, in his extreme instability, a condition of his being able to function at all – just as the violence of his determination to find the answer to the problems of society and a defence against the forces that plagued him in the programme of an imperialist government was evidently directly related to the violence of desperation of his need.

But now both of these shelters he had built himself – the roof of his family life, the confidence of his political idealism – were suddenly to be broken down.

In 1914-18, the British Empire collided with a competitor. All England went to war, including Kipling's only son. The boy, not yet out of his teens, was killed in an attack before Loos in September, 1915, and his body was never found. John Kipling had at first been reported missing, and his father waited for months in the hope of getting a letter from Germany announcing that he had been taken prisoner.

These war years left Kipling defenceless. It had been easy to be grimly romantic on the subject of the warfare in India when Kipling had never seen fighting; it had even been possible, as a reporter at the front, to Meissonier the campaign in South Africa in the bright colours of the new twentieth century. But the long systematic waste of the trench warfare of the struggle against Germany discouraged the artistic exploitation of the cruelties and gallantries of battle. The strain of the suspense and the horror taxed intolerably those attitudes of Kipling's which had been in the first instance provoked by a strain and which had only at the cost of a strain been kept up.

From even before the War, the conduct of British policy had been far from pleasing to Kipling. He saw clearly the careerism and the venality of the modern politician; and he was bitterly opposed on principle to the proposals of the Radicals and Liberals. In May, 1914, when civil war with Ulster was threatening, he delivered at Tunbridge Wells and allowed to be circulated as a penny leaflet a speech against the Home Rule Bill of a virulence almost hysterical. The attempt to free Ireland he excoriates as on a level with the Marconi scandals.

The Home Rule Bill [he declares] broke the pledged faith of generations; it officially recognized sedition, privy conspiracy and rebellion; it subsidized the secret forces of boycott, intimidation and murder; and it created an independent stronghold in which all these forces could work together, as they have always and openly boasted that they would, for the destruction of Great Britain.[35]

This was to remain Kipling's temper in public questions. The victory of the Bolsheviks in Russia of course made the picture blacker: one sixth of the area of the globe, he said, had "passed bodily out of civilisation."[36]

> Our world has passed away,
> In wantonness o'erthrown.
> There is nothing left to-day
> But steel and fire and stone![37]

he wrote when the War began. And when Kipling was sickened and broken with steel and fire and stone, there was little for his spirit to lean on.

Little but the practice of his craft, which now reflects only the twisted fragments of Kipling's exploded cosmos.

These latest stories of Kipling's have attracted meagre attention for reasons that are easily comprehensible. The disappearance in the middle Kipling of the interest in human beings for their own sake and the deliberate cultivation of the excommunicatory imperialist hatreds had already had the effect of discouraging the appetite of the general public; and when the human element reappeared in a new tormented form in Kipling's later stories, the elliptical and complex technique which the writer had by that time developed put the general reader off. On the other hand, the highbrows ignored him, because, in the era of Lawrence and Joyce, when the world was disgusted with soldiering and when the imperialisms were apparently deflated, they could take no interest in the point of view. In their conviction that Kipling could never hold water, they had not even enough curiosity to

[35] [*The Secret Bargain and the Ulster Plot.*]
[36] ["Independence," *A Book of Words.*]
[37] [" 'For all we have and are'," *The Years Between.*]

wonder what had happened to an author who must have en-
chanted them in their childhood. And in a sense they were, of
course, correct. Kipling *had* terribly shrunk; he seemed a man
who had had a stroke and was only half himself – whereas Yeats
was playing out superbly the last act of a personal drama which he
had sustained unembarrassed by public events, and Henry James
was now seen in retrospect to have accomplished, in his long
career, a prodigy of disinterested devotion to an art and a criticism
of life. Where there was so much wreckage around, political,
social and moral, the figure of the disinterested artist commanded
especial respect.

Yet the Kipling who limped out of the wreckage, shrunken
and wry though he looks, has in a sense had his development as
an artist. Some of these stories are the most intense in feeling as
they are among the most concentrated in form that Kipling ever
wrote; to a writer, they are perhaps the most interesting. The
subjects are sometimes hard to swallow, and the stories themselves – through a tasteless device which unfortunately grew on
Kipling as he got older – are each preceded and followed by
poems which elaborate or elucidate their themes in the author's
synthetic verse and which dull the effect of the excellent prose.
But here Kipling's peculiar method, trained with deadly intention,
scores some of its cleanest hits.

Let us, however, first consider the subjects of these final
collections of stories (*A Diversity of Creatures*, *Debits and Credits*,
and *Limits and Renewals*). The fragments of the disintegrated
Kipling fall roughly into five classes: tales of hatred, farces based
on practical jokes, studies of neurotic cases, tales of fellowship in
religion, and tales of personal bereavement.

The tales of hatred – hatred of Americans and the Germans:
"Sea Constables" and "Mary Postgate" – become murderous at
the time of the War (though they give place to other kinds of
themes later). The hatred of democracy – in the satire called "As
Easy as A.B.C." (which appeared in 1912) – is carried to lengths
that would be Swiftian if Kipling had subjected the whole human
race to the death ray of his abstract contempt, but which – as
Edward Shanks points out – is rendered rather suspect by the
exemption from the annihilating irony of a group of disciplined
officials. The morals of these stories are odious and the plots

mostly contrived and preposterous; yet they acquire a certain dignity from the desperation of bitterness that animates them.

Then there are the practical jokes – a category which includes the comic accidents: practical jokes engineered by the author. These have always been a feature of Kipling. His addiction to this form of humour seems to have derived originally from the boobytraps and baitings of Westward Ho!; later, changing sides, he identified them rather with the lickings-into-shape inflicted by regimental raggings. The victims of these pulverising hoaxes fall into two classes: petty tyrants, who humiliate and bully, and who always have to be cads; and political idealists and godless intellectuals, who have to be nincompoops. Kipling likes nothing better than to hurl one of these latter into a hive of bees or, as in one of his early stories, to silence his opinions by a sunstroke. A first principle of Kipling's world is revenge, the humiliated must become the humiliator. One might expect this kind of thing to disappear in the work of the latest Kipling; but the formula becomes instead much more frequent, and it comes to play a special role. The practical joke with its extravagant laughter is a violent if hollow explosion for the relief of nervous strain; and the severity of this strain may be gauged by the prodigious dimensions of the hoaxes in which Kipling now labours to concentrate the complex calculation of an Ibsen and the methodical ferocity of a Chinese executioner.

In some of these stories, the comic disaster is exploited as a therapeutic device. There are six stories of war neurosis in Kipling's last two collections. The situation of the shattered veteran provided him with an opportunity for studying further a subject which had haunted him all his life: the condition of people who seem to themselves on the borderline of madness. Here the sufferers are still perfectly guiltless. In one case, an appearance of guilt, in another, a conviction of guilt, turn out to be actually unjustified. But the picture is now more realistically filled out than it was by the pre-natal occurrences which were the best Kipling could do for motivation for the neurotics of "In the Same Boat." The War supplies real causes for derangement; and Kipling sees that such short-circuits may be mended by going back to the occasion that gave rise to the obsession and disentangling the crossed wires. But his principal prescriptions for saving people from the effects of the horror and the strain of the War are such apropos comic accidents and well-aimed benevolent frauds as, in reality, are rarely possible and which would be of doubtful efficacy if they were. In one story, the fantasy of the sick man turns out to be based on a reading in hospital of a novel by Mrs Ewing (as the soldiers in "The Janeites" find solace in the novels of Jane Austen) – which also gives the veteran, when he recovers, a beneficent interest in life: that of planting wayside gardens. Another ex-soldier is saved by a dog.

Kipling's homeless religious sense resorts to strange fellowships and faiths to bolster up his broken men. He had been made a Freemason in India, and Freemasonry had figured in *Kim* and had seemed to crop up in the guise of Mithraism in the Roman stories of *Puck of Pook's Hill*. Now he invents, for a new series of stories, a circle of philanthropic Masons who meet in the back room of a tobacconist's and who try to help men that have been wrecked by the War. A new ideal – but a new ideal conceived by a tired and humbled man – of a brotherhood which shall not be delimited by the exclusions of a fighting unit or caste begins to appear in these stories. Mithraism figures again in "The Church that was at Antioch"[38]: the young Roman officer turned Mithraist says of his mother: "She follows the old school, of course – the home-worships and the strict Latin Trinity. . . . But one wants more than that"; and he ends by getting murdered by the Jews in revenge for his protection of the Apostle Paul. In another story, "The Manner of Men,"[39] Saint Paul appears again and rescues a neurotic sea-captain: "Serve Caesar," says Paul. "You are not canvas I can cut to advantage at present. But if you serve Caesar you will be obeying at least some sort of law. . . . If you take refuge under Caesar at sea, you may have time to think. Then I may meet you again, and we can go on with our talks. But that is as the God wills. What concerns you *now*," he concludes, in a line that recalls at the same time the Buchmanite and the psychoanalyst, "is that, by taking service, you will be free from the fear that has ridden you all your life."

The Paul of these final stories, so different from his early heroes, may evidently tell us something about Kipling's changed conception of himself. Paul had preached the Word to the

[38] [*Limits and Renewals.*]   [39] [*Op. cit.*]

Gentiles as Kipling had preached the Law to the colonials and the Americans; Paul, like Kipling, is ill-favoured and undersized, "a little shrimp of a man," who has "the woman's trick of taking the tone and colour of whoever he talked to" and who is scarred from old floggings and from his encounters with the beasts of the arena. Paul, like Kipling, is brash and tense; he is dedicated to a mission which has saved him from fear. But observe that, though he advises the shaky captain to take service with Caesar for a time, he has himself gone on to something higher.

This, then, is quite another Kipling. His prophets have an altered message: Kipling is losing his hatred. His captains have been afraid all their lives. His soldiers are no longer so cocky, so keen to kill inferior peoples, so intent on the purposes of the Empire. And officers and soldiers are now closer, as they were in the earliest stories: they are now simply civilians back in mufti, between whom the bond of having been in the War is stronger than the class differences of peace-time. And they are the remnants of a colossal disaster. I shall quote one of the pieces in verse with which Kipling supplements these stories, because, indifferent though it is as poetry, it strikingly illustrates this change:

> I have a dream – a dreadful dream –
> 　A dream that is never done,
> I watch a man go out of his mind,
> 　And he is My Mother's Son.
>
> They pushed him into a Mental Home,
> 　And that is like the grave:
> For they do not let you sleep upstairs,
> 　And you're not allowed to shave.
>
> And it was *not* disease or crime
> 　Which got him landed there,
> But because They laid on My Mother's Son
> 　More than a man could bear.
>
> What with noise, and fear of death,
> 　Waking, and wounds and cold,
> They filled the Cup for My Mother's Son
> 　Fuller than it could hold.

They broke his body and his mind
And yet they made him live,
And They asked more of My Mother's Son
Than any man could give.

For, just because he had not died
Nor been discharged nor sick,
They dragged it out with My Mother's Son
Longer than he could stick. . . .

And no one knows when he'll get well –
So, there he'll have to be.
And, 'spite of the beard in the looking-glass,
I know that man is me![40]

The theme of inescapable illness dominates the whole later Kipling. In some cases, the diseases are physical, but there is always the implication of a psychological aspect. In "A Madonna of the Trenches" and "The Wish House" – gruesome ghost stories of love and death that make "The End of the Passage" and "The Mark of the Beast" look like harmless bogey tales for children – cancer serves as a symbol for rejected or frustrated love. And it is not clear in "Dayspring Mishandled" whether the detestable literary man Castorley is being poisoned by his wife and the doctor or by the consciousness of the wrong he has committed. The strangest of all these stories is "Unprofessional," in which cancer, spasms of insanity, the aftermath of the War, and the influence of the something beyond human life combine in a clinical fantasy on the beneficent possibilities of science. Here the white mice and the London woman convulsed with suicidal seizures, sets toward death periodically imparted by mysterious cosmic tides, are Kipling's uncanniest image for the workings of nervous disorders.

The old great man is back again in the "House of Desolation" at Southsea, tormented unjustly, ill, deserted by those he loves, and with the haunted darkness descending on that world which his determined effort had once enabled him to see so distinctly. In one of the latest of his stories, "Proofs of Holy Writ," he makes Shakespeare speak to Ben Jonson of a man whom Shakespeare describes as "going down darkling to his tomb 'twixt cliffs

[40] ["The Mother's Son," *Limits and Renewals*.]

of ice and iron" – phrases hardly characteristic of Shakespeare but extremely appropriate to Kipling.

It is striking that some of the most authentic of Kipling's early stories should deal with children forsaken by their parents and the most poignant of his later ones, with parents bereaved of their children. The theme of the abandoned parent seems to reflect in reversal the theme of the abandoned child. The former theme has already appeared in "They" (written after the death of Kipling's daughter), associated with the themes of blindness and the deprivation of love; and even before that, in "Without Benefit of Clergy."

Certainly two of these last stories of Kipling's are among the most moving he wrote. There is a passage in "Mary Postgate"[41] like the plucking of a tightened string that is just about to break. The plain and dull English female "companion" is to burn up the belongings of a young soldier – like most of Kipling's children, an orphan – to whom she has stood in a maternal role and who has just been killed in a 'plane. Kipling tells in one of his typical inventories of the items, mainly relics of boyhood sports, that Mary has to destroy; and then: "The shrubbery was filling with twilight by the time she had completed her arrangements and sprinkled the sacrificial oil. As she lit the match that would burn her heart to ashes, she heard a groan or a grunt behind the dense Portugal laurels." *The match that would burn her heart to ashes*: they are the first words that we have yet encountered, the only words that we shall have encountered, that are not matter-of-fact; and here the observation of Kipling, of which George Moore complained that it was too systematic and too technical, making it *Portugal laurels* where another writer would have simply written *shrubbery* – here this hardness of concrete detail is suddenly given new value by a phrase on another plane.

So in that other remarkable story, "The Gardener,"[42] Kipling's method of preparing a finale by concealing essential information in an apparently casual narrative produces an effect of tremendous power. This method, which Kipling has developed with so much ingenuity and precision, serves in some of his stories to spring surprises that are merely mechanical; but it has always had its special appropriateness to those aspects of the English character

[41] [*A Diversity of Creatures.*]   [42] [*Debits and Credits.*]

with which Kipling has been particularly concerned in that it masks emotion and purpose under a pretence of coldness and indifference; and here it is handled in a masterly fashion to dramatise another example of the impassive Englishwoman. The implications of "Mary Postgate" prevent us from accepting it fully: we know too well that the revengeful cruelty which impels the heroine of the story to let the shattered German aviator die is shared by the author himself. But "The Gardener" may conquer us completely. I am not sure that it is not really the best story that Kipling ever wrote. Like the rest of even the best of Kipling, it is not quite on the highest level. He must still have his fairy-tale properties; and we may be disposed to protest at his taste when we find that the Puck of Pook's Hill element is supplied by the apparition of Jesus. But if we have been following Kipling's development, we recognise that this fact is significant. The role that Christ has formerly played in Kipling – as in the poem called "Cold Iron" – has been that of a *pukka Sahib* who knows how to take his punishment. This is the first time, so far as I remember, that Kipling's Christ has shown pity – as Kipling pities now rather than boasts about the self-disciplined and much-enduring British. And the symbol at once bares the secret and liberates the locked-up emotion with a sudden and shocking force. The self-repression and the hopeless grief of the unmarried mother in "The Gardener" speak for the real Kipling. Here he has found for them intense expression in the concentrated forms of his art.

The big talk of the work of the world, of the mission to command of the British, even the hatefulness of fear and disappointment, have largely faded away for Kipling. He composes as a memorial to his son and to the system in devotion to which the half-American boy has died a history of the Irish Guards in the War, in which Lieutenant John Kipling is hardly mentioned. But, meticulously assembling, by the method by which he once seemed to build so solidly, the scattered memories of his son's battalion, he seems merely to be striving, by wisps and scraps, to re-create the terrible days that preceded the death of his child. Even the victory over the Germans can never make that right.

George Orwell

RUDYARD KIPLING*

IT WAS a pity that Mr Eliot should be so much on the defensive
in the long essay with which he prefaces this selection of Kipling's
poetry,[1] but it was not to be avoided, because before one can
even speak about Kipling one has to clear away a legend that has
been created by two sets of people who have not read his works.
Kipling is in the peculiar position of having been a byword for
fifty years. During five literary generations every enlightened
person has despised him, and at the end of that time nine-tenths
of those enlightened persons are forgotten and Kipling is in
some sense still there. Mr Eliot never satisfactorily explains this
fact, because in answering the shallow and familiar charge that
Kipling is a "Fascist," he falls into the opposite error of defending
him where he is not defensible. It is no use pretending that
Kipling's view of life, as a whole, can be accepted or even
forgiven by any civilised person. It is no use claiming, for
instance, that when Kipling describes a British soldier beating a
"nigger" with a cleaning rod in order to get money out of him,
he is acting merely as a reporter and does not necessarily approve
what he describes. There is not the slightest sign anywhere in
Kipling's work that he disapproves of that kind of conduct – on
the contrary, there is a definite strain of sadism in him, over and
above the brutality which a writer of that type has to have.
Kipling *is* a jingo imperialist, he *is* morally insensitive and aes-
thetically disgusting. It is better to start by admitting that, and

* [First published 1942, revised 1945. Reprinted from George Orwell,
Critical Essays, London 1946.]

[1] *A Choice of Kipling's Verse made by T. S. Eliot.* [London 1941. The essay
is reprinted in *On Poetry and Poets*, London 1957.]

then to try to find out why it is that he survives while the refined
people who have sniggered at him seem to wear so badly.

And yet the "Fascist" charge has to be answered, because the
first clue to any understanding of Kipling, morally or politically,
is the fact that he was *not* a Fascist. He was further from being
one than the most humane or the most "progressive" person is
able to be nowadays. An interesting instance of the way in which
quotations are parroted to and fro without any attempt to look
up their context or discover their meaning is the line from "Recessional," "Lesser breeds without the Law". This line is always
good for a snigger in pansy-left circles. It is assumed as a matter
of course that the "lesser breeds" are "natives," and a mental
picture is called up of some *pukka sahib* in a pith helmet kicking
a coolie. In its context the sense of the line is almost the exact
opposite of this. The phrase "lesser breeds" refers almost
certainly to the Germans, and especially the pan-German writers,
who are "without the Law" in the sense of being lawless, not in
the sense of being powerless. The whole poem, conventionally
thought of as an orgy of boasting, is a denunciation of power
politics, British as well as German. Two stanzas are worth
quoting (I am quoting this as politics, not as poetry):

> If, drunk with sight of power, we loose
>   Wild tongues that have not Thee in awe,
> Such boastings as the Gentiles use,
>   Or lesser breeds without the Law –
> Lord God of Hosts, be with us yet,
> Lest we forget – lest we forget!

> For heathen heart that puts her trust
>   In reeking tube and iron shard,
> All valiant dust that builds on dust,
>   And guarding, calls not Thee to guard,
> For frantic boast and foolish word –
> Thy mercy on Thy people, Lord!

Much of Kipling's phraseology is taken from the Bible, and
no doubt in the second stanza he had in mind the text from
Psalm cxxvii: "Except the Lord build the house, they labour in
vain that build it; except the Lord keep the city, the watchman
waketh but in vain." It is not a text that makes much impression

on the post-Hitler mind. No one, in our time, believes in any sanction greater than military power; no one believes that it is possible to overcome force except by greater force. There is no "law," there is only power. I am not saying that that is a true belief, merely that it is the belief which all modern men do actually hold. Those who pretend otherwise are either intellectual cowards, or power-worshippers under a thin disguise, or have simply not caught up with the age they are living in. Kipling's outlook is pre-Fascist. He still believes that pride comes before a fall and that the gods punish *hubris*. He does not foresee the tank, the bombing plane, the radio and the secret police, or their psychological results.

But in saying this, does not one unsay what I said above about Kipling's jingoism and brutality? No, one is merely saying that the nineteenth-century imperialist outlook and the modern gangster outlook are two different things. Kipling belongs very definitely to the period 1885-1902. The Great War and its aftermath embittered him, but he shows little sign of having learned anything from any event later than the Boer War. He was the prophet of British Imperialism in its expansionist phase (even more than his poems, his solitary novel, *The Light that Failed*, gives you the atmosphere of that time) and also the unofficial historian of the British Army, the old mercenary army which began to change its shape in 1914. All his confidence, his bouncing vulgar vitality, sprang out of limitations which no Fascist or near-Fascist shares.

Kipling spent the later part of his life in sulking, and no doubt it was political disappointment rather than literary vanity that accounted for this. Somehow history had not gone according to plan. After the greatest victory she had ever known, Britain was a lesser world power than before, and Kipling was quite acute enough to see this. The virtue had gone out of the classes he idealised, the young were hedonistic or disaffected, the desire to paint the map red had evaporated. He could not understand what was happening, because he had never had any grasp of the economic forces underlying imperial expansion. It is notable that Kipling does not seem to realise, any more than the average soldier or colonial administrator, that an empire is primarily a money-making concern. Imperialism as he sees it is a sort of forcible evangelising. You turn a Gatling gun on a mob of un-armed "natives," and then you establish "the Law," which includes roads, railways and a court-house. He could not foresee, therefore, that the same motives which brought the Empire into existence would end by destroying it. It was the same motive, for example, that caused the Malayan jungles to be cleared for rubber estates, and which now causes those estates to be handed over intact to the Japanese. The modern totalitarians know what they are doing, and the nineteenth-century English did not know what they were doing. Both attitudes have their advantages, but Kipling was never able to move forward from one into the other. His outlook, allowing for the fact that after all he was an artist, was that of the salaried bureaucrat who despises the "box wallah" and often lives a lifetime without realising that the "box wallah" calls the tune.

But because he identifies himself with the official class, he does possess one thing which "enlightened" people seldom or never possess, and that is a sense of responsibility. The middle-class Left hate him for this quite as much as for his cruelty and vul-garity. All left-wing parties in the highly industrialised countries are at bottom a sham, because they make it their business to fight against something which they do not really wish to destroy. They have internationalist aims, and at the same time they struggle to keep up a standard of life with which those aims are incompatible. We all live by robbing Asiatic coolies, and those of us who are "enlightened" all maintain that those coolies ought to be set free; but our standard of living, and hence our "enlightenment," demands that the robbery shall continue. A humanitarian is always a hypocrite, and Kipling's understanding of this is perhaps the central secret of his power to create telling phrases. It would be difficult to hit off the one-eyed pacifism of the English in fewer words than in the phrase, "making mock of uniforms that guard you while you sleep." It is true that Kipling does not understand the economic aspect of the relationship between the highbrow and the blimp. He does not see that the map is painted red chiefly in order that the coolie may be exploited. Instead of the coolie he sees the Indian Civil Servant; but even on that plane his grasp of function, of who protects whom, is very sound. He sees clearly that men can only be highly civilised while other men, inevitably less civilised, are there to guard and feed them.

How far does Kipling really identify himself with the administrators, soldiers and engineers whose praises he sings? Not so completely as is sometimes assumed. He had travelled very widely while he was still a young man, he had grown up with a brilliant mind in mainly philistine surroundings, and some streak in him that may have been partly neurotic led him to prefer the active man to the sensitive man. The nineteenth-century Anglo-Indians, to name the least sympathetic of his idols, were at any rate people who did things. It may be that all that they did was evil, but they changed the face of the earth (it is instructive to look at a map of Asia and compare the railway system of India with that of the surrounding countries), whereas they could have achieved nothing, could not have maintained themselves in power for a single week, if the normal Anglo-Indian outlook had been that of, say, E. M. Forster. Tawdry and shallow though it is, Kipling's is the only literary picture that we possess of nineteenth-century Anglo-India, and he could only make it because he was just coarse enough to be able to exist and keep his mouth shut in clubs and regimental messes. But he did not greatly resemble the people he admired. I know from several private sources that many of the Anglo-Indians who were Kipling's contemporaries did not like or approve of him. They said, no doubt truly, that he knew nothing about India, and on the other hand, he was from their point of view too much of a highbrow. While in India he tended to mix with "the wrong" people, and because of his dark complexion he was wrongly suspected of having a streak of Asiatic blood. Much in his development is traceable to his having been born in India and having left school early. With a slightly different background he might have been a good novelist or a superlative writer of music-hall songs. But how true is it that he was a vulgar flag-waver, a sort of publicity agent for Cecil Rhodes? It is true, but it is not true that he was a yes-man or a time-server. After his early days, if then, he never courted public opinion. Mr Eliot says that what is held against him is that he expressed unpopular views in a popular style. This narrows the issue by assuming that "unpopular" means unpopular with the intelligentsia, but it is a fact that Kipling's "message" was one that the big public did not want, and, indeed, has never accepted. The mass of the people, in the 'nineties as now, were anti-militarist, bored by the Empire and only unconsciously patriotic. Kipling's official admirers are and were the "service" middle class, the people who read *Blackwood's*. In the stupid early years of this century, the blimps, having at last discovered someone who could be called a poet and who was on their side, set Kipling on a pedestal, and some of his more sententious poems, such as "If," were given almost Biblical status. But it is doubtful whether the blimps have ever read him with attention, any more than they have read the Bible. Much of what he says they could not possibly approve. Few people who have criticised England from the inside have said bitterer things about her than this gutter patriot. As a rule it is the British working class that he is attacking, but not always. That phrase about "the flannelled fools at the wicket and the muddied oafs at the goal"[2] sticks like an arrow to this day, and it is aimed at the Eton and Harrow match as well as the Cup-Tie Final. Some of the verses he wrote about the Boer War have a curiously modern ring, so far as their subject-matter goes. "Stellenbosch," which must have been written about 1902, sums up what every intelligent infantry officer was saying in 1918, or is saying now, for that matter.

Kipling's romantic ideas about England and the Empire might not have mattered if he could have held them without having the class-prejudices which at that time went with them. If one examines his best and most representative work, his soldier poems, especially *Barrack-Room Ballads*, one notices that what more than anything else spoils them is an underlying air of patronage. Kipling idealises the army officer, especially the junior officer, and that to an idiotic extent, but the private soldier, though lovable and romantic, has to be a comic. He is always made to speak in a sort of stylised Cockney, not very broad but with all the aitches and final "g's" carefully omitted. Very often the result is as embarrassing as the humorous recitation at a church social. And this accounts for the curious fact that one can often improve Kipling's poems, make them less facetious and less blatant by simply going through them and transplanting them from Cockney into standard speech. This is

[2] ["The Islanders," *The Five Nations.*]

especially true of his refrains, which often have a truly lyrical quality. Two examples will do (one is about a funeral and the other about a wedding):

> So it's knock out your pipes and follow me!
> And it's finish up your swipes and follow me!
> Oh, hark to the big drum calling,
> Follow me – follow me home![3]

and again:

> Cheer for the Sergeant's wedding –
> Give them one cheer more!
> Grey gun-horses in the lando,
> And a rogue is married to a whore![4]

Here I have restored the aitches, etc. Kipling ought to have known better. He ought to have seen that the two closing lines of the first of these stanzas are very beautiful lines, and that ought to have overridden his impulse to make fun of a working-man's accent. In the ancient ballads the lord and the peasant speak the same language. This is impossible to Kipling, who is looking down a distorting class-perspective, and by a piece of poetic justice one of his best lines is spoiled – for "follow me 'ome" is much uglier than "follow me home." But even where it makes no difference musically the facetiousness of his stage Cockney dialect is irritating. However, he is more often quoted aloud than read on the printed page, and most people instinctively make the necessary alterations when they quote him.

Can one imagine any private soldier, in the 'nineties or now, reading *Barrack-Room Ballads* and feeling that here was a writer who spoke for him? It is very hard to do so. Any soldier capable of reading a book of verse would notice at once that Kipling is almost unconscious of the class war that goes on in an army as much as elsewhere. It is not only that he thinks the soldier comic, but that he thinks him patriotic, feudal, a ready admirer of his officers, and proud to be a soldier of the Queen. Of course that is partly true, or battles could not be fought, but "What have I done for thee, England, my England?" is essentially a middle-class query. Almost any working man would follow it up imme-

---

[3] ["Follow Me 'Ome," *The Seven Seas.*]
[4] ["The Sergeant's Weddin'," *op. cit.*]

diately with "What has England done for me?" In so far as Kipling grasps this, he simply sets it down to "the intense selfishness of the lower classes" (his own phrase).[5] When he is writing not of British but of "loyal" Indians he carries the "Salaam, sahib" *motif* to sometimes disgusting lengths. Yet it remains true that he has far more interest in the common soldier, far more anxiety that he shall get a fair deal, than most of the "liberals" of his day or our own. He sees that the soldier is neglected, meanly underpaid, and hypocritically despised by the people whose incomes he safeguards. "I came to realise," he says in his posthumous memoirs, "the bare horrors of the private's life, and the unnecessary torments he endured." He is accused of glorifying war, and perhaps he does so, but not in the usual manner, by pretending that war is a sort of football match. Like most people capable of writing battle poetry, Kipling had never been in battle, but his vision of war is realistic. He knows that bullets hurt, that under fire everyone is terrified, that the ordinary soldier never knows what the war is about or what is happening except in his own corner of the battlefield, and that British troops, like other troops, frequently run away:

> I 'eard the knives be'ind me, but I dursn't face my man,
> Nor I don't know where I went to, 'cause I didn't 'alt to see,
> Till I 'eard a beggar squealin' out for quarter as 'e ran,
> An' I thought I knew the voice an' – it was me![6]

Modernise the style of this, and it might have come out of one of the debunking war books of the nineteen-twenties. Or again:

> An' now the hugly bullets come peckin' through the dust,
> An' no one wants to face 'em, but every beggar must;
> So, like a man in irons, which isn't glad to go,
> They moves 'em off by companies uncommon stiff an' slow.[7]

Compare this with:

> Forward the Light Brigade!
> Was there a man dismayed?
> No! though the soldier knew
> Someone had blundered.

[5] ["The Drums of the Fore and Aft," *Wee Willie Winkie.*]
[6] ["That Day," *The Seven Seas.*]
[7] [" 'The 'Eathen'," *op. cit.*]

If anything, Kipling overdoes the horrors, for the wars of his youth were hardly wars at all by our standards. Perhaps that is due to the neurotic strain in him, the hunger for cruelty. But at least he knows that men ordered to attack impossible objectives *are* dismayed, and also that fourpence a day is not a generous pension.

How complete or truthful a picture has Kipling left us of the long-service, mercenary army of the late nineteenth century? One must say of this, as of what Kipling wrote about nineteenth-century Anglo-India, that it is not only the best but almost the only literary picture we have. He has put on record an immense amount of stuff that one could otherwise only gather from verbal tradition or from unreadable regimental histories. Perhaps his picture of army life seems fuller and more accurate than it is because any middle-class English person is likely to know enough to fill up the gaps. At any rate, reading the essay on Kipling that Mr Edmund Wilson has just published or is just about to publish,[8] I was struck by the number of things that are boringly familiar to us and seem to be barely intelligible to an American. But from the body of Kipling's early work there does seem to emerge a vivid and not seriously misleading picture of the old pre-machine-gun army – the sweltering barracks in Gibraltar or Lucknow, the red coats, the pipeclayed belts and the pillbox hats, the beer, the fights, the floggings, hangings and crucifixions, the bugle-calls, the smell of oats and horse-piss, the bellowing sergeants with foot-long moustaches, the bloody skirmishes, invariably mismanaged, the crowded troopships, the cholera-stricken camps, the "native" concubines, the ultimate death in the workhouse. It is a crude, vulgar picture in which a patriotic music-hall turn seems to have got mixed up with one of Zola's gorier passages, but from it future generations will be able to gather some idea of what a long-term volunteer army was like. On about the same level they will be able to learn something of British India in the days when motor-cars and refrigerators were unheard of. It is an error to imagine that we might have had better books on these subjects if, for example, George Moore, or Gissing, or Thomas Hardy, had had Kipling's opportunities. That is the kind of accident that cannot happen. It was not

[8] 1942. [See above, pp. 17-69.]

possible that nineteenth-century England should produce a book like *War and Peace*, or like Tolstoy's minor stories of army life, such as "Sebastopol" or "The Cossacks," not because the talent was necessarily lacking but because no one with sufficient sensitiveness to write such books would ever have made the appropriate contacts. Tolstoy lived in a great military empire in which it seemed natural for almost any young man of family to spend a few years in the army, whereas the British Empire was and still is de-militarised to a degree which Continental observers find almost incredible. Civilised men do not readily move away from the centres of civilisation, and in most languages there is a great dearth of what one might call colonial literature. It took a very improbable combination of circumstances to produce Kipling's gaudy tableau, in which Private Ortheris and Mrs Hauksbee pose against a background of palm trees to the sound of temple bells, and one necessary circumstance was that Kipling himself was only half civilised.

Kipling is the only English writer of our time who has added phrases to the language. The phrases and neologisms which we take over and use without remembering their origin do not always come from writers we admire. It is strange, for instance, to hear the Nazi broadcasters referring to the Russian soldiers as "robots," thus unconsciously borrowing a word from a Czech democrat whom they would have killed if they could have laid hands on him. Here are half a dozen phrases coined by Kipling which one sees quoted in leaderettes in the gutter Press or over-hears in saloon bars from people who have barely heard his name. It will be seen that they all have a certain characteristic in common:

> East is East, and West is West.
> The white man's burden.
> What do they know of England who only England know?
> The female of the species is more deadly than the male.
> Somewhere East of Suez.
> Paying the Dane-geld.

There are various others, including some that have outlived their context by many years. The phrase "killing Kruger with your mouth," for instance, was current till very recently. It is also possible that it was Kipling who first let loose the use of the word "Huns" for Germans; at any rate he began using it as soon as the guns opened fire in 1914. But what the phrases I have listed above have in common is that they are all of them phrases which one utters semi-derisively (as it might be "For I'm to be Queen o' the May, mother, I'm to be Queen o' the May"), but which one is bound to make use of sooner or later. Nothing could exceed the contempt of the *New Statesman*, for instance, for Kipling, but how many times during the Munich period did the *New Statesman* find itself quoting that phrase about paying the Dane-geld?[9] The fact is that Kipling, apart from his snack-bar wisdom and his gift for packing much cheap picturesqueness into a few words ("Palm and Pine" – "East of Suez" – "The Road to Mandalay"), is generally talking about things that are of urgent interest. It does not matter, from this point of view, that thinking and decent people generally find themselves on the other side of the fence from him. "White man's burden" instantly conjures up a real problem, even if one feels that it ought to be altered to "black man's burden." One may disagree to the middle of one's bones with the political attitude implied in "The Islanders," but one cannot say that it is a frivolous attitude. Kipling deals in thoughts which are both vulgar and permanent. This raises the question of his special status as a poet, or verse-writer.

Mr Eliot describes Kipling's metrical work as "verse" and not "poetry," but adds that it is "*great* verse," and further qualifies this by saying that a writer can only be described as a "great verse-writer" if there is some of his work "of which we cannot say whether it is verse or poetry." Apparently Kipling was a versifier who occasionally wrote poems, in which case it was a pity that Mr Eliot did not specify these poems by name. The trouble is that whenever an aesthetic judgment on Kipling's work

----

[9] 1945. On the first page of his recent book *Adam and Eve*, Mr Middleton Murry quotes the well-known lines:

> There are nine and sixty ways
> Of constructing tribal lays,
> And every single one of them is right.

He attributes these lines to Thackeray. This is probably what is known as a "Freudian error." A civilised person would prefer not to quote Kipling, *i.e.*, would prefer not to feel that it was Kipling who had expressed his thought for him.

seems to be called for, Mr Eliot is too much on the defensive to
be able to speak plainly. What he does not say, and what I think
one ought to start by saying in any discussion of Kipling, is that
most of Kipling's verse is so horribly vulgar that it gives one the
same sensation as one gets from watching a third-rate music-hall
performer recite "The Pigtail of Wu Fang Fu" with the purple
limelight on his face, *and yet* there is much of it that is capable of
giving pleasure to people who know what poetry means. At his
worst, and also his most vital, in poems like "Gunga Din" or
"Danny Deever," Kipling is almost a shameful pleasure, like the
taste for cheap sweets that some people secretly carry into middle
life. But even with his best passages one has the same sense of
being seduced by something spurious, and yet unquestionably
seduced. Unless one is merely a snob and a liar it is impossible
to say that no one who cares for poetry could get any pleasure
out of such lines as:

> For the wind is in the palm-trees, and the temple-bells they say:
> "Come you back, you British soldier; come you back to Mandalay!"

and yet those lines are not poetry in the same sense as "Felix
Randal" or "When icicles hang by the wall" are poetry. One can,
perhaps, place Kipling more satisfactorily than by juggling with
the words "verse" and "poetry," if one describes him simply as
a good bad poet. He is as a poet what Harriet Beecher Stowe was
as a novelist. And the mere existence of work of this kind, which
is perceived by generation after generation to be vulgar and yet
goes on being read, tells one something about the age we live in.

There is a great deal of good bad poetry in English, all of it,
I should say, subsequent to 1790. Examples of good bad poems
– I am deliberately choosing diverse ones – are "The Bridge of
Sighs," "When all the World is Young, Lad," "The Charge of
the Light Brigade," Bret Harte's "Dickens in Camp," "The
Burial of Sir John Moore," "Jenny Kissed me," "Keith of
Ravelston," "Casabianca." All of these reek of sentimentality,
and yet – not these particular poems, perhaps, but poems of
this kind, are capable of giving true pleasure to people who can
see clearly what is wrong with them. One could fill a fair-sized
anthology with good bad poems, if it were not for the significant
fact that good bad poetry is usually too well known to be worth

reprinting. It is no use pretending that in an age like our own, "good" poetry can have any genuine popularity. It is, and must be, the cult of a very few people, the least tolerated of the arts. Perhaps that statement needs a certain amount of qualification. True poetry can sometimes be acceptable to the mass of the people when it disguises itself as something else. One can see an example of this in the folk-poetry that England still possesses, certain nursery rhymes and mnemonic rhymes, for instance, and the songs that soldiers make up, including the words that go to some of the bugle-calls. But in general ours is a civilisation in which the very word "poetry" evokes a hostile snigger or, at best, the sort of frozen disgust that most people feel when they hear the word "God." If you are good at playing the concertina you could probably go into the nearest public bar and get yourself an appreciative audience within five minutes. But what would be the attitude of that same audience if you suggested reading them Shakespeare's sonnets, for instance? Good bad poetry, however, can get across to the most unpromising audiences if the right atmosphere has been worked up beforehand. Some months back Churchill produced a great effect by quoting Clough's "Endeavour" in one of his broadcast speeches. I listened to this speech among people who could certainly not be accused of caring for poetry, and I am convinced that the lapse into verse impressed them and did not embarrass them. But not even Churchill could have got away with it if he had quoted anything much better than this.

In so far as a writer of verse can be popular, Kipling has been and probably still is popular. In his own lifetime some of his poems travelled far beyond the bounds of the reading public, beyond the world of school prize-days, Boy Scout singsongs, limp-leather editions, poker-work and calendars, and out into the yet vaster world of the music halls. Nevertheless, Mr Eliot thinks it worth while to edit him, thus confessing to a taste which others share but are not always honest enough to mention. The fact that such a thing as good bad poetry can exist is a sign of the emotional overlap between the intellectual and the ordinary man. The intellectual *is* different from the ordinary man, but only in certain sections of his personality, and even then not all the time. But what is the peculiarity of a good bad poem? A good bad poem is a graceful monument to the obvious. It records in memorable form – for verse is a mnemonic device, among other things – some emotion which very nearly every human being can share. The merit of a poem like "When all the World is Young, Lad" is that, however sentimental it may be, its sentiment is "true" sentiment in the sense that you are bound to find yourself thinking the thought it expresses sooner or later; and then, if you happen to know the poem, it will come back into your mind and seem better than it did before. Such poems are a kind of rhyming proverb, and it is a fact that definitely popular poetry is usually gnomic or sententious. One example from Kipling will do:

> White hands cling to the tightened rein,
>   Slipping the spur from the booted heel,
> Tenderest voices cry, "Turn again!"
>   Red lips tarnish the scabbarded steel. . . .
>
> Down to Gehenna or up to the Throne,
> He travels the fastest who travels alone.[10]

There is a vulgar thought vigorously expressed. It may not be true, but at any rate it is a thought that everyone thinks. Sooner or later you will have occasion to feel that he travels the fastest who travels alone, and there the thought is, ready made and, as it were, waiting for you. So the chances are that, having once heard this line, you will remember it.

One reason for Kipling's power as a good bad poet I have already suggested – his sense of responsibility, which made it possible for him to have a world-view, even though it happened to be a false one. Although he had no direct connexion with any political party, Kipling was a Conservative, a thing that does not exist nowadays. Those who now call themselves Conservatives are either Liberals, Fascists or the accomplices of Fascists. He identified himself with the ruling power and not with the opposition. In a gifted writer this seems to us strange and even disgusting, but it did have the advantage of giving Kipling a certain grip on reality. The ruling power is always faced with the question, "In such and such circumstances, what would you *do*?," whereas the opposition is not obliged to take responsibility or make any

---

[10] [From "The Story of the Gadsbys," *Soldiers Three.*]

real decisions. Where it is a permanent and pensioned opposition, as in England, the quality of its thought deteriorates accordingly. Moreover, anyone who starts out with a pessimistic, reactionary view of life tends to be justified by events, for Utopia never arrives and "the gods of the copybook headings," as Kipling himself put it, always return. Kipling sold out to the British governing class, not financially but emotionally. This warped his political judgment, for the British ruling class were not what he imagined, and it led him into abysses of folly and snobbery, but he gained a corresponding advantage from having at least tried to imagine what action and responsibility are like. It is a great thing in his favour that he is not witty, not "daring," has no wish to *épater les bourgeois*. He dealt largely in platitudes, and since we live in a world of platitudes, much of what he said sticks. Even his worst follies seem less shallow and less irritating than the "enlightened" utterances of the same period, such as Wilde's epigrams or the collection of cracker-mottoes at the end of *Man and Superman*.

Lionel Trilling

KIPLING*

KIPLING BELONGS irrevocably to our past, and although the re-
newed critical attention he has lately been given by Edmund
Wilson and T. S. Eliot is friendlier and more interesting than
any he has received for a long time, it is less likely to make us
revise our opinions than to revive our memories of him. But
these memories, when revived, will be strong, for if Kipling
belongs to our past, he belongs there very firmly, fixed deep in
childhood feeling. And especially for liberals of a certain age he
must always be an interesting figure, for he had an effect upon
us in that obscure and important part of our minds where literary
feeling and political attitude meet, an effect so much the greater
because it was so early experienced; and then for many of us our
rejection of him was our first literary-political decision.

My own relation with Kipling was intense and I believe
typical. It began, properly enough, with *The Jungle Book*. This
was my first independently chosen and avidly read book, my first
literary discovery, all the more wonderful because I had come
upon it in an adult "set," one of the ten green volumes of the
Century Edition that used to be found in many homes. (The
"set" has become unfashionable, and that is a blow to the literary
education of the young, who, once they had been lured to an
author, used to remain loyal to him until they had read him by
the yard.) The satisfactions of *The Jungle Book* were large and
numerous. I suppose a boy's vestigial animal totemism was

* [First published 1943. Reprinted from *The Liberal Imagination*, London
1951. Professor Trilling has asked me to say that if he were writing on
Kipling now he would do so "less censoriously and with more affectionate
admiration." ED.]

pleased; there were the marvellous but credible abilities of
Mowgli; there were the deadly enmities and grandiose revenges,
strangely and tragically real. And it was a world peopled by
wonderful parents, not only Mother Wolf and Father Wolf, but
also – the fathers were far more numerous than the mothers –
Bagheera the panther, Baloo the bear, Hathi the elephant, and
the dreadful but decent Kaa the python, a whole council of
strength and wisdom which was as benign as it was dangerous,
and no doubt much of the delight came from discovering the
benignity of this feral world. And then there was the fascination
of the Pack and its Law. It is not too much to say that a boy had
thus his first introduction to a generalised notion of society. It
was a notion charged with feeling – the Law was mysterious, firm,
certain, noble, in every way admirable beyond any rule of home
or school.

Mixed up with this feeling about the Pack and the Law, and
perfectly expressing it, was the effect of Kipling's gnomic
language, both in prose and in verse, for you could not entirely
skip the verse that turned up in the prose, and so you were led to
trust yourself to the *Barrack Room Ballads* at a time when you
would trust no other poetry. That gnomic quality of Kipling's,
that knowing allusiveness which later came to seem merely
vulgar, was, when first experienced, a delightful thing. By
understanding Kipling's ellipses and allusions, you partook of
what was Kipling's own special delight, the joy of being "in."
Max Beerbohm has satirised Kipling's yearning to be admitted
to any professional arcanum, his fawning admiration of the man
in uniform, the man with the know-how and the technical slang.
It is the emotion of a boy – he lusts for the exclusive circle, for
the sect with the password, and he profoundly admires the
technical, secret-laden adults who run the world, the overalled
people, majestic in their occupation, superb in their preoccupation, the dour engineer and the thoughtful plumber. To this
emotion, developed not much beyond a boy's, Kipling was addicted all his life, and eventually it made him silly and a bore.
But a boy reading Kipling was bound to find all this sense of
arcanum very pertinent; as, for example, it expressed itself in
Plain Tales from the Hills, it seemed the very essence of adult life.
Kipling himself was not much more than a boy when he wrote

these remarkable stories – remarkable because, no matter how one judges them, one never forgets the least of them – and he saw the adult world as full of rites of initiation, of closed doors and listeners behind them, councils, boudoir conferences, conspiracies, innuendoes, and special knowledge. It was very baffling, and certainly as an introduction to literature it went counter to all our present educational theory, according to which a child should not be baffled at all but should read only about what he knows of from experience; but one worked it out by a sort of algebra, one discovered the meaning of the unknowns through the knowns, and just as one got without definition an adequate knowledge of what a *sais* was, or a *dâk*-bungalow, and what the significance of *pukka* was, so one penetrated to what went on between the Gadsbys and to why Mrs Hauksbee was supposed to be charming and Mrs Reiver not. Kipling's superior cryptic tone was in effect an invitation to understand all this – it suggested first that the secret was being kept not only from one-self but from everyone else and then it suggested that the secret was not so much being kept as revealed, if one but guessed hard enough. And this elaborate manner was an invitation to be "in" not only on life but on literature; to follow its hints with a sense of success was to become an initiate of literature, a Past Master, a snob of the esoteric Mystery of the Word.

"Craft" and "craftily" were words that Kipling loved (no doubt they were connected with his deep Masonic attachment), and when he used them he intended all their several meanings at once – shrewdness, a special technique, a special *secret* technique communicated by some master of it, and the bond that one user of the technique would naturally have with another. This feeling about the Craft, the Mystery, grew on Kipling and coloured his politics and even his cosmological ideas quite for the worse, but to a boy it suggested the virtue of disinterested professional commitment. If one ever fell in love with the cult of art, it was not because one had been proselytised by some intelligent Frenchman, but because one had absorbed Kipling's credal utterances about the virtues of craft and had read *The Light that Failed* literally to pieces.

These things we must be sure to put into the balance when we make up our account with Kipling – these and a few more. To a middle-class boy he gave a literary sanction for the admiration of the illiterate and shiftless parts of humanity. He was the first to suggest what may be called the anthropological view, the perception that another man's idea of virtue and honour may be different from one's own but quite to be respected. We must remember this when we condemn his mindless imperialism. Indians naturally have no patience whatever with Kipling and they condemn even his best book, *Kim*, saying that even here, where his devotion to the Indian life is most fully expressed, he falsely represents the Indians. Perhaps this is so, yet the dominant emotions of *Kim* are love and respect for the aspects of Indian life that the ethos of the West does not usually regard even with leniency. *Kim* established the value of things a boy was not likely to find approved anywhere else – the rank, greasy, over-rich things, the life that was valuable outside the notions of orderliness, success, and gentility. It suggested not only a multitude of different ways of life, but even different modes of thought. Thus, whatever one might come to feel personally about religion, a reading of *Kim* could not fail to establish religion's factual reality, not as a piety, which was the apparent extent of its existence in the West, but as something at the very root of life; in *Kim* one saw the myth in the making before one's very eyes and understood how and why it was made, and this, when later one had the intellectual good luck to remember it, had more to say about history and culture than anything in one's mere experience. *Kim*, like *The Jungle Book*, is full of wonderful fathers, all dedicated men in their different ways, each representing a different possibility of existence; and the charm of each is the greater because the boy need not commit himself to one alone but, like Kim himself, may follow Mahbub Ali into the shrewdness and sensuality of the bazaars, and be initiated by Colonel Creighton into the cold glamour of the Reason of State, and yet also make himself the son of the Lama, the very priest of contemplation and peace.

And then a boy in a large New York high school could find a blessed release from the school's offensive pieties about "service" and "character" in the scornful individualism of *Stalky & Co.* But it was with *Stalky & Co.* that the spell was broken, and significantly enough by H. G. Wells. In his *Outline of History*,

Wells connected the doings of Stalky, M'Turk, and Beetle with
British imperialism, and he characterised both in a way that
made one see how much callousness, arrogance, and brutality
one had been willing to accept. From then on the disenchant-
ment grew. Exactly because Kipling was so involved with one's
boyhood, one was quick to give him up in one's adolescence.
The Wellsian liberalism took hold, and Shaw offered a new
romance of wit and intellect. The new movements in literature
came in to make Kipling seem inconsequential and puerile, to
require that he be dismissed as official and, as one used to say,
intending something aesthetic and emotional rather than political,
"bourgeois." He ceased to be the hero of life and literature and
became the villain, although even then a natural gratitude kept
green the memory of the pleasure he had given.

But the world has changed a great deal since the days when that
antagonism between Kipling and enlightenment was at its early
intensity, and many intellectual and political things have shifted
from their old assigned places. The liberalism of Wells and Shaw
long ago lost its ascendency, and indeed in its later developments
it showed what could never in the early days have been foreseen,
an actual affinity with certain elements of Kipling's own constella-
tion of ideas. And now when, in the essay which serves as the
introduction to his selection of Kipling's verse, Mr Eliot speaks
of "the fascination of exploring a mind so different from my own,"
we surprise ourselves – as perhaps Mr Eliot intended that we
should – by seeing that the similarities between the two minds
are no less striking than the differences. Time surely has done its
usual but always dramatic work of eroding our clear notions of
cultural antagonisms when Kipling can be thought of as in any
way akin to Eliot. Yet as Mr Eliot speaks of the public intention
and the music-hall tradition of Kipling's verse, anyone who has
heard a record of Mr Eliot reading *The Waste Land* will be struck
by how much that poem is publicly intended, shaped less for the
study than for the platform or the pulpit, by how much the full
dialect rendition of the Cockney passages suggests that it was
even shaped for the music hall, by how explicit the poet's use of
his voice makes the music we are so likely to think of as internal
and secretive. Then it is significant that among the dominant
themes of both Kipling and Eliot are those of despair and the

fear of nameless psychological horror. Politically they share an excessive reliance on administration and authority. They have the same sense of being beset and betrayed by the ignoble mob; Kipling invented and elaborated the image of the Pict, the dark little hating man, "too little to love or to hate," who, if left alone, "can drag down the state"; and this figure plays its well-known part in Mr Eliot's poetry, being for both poets the stimulus to the pathos of xenophobia.

Mr Eliot's literary apologia for Kipling consists of asking us to judge him not as a deficient writer of poetry but as an admirable writer of verse. Upon this there follow definitions of a certain ingenuity, but the distinction between poetry and verse does not really advance beyond the old inadequate one – I believe that Mr Eliot himself has specifically rejected it – which Matthew Arnold put forward in writing about Dryden and Pope. I cannot see the usefulness of the distinction; I can even see critical danger in it; and when Mr Eliot says that Kipling's verse sometimes becomes poetry, it seems to me that verse, in Mr Eliot's present sense, is merely a word used to denote poetry of a particular kind, in which certain intensities are rather low. Nowadays, it is true, we are not enough aware of the pleasures of poetry of low intensity, by which, in our modern way, we are likely to mean poetry in which the processes of thought are not, by means of elliptical or tangential metaphor and an indirect syntax, advertised as being under high pressure; Crabbe, Cowper, and Scott are rejected because they are not Donne or Hopkins or Mr Eliot himself, or even poets of far less consequence than these; and no doubt Chaucer would be depreciated on the same grounds, if we were at all aware of him these days. I should have welcomed Mr Eliot's speaking out in a general way in support of the admirable, and, as I think, necessary, tradition of poetry of low intensity. But by making it different in kind from poetry of high intensity and by giving it a particular name which can only be of invidious import, he has cut us off still more sharply from its virtues.

Kipling, then, must be taken as a poet. Taken so, he will scarcely rank very high, although much must be said in his praise. In two evenings, or even in a single very long one, you can read through the bulky Inclusive Edition of his verse, on which Mr Eliot's selection is based, and be neither wearied, in part because you will not have been involved, nor uninterested, because Kipling was a man of great gifts. You will have moments of admiration, sometimes of unwilling admiration, and even wish that Mr Eliot had included certain poems in his selection that he has left out. You will be frequently irritated by the truculence and sometimes amused by its unconsciousness – who but Kipling would write a brag about English understatement? Carlyle roaring the virtues of Silence is nothing to it – but when you have done you will be less inclined to condemn than to pity: the constant iteration of the bravado will have been illuminated by a few poems that touch on the fear and horror which Mr Wilson speaks of at length and which Mr Eliot refers to; you feel that the walls of wrath and the ramparts of empire are being erected against the mind's threat to itself. This is a real thing, whether we call it good or bad, and its force of reality seems to grow rather than diminish in memory, seems to be greater after one's actual reading is behind one; the quality of this reality is that which we assign to primitive and elemental things, and, judge it as we will, we dare not be indifferent or superior to it.

In speaking of Kipling's politics, Mr Eliot contents himself with denying that Kipling was a Fascist; a Tory, he says, is a very different thing, a Tory considers Fascism the last debasement of democracy. But this, I think, is not quite ingenuous of Mr Eliot. A Tory, to be sure, is not a Fascist, and Kipling is not properly to be called a Fascist, but neither is his political temperament to be adequately described merely by reference to a tradition which is honoured by Dr Johnson, Burke, and Walter Scott. Kipling is not like these men; he is not generous, and, although he makes much to-do about manliness, he is not manly; and he has none of the *mind* of the few great Tories. His Toryism often had in it a lower-middle-class snarl of defeated gentility, and it is this, rather than his love of authority and force, that might suggest an affinity with Fascism. His imperialism is reprehensible not because it *is* imperialism but because it is a puny and mindless imperialism. In short, Kipling is unloved and unlovable not by reason of his beliefs but by reason of the temperament that gave them literary expression.

I have said that the old antagonism between liberalism and

Kipling is now abated by time and events, yet it is still worth saying, and it is not extravagant to say, that Kipling was one of liberalism's major intellectual misfortunes. John Stuart Mill, when he urged all liberals to study the conservative Coleridge, said that we should pray to have enemies who make us worthy of ourselves. Kipling was an enemy who had the opposite effect. He tempted liberals to be content with easy victories of right feeling and with moral self-congratulation. For example, the strength of Toryism at its best lies in its descent from a solid administrative tradition, while the weakness of liberalism, arising from its history of reliance upon legislation, is likely to be a fogginess about administration (or, when the fog clears away a little, a fancy and absolute notion of administration such as Wells and Shaw gave way to). Kipling's sympathy was always with the administrator and he is always suspicious of the legislator. This is foolish, but it is not the most reprehensible error in the world, and it is a prejudice which, in the hands of an intelligent man, say a man like Walter Bagehot or like Fitzjames Stephen, might make clear to the man of principled theory, to the liberal, what the difficulties not merely of government but of *governing* really are. And that is what Kipling set out to do, but he so charged his demonstration with hatred and contempt, with rancour and caste feeling, he so emptied the honourable Tory tradition of its intellectual content, that he simply could not be listened to or believed, he could only be reacted against. His extravagance sprang from his hatred of the liberal intellectual – he was, we must remember, the aggressor in the quarrel – and the liberal intellectual responded by hating everything that Kipling loved, even when it had its element of virtue and enlightenment.

We must make no mistake about it – Kipling was an honest man and he loved the national virtues. But I suppose no man ever did more harm to the national virtues than Kipling did. He mixed them up with a swagger and swank, with bullying, ruthlessness, and self-righteousness, and he set them up as necessarily antagonistic to intellect. He made them stink in the nostrils of youth. I remember that in my own undergraduate days we used specifically to exclude physical courage from among the virtues; we were exaggerating the point of a joke of Shaw's and reacting from Kipling. And up to the War I had a yearly struggle with undergraduates over Wordsworth's poem, "The Character of the Happy Warrior," which is, I suppose, the respectable father of the profligate "If."[1] It seemed too moral and "manly," the students said, and once when I remarked that John Wordsworth had apparently been just such a man as his brother had described, and told them about his dutiful and courageous death at sea, they said flatly that they were not impressed. This was not what most of them really thought, but the idea of courage and duty had been steeped for them in the Kipling vat and they rejected the idea with the colour. In England this response seems to have gone even further.[2] And when the War came, the interesting and touching phenomenon of the cult of Richard Hillary, which Arthur Koestler has described, was the effort of the English young men to find the national virtues without the Kipling colour, to know and resist their enemies without self-glorification.

In our day the idea of the nation has become doubtful and debilitated all over the world, or at least wherever it is not being enforced by ruthless governments or wherever it is not being nourished by immediate danger or the tyranny of other nations. Men more and more think it best to postulate their loyalty either to their class, or to the idea of a social organisation more comprehensive than that of the nation, or to a cultural ideal or a spiritual fatherland. Yet in the attack which has been made on the national idea, there are, one suspects, certain motives that are not expressed, motives that have less to do with reason and order than with the modern impulse to say that politics is not really a proper human activity at all; the reluctance to give loyalty to any social organisation which falls short of some ideal organisation of the future may imply a disgust not so much with the merely national life as with civic life itself. And on the positive side too something is still to be said for nations, the case against them is not yet closed. Of course in literature nothing ever is said; every avowal of national pride or love or faith rings false and serves but to reinforce the tendency of rejection, as the example of the

[1] The War over, the struggle is on again.

[2] George Orwell's essay on Kipling deals bluntly and fairly with the implications of easy "liberal" and "aesthetic" contempt for *everything* Kipling stood for.

response to Kipling shows. Yet Kipling himself, on one occasion, dealt successfully with the national theme and in doing so implied the reason for the general failure – the "Recessional" hymn is a remarkable and perhaps a great national poem; its import of humility and fear at the moment of national success suggests that the idea of the nation, although no doubt a limited one, is still profound enough to require that it be treated with a certain measure of seriousness and truth-telling. But the occasion is exceptional with Kipling, who by the utterances that are characteristic of him did more than any writer of our time to bring the national idea into discredit.

II. KIPLING'S "PHILOSOPHY"

Noel Annan

KIPLING'S PLACE IN THE HISTORY OF IDEAS*

I

CRITICISM HAS not yet come to terms with Kipling: the man and his works symbolise a part of British political and social history about which his countrymen have an uneasy conscience. Ever since the turn of the century, when Max Beerbohm began to caricature him with loathing, he has been regarded as a strident geranium, red as a map of the colonies and the antithesis of the green carnations of the 'nineties, and at the root of every assessment of Kipling lies the problem of his morality. In 1941 the two most famous critics in England and America chose quite independently to consider his status. T. S. Eliot, meditating among the bombs in war-time London, asked us to reconsider the fashionable verdict on the great imperialist.[1] He met with an unequivocal response. Raymond Mortimer,[2] Peter Quennell,[3] Graham Greene,[4] G. W. Stonier,[5] Hugh Kingsmill,[6] and *Scrutiny*[7] in the person of Boris Ford echoed each other's disgust; and in America Lionel Trilling[8] denied that Eliot could claim Kipling for the Tory tradition, "a tradition which is honoured by Dr Johnson, Burke, and Walter Scott. . . . he has none of the *mind* of the few great Tories. His Toryism had in it a lower middle-

* [Reprinted from *Victorian Studies*, VOL. III (1959-60).]
[1] *A Choice of Kipling's Verse made by T. S. Eliot*, London 1941.
[2] *Sunday Times*, 14 Sep. 1952.
[3] *The Singular Preference*, London 1952, pp. 159-66.
[4] *The Lost Childhood*, London 1951, pp. 74-5.
[5] *New Statesman and Nation*, XXIII (1942), 10.
[6] *Progress of a Biographer*, London 1949, pp. 27-37.
[7] XI (1942), 23-33.   [8] See above, pp. 85-94.

class snarl of defeated gentility. . . ." Auden[9] and Orwell[10] characteristically refused to sing in harmony but took as proved the usual charges against Kipling's social and moral philosophy; and Desmond MacCarthy's encomium[11] at Kipling's death, though judicious, was restrained.

On the other side of the Atlantic, however, Edmund Wilson, writing at the high-noon of American liberalism, gave a verdict which has become orthodoxy.[12] He found much to praise in the young Anglo-Indian journalist and in the dark stories of Jamesian complexity written in his last years – "the Kipling that nobody read." But the praise was combined with a devastating judgment on the mature man, whose morality Wilson found repulsive. In a brilliant piece of conjectural biography he reconciled the two Kiplings and explained how this lively and sympathetic young man, who wrote with equal understanding of Englishmen and Indians, became the champion of authoritarian upper-middle-class rule: yet eventually with the loss of his son in the First World War, which led to the collapse of Kipling's ideal of Imperial Britain ruling the world, was purged of his sins through suffering and emerged as an Oedipus Coloneus.

Kipling has always had, of course, his defenders among the clerisy: professors, such as Bonamy Dobrée,[13] who has lived in the East, or G. M. Trevelyan,[14] who admires his historical imagination; biographers, such as Edward B. Shanks[15] or Hilton Brown,[16] and, in particular, the Imperial historian C. E. Carrington,[17] whose official biography disposes, if anything can dispose, of Wilson's conjectures. But Carrington is no critic and the now aging generation that read Kipling in boyhood spend so much of the fight in protesting that Kipling has been misunderstood that they look like a boxer milling on the retreat. Now they have been joined by Miss J. M. S. Tompkins, a past member of the English staff at two of the women's colleges of London University. Her

[9] "The Poet of the Encirclement" in *Literary Opinion in America*, ed. M. D. Zabel, New York 1951. Repr. from the *New Republic*, CIX (1943), 579-81.   [10] See above, pp. 70-84.

[11] *Memories*, London 1953, pp. 76-82.

[12] See above, pp. 17-69.   [13] *Listener*, XLVII (1952), 967-78.

[14] *A Layman's Love of Letters*, London 1954, pp. 27-35.

[15] *Rudyard Kipling*, London 1940.

[16] *Rudyard Kipling*, London 1945.   [17] *Rudyard Kipling*, London 1955.

book[18] is an immensely thorough study of what Kipling wrote and has several great merits. She explains his work in the light of his explicit intention. Indeed she often uses the very terms that Kipling used in describing how he wrote – the Pre-Raphaelite words of his uncle Burne-Jones, colour, tone, "heavy strokes" – so that, whatever one thinks of these terms, one knows what Kipling was at and how he saw himself compose. Thus she draws attention to the intricacy and economy of Kipling's stories, which are usually asserting a number of things simultaneously. She shows how the verse relates to the stories and she pays the minutest attention to the texture of his tales: in so doing she weaves the pattern of the development of his technique as an artist. She also isolates the important themes in his work: the notions of Laughter, Hatred, Revenge, Healing, and man's relation to the unseen and incomprehensible.

But the problem of placing Kipling remains. Miss Tompkins is not a modern critic. She is concerned with the texture of the stories but not with the texture of Kipling's *language*, and Kipling's craftsmanship occupies her attention rather than his total response to life. She candidly admits that her book is not a "a formal assessment of his achievement" nor "a critical enquiry in the strictest sense of the term"; and, though in fact she establishes that contemporary criticism is based on a superficial reading of his works and in the course of the book implicitly meets many of the common strictures, she ignores from the outset the main moral and political challenge which Kipling's work has always made. Her honest disavowal does her all the more credit, but this book convinces me that the riddle of Kipling cannot be answered wholly in literary, or still less in biographical, terms. Part of the answer, I believe, lies in Kipling's peculiar analysis of how society works. From this analysis came a conception of history and politics far more disturbing than that of the imperialism which is supposed to be the compass of his imagination. Despite the multitude of characters in his stories, he is less interested in people than in social realities and that is why his morality appears to be distorted. The centre of Kipling's world is society itself, and he related man to society in a way different from that of any other late Victorian writer. His understanding

[18] *The Art of Rudyard Kipling*, London 1959.

of society resembles that of a sociologist – and, what is more odd, it owed nothing to the theories of society then current in England. He is indeed the sole analogue in England to those continental sociologists – Durkheim, Weber, and Pareto – who revolutionised the study of society at the beginning of this century. The same problems which forced them to invent new methods of analysing human behaviour led him to conclusions similar to theirs.

2

Nothing marks the break with Victorian thought more decisively than modern sociology. The new sociologists in Europe broke with philosophy and historicism, whether Positivist, Idealist, or Marxist. They saw society as a nexus of groups; and the patterns of behaviour which these groups unwittingly established, rather than men's wills or anything so vague as a class, cultural, or national tradition, primarily determined men's actions. They asked how these groups promoted order or instability in society, whereas their predecessors had asked whether certain groups helped society to progress. Weber did not consider whether religion was true or good. He accepted it as a social fact and argued that different religions produced different codes of conduct which affected the politics and economy of the society in which they flourished. Durkheim showed concretely how people's behaviour was determined by the society in which they lived. In his famous analysis of suicide he deduced which groups constantly had the highest rate and argued that one important factor was the degree to which the individual was integrated within his group and accepted the code of communal behaviour. He saw the individual as a bolt which might snap if the nut of society held it too tightly or too loosely. Excessive integration, as in the army officer caste, with its strict code of behaviour which sometimes ran counter to the morality of the community as a whole, could be as dangerous as imperfect integration. Institutions could never be explained solely in terms of their utility: they could be understood only by discovering how they corresponded to the general needs of society. Durkheim thus explained in a new manner the existence of order and of the deviations from the norms in society. Men did not so much search for goals to pursue but accepted those which their group or class in society chose for them. The dichotomy between the individual and society he pronounced to be largely false; for though men might act, and be judged to be acting rightly, against the moral consensus of society, without such a moral consensus they could not act at all. A society without moral consensus or rituals and sacred objects would disintegrate.

These insights are commonplace to-day, and indeed we are more aware of the questions which these great innovators left unanswered than of those they settled. But to an historian the striking fact is that for long they were virtually ignored in England. Paradoxically in the land which prides itself on approaching political problems empirically, society continued to be studied in terms of ethics and philosophy.[19] Kipling prided himself, however, on describing what Durkheim called social facts and on despising talk of individual rights, sanctions, and contracts. He did not, of course, analyse social processes in the manner of Durkheim and Weber: he was an artist working through his sensibilities and had no use for deductive systems of thought. While for most writers society is the background, or provides the interests for, or is a positive threat to their characters, for Kipling the very existence of society is a problem. Like the new sociologists he was fascinated by the problem of social order. His English contemporaries, living in a society untouched for generations by civil war or revolution or economic or spiritual disaster were never forced to consider why society still continued to hang together. But Kipling was forced to consider it. He had been born and began to work in India and belonged to one of the many groups, each with its own customs, conventions, and morality, that flourished on the sub-continent. Only thirty years before he began to write, the caste to which he belonged, Anglo-India, had faced annihilation in the days of the Mutiny. Like Maine or Fitzjames Stephen, Kipling perceived the contradictions between what Englishmen were taught to believe about society and what actually existed in India; and when he asked what forces kept the groups in this bewildering society

[19] I have suggested some reasons why this was so in my Hobhouse Memorial Lecture, *The Curious Strength of Positivism in English Political Thought*, London 1958.

together, he found the answer, as Durkheim had, in the forces of
social control. Then again his notion of the "Law" is not an
ordinary idea: it is the same as the anthropologists' *culture*. The
impression which his work as a whole gives is that of a man who
sees human beings moving in a definable network of social
relationships which impose upon them a code of behaviour
appropriate to their environment.

3

The picture of India which Kipling painted in his first four
volumes of short stories and in his earliest verse is that of a
society which politically, nervously, physically, and spiritually
quivered on the edge of a precipice. None of the conditions of
life resembled those of England. Here Nature was inconceivably
hostile. The pitiless sun spread famine and the rain floods, and
cholera, fever, reptiles, and wild beasts brought death. Death
was always at a man's elbow, and Anglo-Indians in remote
villages met regularly to prove to each other that they were still
alive. The very flowers, the hateful marigolds, were symbols of
heat and death. Kipling did not personify Nature like Hardy:
like a sociologist he took the environment as given and noted its
effect upon men. In such a climate love was almost impossible.
Young men slaving to save money in order to bring out girls
from England denied themselves the company or diversions
which they needed in order to survive: either they died themselves, or the girl succumbed, or their children were the victims
of the carelessness of their *ayah*. As often as not the girl in
England had forgotten them long before they could pay her fare.
So they turned to other men's wives or to the few daughters of
their superiors. Yet what romance could blossom when everyone knew to the last rupee everyone else's income and prospects
in this salaried class? Besides, in this world one could easily
propose to the wrong girl in a dust-storm. Those who married
fretted their hearts out as they saw their wives pine in the plains
tortured by heat and illness. Or they sent them to Simla – to
the scandal and adultery which boredom bred, a boredom in
which adultery lost its romance and was founded on delusion.
For what was there to talk about? In this world there was no

art, no music, no books; there was only India.[20] Marriage frequently brought disaster. Those, like Captain Gadsby, who had private means, however loyal to their regiment, in the end sent in their papers for the sake of their wife and family. Those who had not, necessarily cut themselves off from the Indians: Strickland, the omniscient police officer, married, and now "he fills in his Departmental returns beautifully."[21] In this world marriage halved a man's efficiency in his work.

Kipling then cast an admiring but piercing eye upon this work – the work of governing India. In England government, whatever its faults, achieved results. Did it in India? Come to Simla and see the high-ups entirely lacking that intimate knowledge which was needed to govern a country – men whose very children, like Tod, could better amend legislation because they mixed with Indian servants and knew more facts. Come to Simla and see the wives of the high-ups placing their fancy-men in the Secretariat at the expense of those who accumulated experience and knowledge in the Provinces. Come to Simla to see the full corruption of love, of marriage, of administration. Yet perhaps Simla was right. Not to take one's work too seriously was the only way of retaining sanity. Overwork, the endemic disease of the Indian civil servant, led to the collapse in health which spelt death; and why overwork when Pagett, M.P., appeared from Home to tell you in the heat of summer that you were overpaid? Overwork led to the mania whereby an official would spend weeks in plotting revenge upon another who had chaffed him for buying a crock of a horse. Why overwork administering justice in a country where witnesses to a murder could be bought for a few rupees, where the native police were frequently bribed, and where an English attempt to be "moral" could be defeated by a mixture of black magic, debt, and the virtual slavery of women which were integral to Indian life? Nothing changed in India "in spite of the shiny top-scum stuff that people call 'civilisation'."[22] The Army was full of fine

[20] There were highly intelligent and able men in the Indian Civil Service; but their intelligence was brought to bear exclusively on their work or on their hobbies, rarely on general ideas.

[21] "Miss Youghal's Sais," *Plain Tales from the Hills.*

[22] "The Bisara of Pooree," *Plain Tales from the Hills.*

young officers, yet in the arithmetic of the frontier "two thousand pounds of education drops to a ten-rupee jezail"[23]; and was not the campaign likely to be mismanaged when the brigadier was out for a knighthood and the colonel for a medal and the Government wanted to spend as little money and excite as little comment as possible? The life of the private soldier was spent in early morning drill in cantonment followed by hours of insufferable *cafard* broken by a little quiet looting and torturing of Indians when the drink was in him; and it ended perhaps on a gallows hanged for a murder to which he had been driven by heat or by delusion. In this world delusion, not truth, made men act – the delusion that they were doing good, or fulfilling some mission, or giving someone his just deserts.

Kipling perceived that if the normal criteria of the Victorian novelist did not apply to Anglo-India, they applied still less to the Indians. Indians lived lives incomprehensible to white men because custom and religion imposed a code of behaviour different from theirs: the duty to kill another man in a blood-feud was called by the English murder and when the English imposed their culture in addition to their rule – when they sent missionaries to a village – confusion and resentment followed on both sides. Anglicisation of Indians was a delusion. British justice was an efficient machine which enabled the money-lender and landlord the keener to oppress the poor. Finally Kipling declared that no native could be trusted to rule because "he is as incapable as a child of understanding what authority means, or where is the danger of disobeying it."[24]

4

What then prevented such a society from going over the precipice? Kipling answered: religion, law, custom, convention, morality – the forces of social control – which imposed upon individuals certain rules which they broke at their peril. Conventions enabled men to retain their self-respect and even to live together under appalling circumstances. In "A Wayside Comedy" (*Wee Willie Winkie*), at a remote outpost inhabited by two Anglo-Indian couples and a bachelor, the first wife hates the bachelor

---

[23] "Arithmetic on the Frontier," *Departmental Ditties*.
[24] "His Chance in Life," *Plain Tales from the Hills*.

for trying to seduce her; the second wife hates the first for rejecting the man who was her lover but has now left her; but the
husbands see that life in this place and situation is possible only
if everyone obeys the trivialities of existence. They have created
a hell from which there is no escape; this is the only way to
alleviate the torment. As a corollary, punishment must fall on
those who break the conventions, and this partially explains why
so many of Kipling's stories are concerned with scenes in which
the individualist, the eccentric, the man who offends against the
trivial rules of the club, are tarred and feathered with gleeful
brutality. If the offender is not brought to heel, society will
suffer. What brought about the situation described in "A Wayside Comedy"? The absence of one of the forces of social
control: "all laws weaken in a small and hidden community
where there is no public opinion." Kipling's favourite themes
are those in which punishment falls on those who break the rules
and disaster on those who do not know them.

He was hardly interested whether the customs or morality or
religion were right or wrong. For him all that mattered was that
they existed. The old sociologists, Comte and Spencer, informed
him that science was true and religion false, and Kipling de-
nounced them in "The Conversion of Aurelian McGoggin"
(*Plain Tales*). In India God and souls existed because the culture
and assumptions of the Indians were based on their existence.
Religion was a social fact. One tenet of the liberal atheists, said
Kipling, paraphrasing W. K. Clifford, "seemed to be that the one
thing more sinful than giving an order was obeying it."[25] But
in India order rested on hierarchy and authority, and "the climate
and the work are against playing bricks with words." Comte's
Humanity bore no relation to the raw, brown, naked humanity
which surrounded Kipling, who understood the social significance
of religion in one sense far better than his great contemporary,
the author of *The Golden Bough*. Writing in the afterglow of
evolutionary theory, Frazer saw religion and magic as a kind of
primitive science which would ultimately vanish as scientific
knowledge spread. Kipling, on the other hand, like Weber,
regarded the truth of religion as irrelevant because religion was
a medium through which men expressed their aspirations and

[25] Cp. W. K. Clifford, *Lectures and Essays*, 3rd edn, London 1901, II, 44.

found solace when frustrated. There were many gods, and men changed and discarded them, as Weland Smith discovered, and as Krishna warned his fellow deities. The forces of social control preserved man by constraining him.

The second part of Kipling's social theory emerges most clearly in the stories of his middle period. The forces of social control are harsh, but the burden of conformity can be alleviated by belonging to in-groups which protect their members from the outsiders who want to invade their privacy, and differentiate them by stamping them with the individuality of the group. Men belong involuntarily to their family or their school and choose other in-groups such as their craft or profession voluntarily. Each in-group teaches the rules by which society is governed. For Kipling, as for nearly all Victorians, the greatest of all involuntary in-groups is the family, the great protector against the world's hostility and the inculcator of love and decency. How closely (and absurdly) Kipling thought the well-being of the family was connected with the good of society may be deduced from one of the most dreadful sentences he ever wrote. When that paragon of virtue, the Brushwood Boy, returns to his ancestral home, his mother, wishing to spy out his intentions as regards marriage, takes him aside. "They talked for a long hour, as mother and son should, if there is to be any future for our Empire."[26] The dispensations of the family were too sacred to be recorded. The parting of children from their parents, the common lot of Anglo-Indians, was a blasphemy to Kipling, who remembered his own suffering. The family was the only place where affections between human beings could *safely* be displayed. His personal life, so carefully hidden in his autobiography, existed first within the orbit of his parents and his sister, to whom he was devoted, and then within that of his wife and children. Such happiness acquired the characteristics of a taboo and could not be profaned in speech.

The second involuntary in-group was the school, which showed men what society was like. Kipling emphasised that this education was implicit and impersonal, not explicit and pedagogic. In *Stalky & Co.* the distinction is continually drawn between appearance and reality. The good-form, herd schoolboy is

[26] "The Brushwood Boy," *The Day's Work.*

opposed to Stalky. The heavy priggish housemaster, Prout, with his self-conscious encouragement of games and house spirit is set against the realists Hartopp and the Chaplain, who expect boys to crib and bully. King, the best teacher (in the academic sense), with his passion for the Latin authors and the respectable English poets is regarded cynically by the heavy-lidded boys who know that he is hired to cram them for Sandhurst and that "all the rest's flumdiddle." Whereas King's ambition is to raise the standard and manners of the place to those of the great public schools, the common sense of the Head and the boys tells them that the Imperial Service College is a minor public school and "a limited liability company paying four per cent." The real patriot is the subaltern Toffee Crandall, not the Jelly-Bellied Flag-Flapper; the real enthusiasm for letters is not to be found among the Sixth Form swats, but in Beetle, avidly reading his way through the Head's French yellow-backs and the metaphysical poets. Real education is what the boys teach each other in ways which the masters cannot. The in-group teaches spontaneously the way society works. The masters are powerless to diminish vice unless they work subtly unobserved through the boys' collective sense of rightness. Appeals to individual conscience are ineffective because they are "unreal," being based on an ideology – the ideology of public school "good form" be-haviour – that does not spring from social facts, but is imposed from without by abstract moralisers. Even the individuality of Stalky, M'Turk, and Beetle does not grow from themselves, but from the fact that they form an in-group within the macrocosm and are thus able to protect and assert themselves. As the self-made father of Harvey in *Captains Courageous* tells his son, school-ing gives men the means to hurt their enemies more effectively. To acquire this power is a painful process, and Kipling signi-ficantly describes it as learning "all the Armoured Man should know, Through his Seven Secret Years . . ."[27] It consists in hardening the shell. Not to expect fairness was the mark of the "educated" man.[28] Stalky earned his name by seeing the facts as

[27] "The Totem," *Limits and Renewals*.

[28] Who need not have been to a public school. Cp. Ortheris's scorn when, in "His Private Honour" (*Many Inventions*), he rejects the suggestion that he could have stood on his right to get the officer who struck him

they were: by not being blinded by emotion or resentment, as Beetle frequently was, by never being "drawn" either by King or the Viceroy, and by rejecting the ideology of the public school or the Army, which is a gloss put upon the facts by moralists who try to conceal the harsh truth about social relationships.

The true spirit of the public school or the Army was not expressed in precepts and regulations. On the one occasion when Stalky abandoned his principles and on an emotional impulse took the lead in joining the volunteer cadet corps because he wanted to play at being a regular soldier, he was so disintegrated by the speech of the Jelly-Bellied Flag-Flapper that he broke up the cadet corps and burst into tears because he knew that he had been an instrument in profaning the sacred. Malinowski observed that precisely because savages understood that no magic or ritual could bring the dead back to life, the need for regulating emotion by ritual was all the stronger: death inspired such violent emotions that the tribe would be exposed to the danger of the frenzied grief of the bereaved unless such grief were canalised. Kipling similarly suggested that emotion which gushed uncontrolled was a menace permissible only to those who had no roots.

> Unless you come of the gipsy stock
> That steals by night and day
> Lock your heart with a double lock
> And throw the key away . . .[29]

The voluntary in-groups repeat these lessons. The practical jokes in "The Rescue of Pluffles" or "Watches of the Night" (*Plain Tales*), exemplify the way in which the in-group educates. And they teach another. Self-discipline is needed to master a craft. Dick Heldar in *The Light that Failed* was in danger of valuing success instead of his craft and had to learn the wisdom of the Maltese Cat or Mahbub Ali. Knowledge comes only to those who acquire it for its own sake. Kipling seems to suggest that he who had mastered a craft would possess insight into the workings of the world; or rather that discipline would regulate

cashiered. Kipling wrote *Stalky & Co.* on his return from America after the row with his brother-in-law in which he had stood on his rights and expected fairness.   [29] "Gipsy Vans," *Debits and Credits*.

the mind and purge it of fancies and conceit so that it would in-tuitively distinguish the true from the false. This was why he so admired the "crafty" and desired to be on the inside, why he displayed his knowledge by throwing off aphorisms and proverbial wisdom, and why he was able through his gift of turning a casual acquaintance inside out to convey to his reader the technique of the forester, the engineer, the soldier, or the horse-coper. He was astonished on his return to London from India to find that his fellow-writers ignored contemporary French fiction, an essential instrument for mastering their craft. The knowledge learnt first-hand from the involuntary in-group or second-hand from those who discovered the secrets of other in-groups was the clue to social adjustment.

5

There remains the last part of his sociology, the doctrine of the Law. All cultures exhibit common features, and men in all ages have recognised that different societies owe obligations to each other. Although Kipling was not concerned with the rightness of the codes of in-groups or societies, he was not a moral rela-tivist. British culture was superior to Indian only by virtue of its superior techniques and ability to rule: as Bagehot said, the British were superior because "they can beat [them] in war when they like; they can take from them anything they like, and kill any of them they choose."[30] Kipling, who had little love for the Christianity of the churches, implied that the Indians were as superior to the British in religion as the British were to them in material power. Civilisation in all of its forms rested upon knowledge of the Law which transcended individual cultures. The Law, which appears in the form of a fable in the *Jungle Books*, consisted of those rules of conduct – the keeping of promises, loyalty to friends, bravery, generosity, respect for parents, and so on – which restrained men's egotism, which all races and creeds held were good, and which enabled the British soldier to recognise that Gunga Din was a better man than he. It follows that those who broke the Law were outside the pale of civilisation.

This theory of society contains within it two interesting modu-

[30] Walter Bagehot, *Physics and Politics*, London 1872, p. 207. (He was referring to Australian aborigines.)

lations in the Conservative tradition. Ever since Burke, conservative political thinkers have attacked deductive or "rationalist" political philosophy and in the past hundred years have often used Kant's distinction between pure and practical reason as the foundation of their critique of knowledge. The argument is familiar. *Real* knowledge about things that matter – morals, behaviour, politics, and personal relations – is incapable of scientific analysis and can be acquired only by experience. To express a tradition of behaviour in rules or precepts is to devitalise it. Thus the folk-lore of Pook's Hill is a better guide to the feelings and needs of common people than abstract treatises on their rights or sanctimonious schemes for their improvement. Kipling suspected any belief that purported to have been formed by rational conviction and delighted in showing that such beliefs were either held for disreputable motives or were mere repetitions of formulae. An Indian's conversion to Christianity could never be more than skin-deep, and a sophisticated Moslem's agnosticism would vanish at the sound of a religious riot. Social well-being depended not on abstract notions of justice but on the administration of people. The hard-bitten district officers such as Orde and Tallantire, who knew all the gossip of the area under their administrations, were contrasted with the bureaucrats and Radical politicians. To Kipling, Josephine Butler's struggle for women's rights was an instance of abstract morality that had increased the rate of venereal disease in the Army by forcing the military authorities to discontinue the medical inspection of prostitutes in licensed military brothels. Democracy and popular education were suspect in that they enabled people to cut loose from the conventions of their class which gave them stability and dignity. Whereas liberals regard class distinctions as fetters forged by society which prevent equals from shaking hands, conservatives regard them as valuable hall-marks enabling men to recognise how they stand in relation to each other. "Without Benefit of Clergy" (*Life's Handicap*) showed Kipling writing with sympathy of a *liaison* between an Englishman and an Indian woman; but the idyll ends with the death of wife and child and the demolition of the very house which they inhabited. The demolition symbolises the impossibility of fusing British and Indian culture through love. Love is not a supra-social attribute: as Malthus argued, it is socialised by the institution of marriage. Since marriage in this case is impossible, the separate cultures cannot be bridged by love. Nor could the English genius for government be transmitted by bureaucratic fiat to the Indians: only on the level of the Law where strength recognised strength could East and West meet.

Implicit, however, in the conservative theory of knowledge runs a deep distrust of science and the scientific method, which in late Victorian times was riding high on the crest of positivist philosophy and radicalism. Here Kipling added something new. As the bard of the engineer and protagonist of the new technology, he would have nothing to do with the reactionary cant which maintains that science itself is an evil. The evil lay only in claiming more for science than it can perform. It was a marvellous craft whose discoveries Kipling continually set in contrast to the as yet undiscovered. In "Wireless" (*Traffics and Discoveries*), the transmission of the human voice by the new invention was dwarfed by the extraordinary transferences in the thought of the tubercular chemist's assistant who spoke Keats's poetry. Science could never challenge "true" knowledge because it was true only for its own time and our science would appear to future generations as astrology did to us: discoveries in fact might be made too early and, as in "The Eye of Allah" (*Debits and Credits*), might have to be suppressed because society was not yet able to assimilate them. The close connexion between science and society was again picked up in "Unprofessional" (*Limits and Renewals*), where Kipling stressed that a new discovery in science would create a new social problem: Mrs Berner tried to commit suicide *after* she was cured, a moral to those who imagined that a problem has only to be scientifically examined for the "correct" solution to be found. If Kipling admired the strides made in psychology and medicine and engineering, he also intended to demonstrate how limited were their potentiality and accuracy.[31]

The second modulation that Kipling made was in breaking with the older English conservatism which placed its trust in

[31] For similar reasoning about the place of science in history and thought by two modern conservatives see: Herbert Butterfield, *The Origins of Modern Science*, London 1949, and Michael Oakeshott, "Rationalism in Politics," *Cambridge Journal*, I (1947), 81-98, 145-57.

leadership by an aristocracy of birth. He belonged to the new conservatism of imperial adventure and to the new class of skilled workers, technicians, engineers, and public servants, products of the rapid class-differentiation in the second phase of the Industrial Revolution. His genius in describing the emotions of this class towards their work has diverted attention from his delight in the mess of cotton waste and oil and clinker generated by engines; his tramp steamers are held together by the proverbial piece of string and coaxed along by their engineers. This adds to his picture of society as ordered by laws but nevertheless as dynamic, bursting at the seams, untidy, full of rascals and shrewd men operating on a shoestring and ready to exploit any sucker. A world without hardness, a world in which fairness, in which men's rights were scrupulously weighed, would be for Kipling a devitalised world. Miss Tompkins points out that in Kipling's most famous anti-democratic tract, "As Easy as A.B.C." (*A Diversity of Creatures*), the utopian world governed by five dictators in which peace and plenty reign is afflicted by too much happiness and "the basic energy of life is failing in a world where men do not struggle and suffer to their full scope."[32] Action, then, has a positive merit. The natural conflict of social forces within the State is to be regarded as a blessing, not as a curse, and happiness is only one of the many goals in life. Liberals regard men's happiness as the ideal to which all the sciences and arts minister: the forms of government which ensure his freedom, the drugs and psycho-analysis which cure his diseased body and mind, the economics which shows how the plenty which the applied sciences make possible can best be produced and distri-buted, are all called into being to increase his happiness. The conservative distrusts this word. In his worst moods he is apt to argue that the abolition of slavery is a piece of legislative legerdemain which in no way increases happiness because it does not change those social processes which determine whether a man is free in more than name: or he plays the game of *tu quoque*, observing, like Kipling, that those who protested most loudly about British oppression of Indians were those most given to oppressing their housemaids.[33] But even when he admits that happiness is a reality, he defines it as a state of mind which

---

[32] Tompkins, *op. cit.*, p. 96.   [33] *Something of Myself*, Chapter Four.

comprehends where the self fits into the scheme of things and realises that spring cannot for ever be spring and that winter succeeds autumn. Men are, however, incurably full of illusions and seldom contented with their lot. They should therefore be taught the terms on which they are allowed to rise and the upstart should be subjected to a course of indoctrination which will bring his ambition within bounds, and turn his children into gentlemen. A sequence of stories, from "The Walking Delegate" (*The Day's Work*) to "The Tie" (*Limits and Renewals*), all emphasise the necessity for men or animals to find their place and, if they have come up in the world, to be taught it. But when the individual has proved himself in his in-group, and so long as he is not, in the strict sense of the word, an eccentric, then the more daring his behaviour and the more abundant his action, the greater is the addition of joy in the world. The baby of the mess could score off the Senior Subaltern, a scoundrel such as Dana Da could perpetrate monstrous deceptions, and Stalky could tweak the nose of authority. Stalky was the prototype of this socialised individualism. He acted beyond the formal law of Army regulations and possessed the gift of seeing himself from the outside – in relation to society.[34] In Kipling's world the joy in action and its revitalising influence were the obverse of the suffering it caused. And suffering was inevitable. Political action is often not a choice between good and evil but between lesser and greater evil. This is one of the lessons, Miss Tompkins notes, that Puck teaches Dan: "We cannot judge men for what they do under duress; nor can we judge the Lord for imposing the duress by which such actions are enforced."[35]

Puck of Pook's Hill is a study in the dynamics of culture and its tales are deliberately arranged unchronologically to illustrate the connexion between social order and civilisation. The main theme is that the Sword led men to the Treasure, and the Treasure gave the Law. The two symbols of Power are civilised by the Law.

[34] Kipling was surprised when Dunsterville (Stalky) dispassionately admitted that the War Office was justified in dispensing with his services after he had pitched in a particularly hot letter on his return to England at the end of the Dunsterforce expedition (*op. cit.*, Chapter Two).

[35] Tompkins, *op. cit.*, pp. 73, 84.

The Norman stories present the picture of an England smitten by rebellion, and riven between Norman and Saxon. How had order and civilisation collapse? The Roman stories provide the answer: the Wall, the symbol of civilisation, was then about to fall because Rome had lost its genius for government. The Norman De Aquila by his cunning and political wisdom is trying to unite the country. He marries his young knights to the conquered and does not hang but uses the rebels Fulke and Gilbert. " 'I am too old to judge or to trust any man,' he said. . . . De Aquila was right. One should not judge men." And this theme is repeated in "Hal o' the Draft" where the shrewd J.P. lets the smugglers go scot-free: he does not want civil war in Sussex and a lot of nonsense talked about traitors. The last story cuts back to Magna Carta, the formal pronouncement of the English Law. Here Kipling introduces the theme of the Jew who alone understands money, the dangerous solvent of society. When the Danes returned from Africa with the Gold, all except the landless Thorkild of Borkum were infected by its presence. "Gold changes men altogether." But the rootless Jew knows that Gold is stronger than the Sword and can make and break kings. "That is *our* God in our captivity. Power to use!" And Kadmiel uses it to benefit his race by getting the barons to include even Jews under the provisions of Magna Carta.

Four orders of men appear: those like the Picts, slaves by Necessity, ground between the grindstones of Rome and the Winged Hats, and also slaves by nature, "too little to love or to hate"; the craftsmen of England, Hal the painter and Hobson the yeoman; the officers or administrators, Parnesius and Pertinax (the Ordes and Tallantires of yesterday), who know their province and their people; and Maximus and De Aquila, the politicians and governors. To test Parnesius' flexibility Maximus orders him to execute a soldier for trivial disobedience; he refuses, and Maximus tells him that he will never be a staff-officer or rule a province, for he lacks the will to please his superiors. Meanwhile the fairy theme illuminates a different order of reality. The fairies, gods of a bygone age who have come down in the world and learnt humility through misfortune, were worshipped in the days when man was the child of Nature. But when he discovered iron and believed himself to be her master, they fell; and when the

Reformation turned Englishmen's religion into hate they flitted. Now they are gone – but Puck bestowed a gift upon the descendants of the widow who gave them her blessing and the means to flit: in each generation one of her family will be a simpleton and blessed with the gift of insight into the ways of Nature to preserve the immemorial wisdom of the country and the rituals which descend from the runes on the sword and Mithraism through the religion of Freemasonry.

The presence throughout of the children conveys the hope for the future. For beneath the solid trappings of Edwardian affluence Kipling scanned the future with anxious eyes. Would the Wall fall again before the democratic hordes of little men and the Prussian Winged Hats? Were not the younger rulers, F. E. Smith and the renegade conservative Winston Churchill, tainted by the ambition of Maximus? Were not the financiers manipulating trade and industry to their own ends – were not luxury and wealth corrupting the ruling class and turning their children into flannelled fools at the wicket? What then was the fate of England – an England rent by class warfare and in a few years time to be meditating civil war in Ireland? Critics have pointed out that other writers also scanned the future.[36] *Heartbreak House*, *Howard's End*, and *Puck of Pook's Hill* are the attempts by a socialist, a liberal, and a conservative to discern England's destiny.

6

Such I believe to be Kipling's theory of society; and it is important, not only for what it is, but because he had worked it out so thoroughly. This, he says with relish in his stories of hatred and revenge, is how men and women behave, and how they must behave, under the pressure of social forces. Almost everything in Kipling, as in Malinowski, has its *function* – whether it is laughter or ritual. But the theory is not the whole story, and Miss Tompkins's book is one long refutation of the simple liberal interpretations that have been made of his work. His stories have so many layers (as distinct from, in greater writers, unconscious levels) of meaning that nearly always a multitude of things

[36] F. E. W. McDowell, "Technique, Symbol and Theme in Heartbreak House," *P.M.L.A.*, LXVIII (1953), 335-56; Lionel Trilling, *E. M. Forster*, London 1951, p. 102.

are being asserted. (The analysis of *Puck of Pook's Hill* above by
no means covers all that is being said.) The most revealing
testimony which Miss Tompkins provides is her analysis of the
theme of healing. Like Durkheim in his essay on suicide, Kipling
realised that men break under the strain which society imposes
upon them and that the protection afforded by the normal in-
groups is insufficient. Freemasonry can heal them: "Ritual's a
natural necessity of mankind," says one of the Brothers in the
Lodge, "the more things are upset, the more they fly to it."[37]
Science or communion with Nature, rascals, laughter, and dogs
can heal them. The worst disease of all, introspection and self-
pity – the refusal to accept Necessity – can be cured only by
contact with mirth, vitality, and love. Kipling's sense of his own
social theory prevents him from self-contradiction. He shows
how suffering can be alleviated but also shows the Limits of
Renewal. Miss Tompkins cites "Fairy Kist" (*Limits and Renewals*) where one character is saved outright but another has
"been tried too high." Some, such as Helen in "The Gardener"
(*Debits and Credits*), will never be freed from their burden, though
the pain may be lightened; some, such as Grace Ashcroft, are
cleansed by their suffering, though doomed to disease; others,
like the scientist Wilkett, are cured psychologically of their
obsessions, but not morally. The whole of Edmund Wilson's
case hung on the assertion that the brutally insensitive authoritarian of the middle years is replaced by the compassionate figure
of the post-1918 period. Miss Tompkins has no difficulty in
showing that the theme of healing appeared long before the last
two volumes, in "Baa, Baa, Black Sheep" (*Wee Willie Winkie*),
"Marklake Witches" (*Rewards and Fairies*), "A Doctor of Medicine," "An Habitation Enforced" (*Actions and Reactions*), "My
Son's Wife" (*A Diversity of Creatures*), and "In the Same Boat"
(*Actions and Reactions*). Nor of healing alone: the theme of forgiveness emerges in "The House-Surgeon" (*Actions and Reactions*), of alleviation of suffering in "They" (*Traffics and Discoveries*), of pity for the doomed in "The Disturber of Traffic"
(*Many Inventions*) and "A Matter of Fact" (*Many Inventions*), with
its eerie description of the death of the sea-monster blinded by

[37] "The Interests of the Brethren," *Debits and Credits*, quoted by Tompkins,
p. 175.

the under-water explosion. I would also add that Kipling no less than the modern Roman Catholic novelists understood the meaning of repentance – its apparent futility and its ultimate importance. The characters of *Soldiers Three* appear at first to be stock local figures, the Cockney, the Yorkshire tyke, and the Irishman. But Mulvaney is not a stage Irishman. He knows that he is sentenced to the life of a private soldier by his slavery to drink; he knows that he has condemned his wife to the lowest station by his addiction; he knows that he will again get roaring drunk and again repent; he knows that only he can keep up his comrades' spirits during the stifling Indian nights, and does so suffering greater torments than they. The themes of spiritual terror, of disintegration of the personality, and of the unknown all appear in the earlier work. And the real refutation of Edmund Wilson's essay lies in *Kim*.

Wilson disposes of Kipling's novel by arguing that there must be an inescapable conflict between the Indians and British. Kim, the white orphan, has escaped into native life and becomes simultaneously a neophyte in the British secret service and the disciple of the Lama. "Now what the reader tends to expect is that Kim will come eventually to realise that he is delivering into bondage to the British invaders those whom he has always considered his people."[38] But, he complains, the conflict never materialises, and the discrepancy between the Lama's search for salvation and Kim's disreputable mundane activities remains unresolved. No doubt this is what a courageous liberal writing at a time when Gandhi and Congress were struggling for Indian independence did expect, but such a conflict is imposed by the critic on the novel. No doubt the future life of a young agent would have entailed confounding Indian resistance to the British, but this is an *ex post facto* judgment, and in the novel such a career is depicted as the maintenance of that minimum of order such as is necessary to prevent foreign intrigue, frontier invasions, and injustice by native princes and to permit the joyous, noisy, pullulating mess of Indian life on the Great Trunk Road to continue. Secret services in general since the rise of Communist and Fascist regimes, and the British secret service in particular since Buchan, "Sapper," and other best-sellers for many weary

[38] See above, p. 30.

years used it as a vehicle, have little to recommend them in the eyes of the liberal: unhappily they are necessary, and in Kipling's India the secret service formed part of that ideal of minimal government – of a handful of officials and a few brigades of troops – which is some degrees better than a full-scale military occupation and a bureaucracy of spies coming not as single sorrows but in M.V.D. battalions. This conflict cannot arise within the terms of the book because the hierarchy of religion and life which is implicit in every description of Indian or English society allots a place to each character which he is compelled to occupy. Born white, Kim can no more become an Indian than the Lama can reverse the Wheel of Life and become a merchant. Just as Tolstoy's characters in *War and Peace* find rest when they realise their essential being and their place and duties, so Kim has to discover the exact slot into which his own tiny personality must fit in the bewildering variety of human beings who pass their transitory lives in the Indian sub-continent.

There can then be no conflict in deciding what role to play in life. Kim and the Lama each has his vocation. Kim to govern, the Lama to achieve Nirvana. These vocations are not contradictory but complementary. Kim and the Lama are the two sides of the coin of man's duty on earth. Both are engaged on a search for reality through knowledge, Kim to find his niche on earth and to discover what he really is, the Lama to find the sacred river on whose banks he will be freed from sin. Both have much to learn. Kim has to endure the humiliation and boredom of being transformed into an Englishman in cantonment and school and has then to master the mysteries of his craft. The Lama, who has realised that God cannot be approached solely through adherence to the reformed laws of his monastery in Tibet, has to experience what other people are and what position they occupy on the Wheel of Life; and whereas at the beginning of the story he blessed the Amritzar courtesan for her alms – "She has acquired merit. Beyond doubt it was a nun" – he has learnt much by the end.

The conflict lies elsewhere, and the fact that it materialises late and is not inevitable is the weakness of the book. The conflict is born of the loyalty of Kim and the Lama to their separate vocations and of their love for each other. When Kim and the Babu have thwarted the two foreign spies, Kim is faced with the dilemma, on the one hand, of being loyal to his trust, delivering the papers speedily and safely to his chiefs, and helping his fellow agent the Babu; and, on the other, of succouring the Lama, who is exhausted by the realisation that he has sinned through pride in his prowess in climbing among the hills and through anger against the Russian officer who struck him. Under this physical and mental strain Kim breaks down and, weak with illness, staggers out to sleep in the life-giving dust. When he wakes, the cog-wheel of his soul has fallen into place and connects with the Wheel of Life on which he and all other beings are bound. Meanwhile the Lama, too, has been torn with conflict. For while Kim was ill, he stumbled into a brook and found at last his sacred river. In a trance he left the illusions of Time and Space and saw the whole world within the Soul and drew near the Great Soul.

> "Then a voice cried: 'What shall come to the boy if thou art dead?' and I was shaken back and forth in myself with pity for thee; and I said: 'I will return to my *chela* lest he miss the Way.' Upon this my Soul . . . withdrew itself from the Great Soul with strivings and yearning and retchings and agonies not to be told . . . I pushed aside world upon world for thy sake."

At that moment of union with Nirvana, the Lama renounces for love his soul's desire.

Kim and the Lama each pursue different kinds of knowledge and neither desires or pretends to understand the other's mind. Both find enlightenment and freedom – the comprehension of the order of things – through love. Kim's love for the Lama makes the Sahiba, the woman of Shamlegh, and Mahbub Ali all love him; the Lama's love for Kim makes Mahbub Ali, who despises the Lama as an unbeliever and a madman, resist the temptation to pillage the Sahiba's household. But the Babu – the only babu whom Kipling drew with affection – does not know love: he is "too good Herbert Spencerian." For only those who are loyal to people, as distinct from ideas, can love.

Such was Kipling's scheme of things. It rests on a highly articulated functional analysis of society in which none but socialised individuals exist. From the analysis proceeds a conservative theory of human existence and political life. This in turn is modified by an awareness of spiritual facts such as repentance, forgiveness, love, and supernatural (or inexplicable) forces which can mitigate the harshness of existence, however little Kipling is willing to allow his readers to forget the harshness. Kipling is almost the sole analogue in England at the turn of the century to Durkheim and Weber and the German and Italian thinkers (whom H. Stuart Hughes treats in his book *Consciousness and Society*) who were in revolt against mid-nineteenth-century constructs of the individual and society. He was not a social Darwinist, as Wells argued; his understanding of social forces was original and was not as superficial as has been imagined. The charge that he has no mind must be mitigated.[39] He was one of the *cleverest* of Victorian writers.

7

But none of this solves the problem that faces the literary critic. To say "this, and not that, is what the artist *meant*," evades the central question, "What in fact does the artist communicate?" Miss Tompkins is concerned with Kipling's intention rather than with communication, and she has made me revise, for instance, my reading of "Mary Postgate" (*A Diversity of Creatures*). I had taken this story to mean that Kipling, like Vercors in *Le Silence de la mer*, held Germans in time of war to be beyond the pale of the Law and not entitled to be treated as human beings: to treat them as such would be to endanger society itself. But even if we accept that Mary Postgate's starved spirit, fiercely conventional mind, and unspoken love for her insensitive charge had to express itself by refusing to give water to the dying German pilot, there is in this story and a dozen others a notorious ambiguity (in a non-Empsonian sense). Time and again we feel that Kipling is either trying to *prove* his social theory so that the suspension of disbelief, which the greatest writers compel, disappears; or that he is connecting his characters to his social theory through a series of clever, but fatal, contrivances instead of connecting them imaginatively. Often he has to translate his deepest emotions feebly into fables. Kipling is the Regius Professor of the

[39] H. G. Wells, *The Outline of History*, London 1924, p. 661. Cp. Auden, p. 262.

voulu. Then, again, his very cleverness perpetually betrays him into taking up clever ideas, the trivial fashionable ideas of the 'nineties which people express by saying "Wouldn't it be fun if . . .?" Ghosts or thought-transference need not be treated as titillating puzzles, nor did Kipling always so treat them; Bella Armine's ghost is as real to Sergeant Godsoe as Catherine Earnshaw's was to Heathcliff; the real curse on Dinah Shadd or the imagined curse in "The House Surgeon," or even the extraordinary metaphysical experiments of the astronomer or biologist in "Unprofessional" are acceptable because, like Kipling's symbolic use of cancer and wasting disease, they are images of deeper spiritual crises. But the transmigration of souls in "The Finest Story in the World" and the ghostly regiment in "The Lost Legion" (*Many Inventions*), the thought-transference in "Wireless" or the exchange of dreams between the drug-addicts in "In the Same Boat," or the dream which visits the Brushwood Boy and his soul-mate, are all "ideas" which have momentarily taken Kipling's fancy; and when a writer self-consciously draws our attention to the existence of Higher Things he usually ends merely by making them rum. That he was didactic is not his undoing: he was not the only schoolmaster abroad at the time – there were Shaw, Wells, Chesterton, Forster, and that *guru* of café society, Somerset Maugham, who, though not in the same class as a writer, has seen fit to patronise Kipling.[40] To say that he was at times vulgar and theatrical is not fatal: his manners can remind one of Dickens as well as Browning and Ruskin. But in order to hammer home the tenets of his creed he would strain his voice and bully or cajole or claim inside knowledge to justify his conclusions: the importance of knowledge became an external adjunct instead of remaining an internal condition.

Kipling lacked a gift, which greater writers possess, the gift of understanding intuitively the *consequences* of holding a particular theory of human destiny. A conservative must be aware of the consequences of his creed: if he does not, he degenerates into a complacent defender of anything that actually exists. He must find reasons to persuade his reader to accept the existence of evil in the world and reconcile him to the impossibility of eliminating

[40] *A Choice of Kipling's Prose: selected and with an introductory essay* by W. S. Maugham, London 1952,

it. To do this he may turn to the Christian doctrine of original sin as a concept which dramatises the hopeless chasm between man's endeavours and his achievement; and he will point to the tragic spectacle as the justification of his faith. Or he can draw a picture of the struggle between naked human egos which in Hobbes and Balzac reaches a terrifying pitch of intensity. Or, like Stendhal, he can revel in the corruption of political life and suggest ways in which he who chooses to live outside it can exploit the exploiters and refine his sensibilities. Or, like Scott in the Midlothian novels, he can call on his sense of the past to show how all parties in a great political conflict are to be pitied in the light of history, in particular those men in whom reposed the nobler virtues of a more simple and heroic culture and whose fate it was to be overwhelmed by modern change. Kipling's mind was not destitute of such apprehensions but he could not transmute them into a vision of life: and that is partly why his "views" and his morality have received such harsh treatment. His social theory is so clear that it stands open to many of the objections that have been brought against Pareto's system of *élites* or against Durkheim's personification of Society. There is more to be said for Bentham's conception of society consisting of individuals satisfying their own interests – though of course creating in given individuals interests that it must satisfy at its peril – than the functional sociologists allowed.

The question which Kipling asked, "What holds society (or an organisation) together?" is exceedingly rarely asked in literature. Equally rarely do creative writers concern themselves with the problem of authority in society. But Kipling's originality in choosing these problems is vitiated by the terms of his solution. He fell into somewhat the same error as Durkheim, who ended by personifying society. Kipling uses the concept as a *deus ex machina*; and in his schematic presentation of life we feel that not only is everything to be explained in terms of social processes and relationships, but that when he introduces those alleviations of social pressures upon men, such as laughter, mirth, vitality, or love, he is thinking of them equally as social forces existing apart from the individuals who experience them. A writer who treats human beings in such exclusively social terms falls into a great error, for he is implicitly dealing with the total human situation even if he chooses to write about only one minute portion of human activity. He cannot – except at the risk of offending our sense of the complexity of human nature and life – accept unreservedly the utilitarian theory that the rightness of actions is a derivative concept and depends upon the goodness of a state of affairs, nor yet the Kantian theory that the rightness of actions is the primary concept and that ethics is concerned with answering "What is it my duty to do?" Similarly he cannot, as Kipling does, conceive of morality as being a derivative of the social process, embodied in the Law and in the operations of groups which transmit it to the individual. Kipling is, indeed, seldom interested in the individual as such. He hardly ever shows how the social process or social morality affects the individual – how men's characters develop, are corrupted or ennobled. Forster, as well as Kipling, says that India upsets the tidy morality and cosmology of Western men and women; but he not only states this, he shows what happens to these men and women when struck by this fact. Kipling relishes revealing the social process: then he steps back and audibly refrains from comment.

It is at this point that his liberal critics have been at fault. They object to his analysis of the social process. Edmund Wilson and other critics have been outraged by the cruelty of the scene where Stalky & Co. turn the tables on the two school bullies by trapping and bullying them with the connivance of the headmaster and the chaplain. But to assert that boys in every age educate each other by cruelty is unexceptionable, and Stalky's comment on the overt moralising of Dean Farrar's classic tales of school life, "We want no beastly Erickin' here," is the cue-line to Kipling's thesis that precepts and preaching are ineffective and unctuous ways of teaching boys what is right. The weakness in Kipling's notion of morality does not lie in his assertion that society is as it is. It lies in the connexion which he makes between society and the individual, and in his assumption that morality is an entirely social product.

The disparity between the social process and the concrete predicament of the individual caught up in this process is too glaring to escape the reader's attention. Just as we cannot believe that the future of the Empire depended on the degree of intimacy between the Brushwood Boy and his mamma, so Kipling's solution of the problem of maintaining order and decency in a school is too slick and trite. Compare Kipling's story with Gorki's treatment of cruelty in his autobiographical trilogy. Kipling does not show us what the effect is of the social process on the individual, nor does he see that the writer creates a world peopled with characters who necessarily act and feel as isolated individuals as well as political animals. And so, when we return to the vexed question of Kipling's morality, perhaps it is not stretching the analogy to sociology too far to say that he is unaware of the problem set by the concept of roles. Man, not in his time but simultaneously, plays many parts – and having to play these roles arouses moral conflict within him. In the typical Kipling story this conflict is either never admitted or it is submerged under the all-embracing concept of the Law. He brilliantly sets out the conflict between different cultures, but he evades for the most part the conflict within the individual himself.

In a fashion, this is to say that his social theory does not go nearly deep enough – it is too often the kind of popularisation that a journalist picks up and transmits. It leaves the same taste in the mouth as a reading of Burnham. It has some of the characteristics of the neo-Machiavellians, such as Michels and Pareto, but lacks their deadly, serious destructiveness. Kipling's smartness and knowingness, his delight in telling his readers what is what, in underlining brutality and harshness and the importance of codes of conduct, his in-group theories, including for example his anti-Semitism, offend because they are too simple-minded – and perhaps that is one of the reasons why so many of his admirers were men of action, businessmen and administrators, who were used to accepting a "realist" theory of society and rarely reflected on how complex society is. The journalist's device of heightening his effects, of popularising his message, and of shocking and exploiting the reader's emotion can also be found, I believe, in the texture of his prose – in the laying on of all those "heavy strokes."

It is in the study of the texture of his prose that the next advance in understanding him must be made. In the reflexions above I have already overstepped my competence as an historian of ideas and have been usurping the function of the literary critic. Like Miss Tompkins, I believe that until now the critics have underestimated and misunderstood the nature of Kipling's work.[41] She has now given them a professional and learned guide to it. She is the first of his defenders to state Kipling's intentions without turning to execute his hostile critics. It is now up to the critics to reciprocate and reconsider the matter. *Que MM. les assassins commencent.*

[41] It was, however, Trilling who said that from the *Jungle Books* a boy would get "his first introduction to a generalised notion of society." I should also here acknowledge with gratitude the most helpful comments of George Homans, who read an early draft of this article.

George Shepperson

THE WORLD OF RUDYARD KIPLING

"THE MOST popular modern British poet in Moscow is Kipling," declared the young Soviet writer, Evgeni Evtushenko, to a newspaper interviewer during his visit to Britain in 1962. "But Kipling was an imperialist," disclaimed the interviewer. "The Russian smiled and quoted Kipling in Russian with evident approval."[1]

One might speculate on the qualities which Soviet readers to-day find attractive in Kipling and, in cataloguing them, one can see that many are qualities which for most people in the West would have a distinctly nineteenth-century ring: the gospel of work; the hymn to technology; the call to sacrifice and leadership; the challenge of Progress; the Darwinist, evolutionary imagery; the bold use of contemporary speech, slang, and rhyme, and the evocation of popular ballads and songs. This nineteenth-century note is worth examining; for although Kipling spent half his life in the twentieth century, his roots were in the nineteenth, and many of the complexities which critics find in his later work may be appreciated as the unresolved conflict of these two periods; and in its nineteenth-century roots is to be found much of the strength as well as the weakness of his writing.

The almost conditioned reflex, "imperialist," of Evtushenko's interviewer illustrates the stock response to the name "Kipling" amongst most British and American readers to-day – a response which shows that they have seized upon at least part of the major weakness of his nineteenth-century inheritance. It is a weakness which must be faced frankly by admirers of Kipling if his true and enduring greatness is to emerge. And in this weakness, it is not so much the elements of territorial or economic expansion

[1] *Sunday Times*, London (6 May 1962), p. 29.

in his imperialism which matter to-day but the racialism, the worship of the "White Man," which informs it.

Two generations of over-simple economic interpretations of the great wave of empire-building which swept over Britain, Europe, and the United States in the last twenty years of the nineteenth century have tended to disguise the importance of racialism as a primary force in this imperialism. Recently, however, scholars have emphasised its all-pervading nature[2] in the experience of white peoples in this period and have suggested that it was not simply a reflexion of an economic necessity. Whatever the reasons for its sharp rise at this time, Kipling shared this racialism with his contemporaries – of the left as well as of the right, as can be seen by glancing through *The Mutiny of the "Elsinore,"* a shabby and falsely romantic novel of white supremacy by the revolutionary socialist, Jack London.

When, for example, Kipling wrote such lines as "Well for the world when the White Men drink to the dawn of the White Man's day,"[3] their implications cannot be obliterated by recalling that Gunga Din for "all 'is dirty 'ide . . . was white, clear white inside" and that "in the eighteen-nineties, the phrase, 'a white man', did not only mean a man with an unpigmented skin; it had a secondary symbolic meaning: a man with the moral standards of the civilised world."[4] Kipling's admired type of non-white was, in fact, the servant or subordinate such as Gunga Din or the Gaelic-speaking Nova Scotian Negro in *Captains Courageous,* "the coal black Celt with the second-sight." Where the non-white was dissatisfied with his subordinate status, and there was no poetry of the primitive with which to invest him, Kipling found little grounds for admiration – as is clear from his portrayal of early Indian nationalists in "The Enlightenments of Pagett, M.P."[5]

Of course, as a major writer with the gift of supreme imagina-

[2] *E.g.* Hannah Arendt, *The Origins of Totalitarianism*, London 1958; Richard Hofstadter, *The Age of Reform*, New York 1961, pp. 77-83, etc.; A. E. Campbell, *Great Britain and the United States*, London 1960, pp. 195-201, 209-11, etc.

[3] "A Song of the White Men" (1899).

[4] Charles Carrington, *Rudyard Kipling*, London 1955, p. 275.

[5] *Contemporary Review*, LVIII, London 1890, pp. 333-55. Cp. also the picture of the American Negro servant in *From Sea to Sea*.

tion and empathy, Kipling sometimes transcended these racialist limitations, as when he showed that what really matters are not the colours without but the colours within,[6] or when, crossing for a moment the racial fence, he saw that the white man's "We" was "They" to the non-white.[7] Yet both of these examples suggest that even when Kipling transcended the racial barrier there was a profound limitation in his approach. The first comes from his moving story about imaginary children, "They"; the second is from a poem in which a child is speaking: Kipling knew well that "in the hearts of children there is neither East nor West."[8] But the child, alas, is not father to the man when it comes to racial prejudice – rather the reverse. When children grew up – that process which Kipling, for all his cult of adult masculinity, dreaded most – in his nineteenth-century world, they took their badges of colour and caste in separate communities. And if he wrote that

> . . . there is neither East nor West, Border, nor
> Breed, nor Birth,
> When two strong men stand face to face, though they
> come from the ends of the earth[9]

here is a further limitation: that the boundaries of colour-caste may be crossed only by exceptional individuals. All children and a few determined grown-ups are exempt from the restrictions of race; but communities of adults are fixed firmly within their ethnic embraces – on this earth at least, although Kipling presumably envisaged the breakdown of these boundaries "at God's great Judgement Seat." He himself was capable – as much of his best work shows – of profound imaginative sympathy and understanding for Indians of many kinds, and in Freemasonry he glimpsed the possibility of a brotherhood transcending the barriers of race, class, and religion. In the Lodge to which he was inducted at Lahore he "met Muslims, Hindus, Sikhs, members of the Araya and Brahmo Samaj, and a Jew tyler, who was priest and butcher to his little community in the city." But there was

[6] See "They," *Traffics and Discoveries*.
[7] "We and They," *Debits and Credits*.
[8] "To James Whitcomb Riley" (1890).
[9] "The Ballad of East and West", *Barrack-Room Ballads*.

no possibility of that brotherhood within the Lodge being carried over to society at large: the "Inside: Outside" antithesis is absolute even in his nostalgic poem "The Mother-Lodge," and there is no suggestion that he would wish it to be otherwise.[10] A few intellectuals of the late nineteenth century considered race as a prelude to a wider bond of human association: "the ideal of human Brotherhood, gained through the unifying ideal of Race,"[11] as one of them put it. Kipling cannot be classed with such writers.

He may "have drunk with mixed assemblies, seen the racial ruction rise"[12] but it did not shake his conviction of the superiority of the white, English-speaking peoples. If, unlike his mentor, W. E. Henley, he may never have used such phrases about them as "the master race of the world,"[13] Kipling had no doubt about the virtues of their "dark enduring blood."[14] If he could sometimes write charitably on racial mixtures, as he did in "Without Benefit of Clergy" about the British civil servant whose Indian mistress bears him a child, once again it was only the individual crossings of the colour-caste lines, the transient, romantic unions that gained his approval. Where these assumed substantial proportions, the Law – in all of Kipling's personal, metaphysical understanding of that capitalised proposition – had been broken and chaos could come again. This was clear in his uneasiness about the Eurasians in India, especially when there was any question of a sahib being foolish enough to want to marry one. It is equally evident from his feelings about the Portuguese, "a once great empire" which could not stand up to the stresses of the Scramble for Africa in the eighteen-eighties and -nineties, "lacking men or money, still in the conviction that three hundred years of slave-holding and intermingling with the nearest natives gave an inalienable right to hold slaves and issue half-castes to all eternity."[15]

[10] *Something of Myself*, Chapter Three; "The Mother-Lodge," *The Seven Seas*. I am indebted to Mr Andrew Rutherford for this point and some others in this essay.

[11] W. E. Burghardt Du Bois, *The Souls of Black Folk*, London 1905, p. 11.

[12] "Et Dona Ferentes," *The Five Nations*.

[13] John Connell, *W. E. Henley*, London 1949, p. 175.

[14] "The Song of Seven Cities," *A Diversity of Creatures*.

[15] "Judson and the Empire," *Many Inventions*.

Not only does Kipling's distaste for mixed breeds emerge in his reference to miscegenation of white and coloured. He also feared the unsettling effect of "the Semitic strain"[16] and other non-Anglo-Saxon elements which the great flood of emigrants had brought to the United States from Eastern Europe and Italy in the last two decades of the nineteenth century. And he gave rather unpleasant expression to that fear towards the end of his life, when he wrote that "it was then [the period 1892-6, when he was living in the United States] that I first began to wonder whether Abraham Lincoln had not killed rather too many autochthonous 'Americans' in the Civil War for the benefit of their hastily imported Continental supplanters."[17]

In at least one place in the Kipling corpus, however, there is an episode which, while seeming on the surface to be a typical expression of his distaste for mixed breeds, actually suggests that his attitude to them and to the coloured races in general may be more complicated than is at first apparent. It is Kipling's description in *The Light that Failed* of the woman passenger who served as a model for his artist hero, Dick Heldar, on a voyage on a dirty old ship from Lima to Auckland. She was "a sort of Negroid-Jewess-Cuban, with morals to match." If *The Light that Failed* was not riddled with all kinds of personal symbolism, one might dismiss, as a half-humorous aside, his remark that "the woman served as the model for the devils and the angels both [in Heldar's picture] – sea-devils and sea-angels."[18] But it is so endowed and we must take its symbolism seriously. The implications of the sea imagery in this quotation from this novel of unconsummated love may be left to others to unravel – though Herman Melville's remark, "Healed of my hurt, I laud the inhuman sea," may supply a clue – but the reference to this half-caste woman serving as a model for both devils and angels calls to mind the famous image in the "The White Man's Burden" ("Your new-caught sullen peoples, Half devil and half child") and suggests that, if imagery is organic rather than decorative in the works of a major writer, Kipling's association of the non-whites with devils and children has some significance for his

[16] *Something of Myself*, Chapter Five.
[17] *Ibid.*
[18] *The Light that Failed*, Chapter Eight.

approach to racial issues. Not only does it suggest a kind of nineteenth-century elaboration of the ambivalence of the noble and ignoble savage conceptions of "the fluttered folk and wild" which had beset European thought from the sixteenth century at least – and which has been well discussed in O. Mannoni's essay on the psychology of colonisation, *Prospero and Caliban* – but it would seem to contain elements of a more personal nature. One ought not to dismiss as paternalistic only the comparison to children of the peoples newly brought into the British Empire. More than one critic has noted the special value that Kipling set on the children's world; and to use this as his image for non-European peoples might be taken as much in a subconsciously complimentary as in an overtly paternalistic sense. Similarly, as the second part of Goethe's *Faust* suggests, the Devil is not always a destructive image. For all Kipling's belief in the superiority of his own people, he had grave doubts about their ability to rise to the new challenge of Empire in the 1890s; and he clearly envied the energy, however demonic, of the best of the native races. To compare them to devils was certainly to evoke their potential destructiveness, but it also expressed an element of admiration. "For God's sake hush, you little devil," the truly devilish Aunty Rosa shrieked at Punch in "Baa, Baa, Black Sheep," and that history of diabolic persecution in the name of religion would account for an ambivalence, a partial transposition of values in Kipling's use of the term – for his awareness, very clear in some of his tales of the supernatural, that devils – like natives – may have their share of primitive virtue. Is there not something of this feeling in Kipling's reference to "the more than inherited (since it is also carefully taught) brutality of the Christian peoples, beside which the mere heathendom of the West Coast nigger is clean and restrained"?[19]

This has something in common with a passage by J. M. Robertson, an anti-imperialist and a fierce critic of Kipling, who wrote in 1900:

> To civilize the tropics! With our own race riddled with the leprosy of decivilization, presenting to the eyes that will see, in a warren after warren of putrid misery, a life that the

[19] "They," *Traffics and Discoveries*.

zoologist declares to be immeasurably more ignoble than that of the lowest savage whose ways he has scanned![20]

Kipling, indeed, shared an idea of the white man's civilising mission with many of his contemporaries, but his was not an unsophisticated conception. He could speak, through the mouth of one of his characters, of the working classes for whose salvation he looked, like Cecil Rhodes and Friedrich Nietzsche, to the colonisation of the Empire, as "diseased, lying drinking white stuff";[21] and could paint a terrible, if melodramatic, picture of the effects of drink on the London working class in "The Record of Badalia Herodsfoot" in *Many Inventions*. If this sometimes reads like the old Victorian music-hall song, "Father, Dear Father Come Home," one should remember that this ballad was not intended as the caricature which it has often become in present-day music-hall revivals but was a realistic picture of life in many working-class homes at the turn of the century. And, higher up the social scale, he could attack the pretentious patriotic propaganda of "an M.P., an impeccable Conservative," who discredits and debases the very values Kipling himself professed.[22] Indeed, in spite of his belief in the soundness of the service classes – the men of the Army and the Indian Administration – Kipling's whole idea of the civilising mission of the white man was shot through with mistrust and sometimes despair, as "One View of the Question" in *Many Inventions* indicates; and it might be said of him, as Lord Hailey has recently remarked of himself at the time of Queen Victoria's Jubilee in 1887, that under a sense of mission "many of us went to India, perhaps not quite sure exactly what the mission was."[23] The immediate tasks were clear enough: it was the ultimate aims that seemed disturbingly uncertain.

Year by year [to quote Kipling's own formulation of this problem] England sends out fresh drafts for the first fighting-line, which is officially called the Indian Civil Service. These die, or kill themselves by overwork, or are worried to death, or broken in health and hope in order that the land may be

[20] J. M. Robertson, *Patriotism and Empire*, London 1900, p. 193.
[21] "The Comprehension of Private Copper," *Traffics and Discoveries*.
[22] "The Flag of their Country," *Stalky & Co.*
[23] Quoted in *East Africa and Rhodesia*, London (22 Feb. 1962), p. 614.

protected from death and sickness, famine and war, and may
eventually become capable of standing alone. It will never
stand alone, but the idea is a pretty one, and men are willing
to die for it, and yearly the work of pushing and coaxing and
scolding and petting the country into good living goes forward. If an advance be made all credit is given to the native,
while the Englishmen stand back and wipe their foreheads. If
a failure occurs the Englishmen step forward and take the
blame. Overmuch tenderness of this kind has bred a strong
belief among many natives that the native is capable of administering the country, and many devout Englishmen believe
this also, because the theory is stated in beautiful English with all
the latest political colour.

There be other men who, though uneducated, see visions
and dream dreams, and they, too, hope to administer the
country in their own way – that is to say, with a garnish of
Red Sauce.[24]

The existence of these "other men" clearly justified the actions
of the Supreme Government for the time being, but unmistakably
present in this passage is Kipling's unease over the future and
long-term purpose of British India.

One may understand something of his dilemma on the prospect
before British imperialism if one ponders the statement made
recently by two Cambridge historians: "There are good reasons
for regarding the mid-Victorian period as the golden age of
British expansion, and the late Victorian as an age which saw the
beginnings of contraction and decline."[25] The age, in fact, which
was opening for the British Empire at the time when Kipling left
England for India in 1882, for all its pomp and circumstance, was
not the first fine careless rapture of a new empire but rather the
start of the last fine but certainly not careless rupture of the old.
For all its sudden extension of boundaries in the last decade and a
half of the nineteenth century, it is possible to see now that this
was the start of an intricate process of imperial offensive-defence;
the creation, as it were, of an "Inner Ring"[26] of Empire which

[24] "On the City Wall," *Soldiers Three.*
[25] Ronald Robinson and John Gallagher, *Africa and the Victorians,* London
1961, p. 471.
[26] I am using the phrase "Inner Ring" here partly because I want to draw

was to start to crumble almost as soon as it had been built. There is something prophetic in Kipling's "Far-called, our navies melt away" in his "Recessional" of 1897. And there is an element of the visionary, as can be seen now after nearly three quarters of a century of nationalist and anti-British agitation within the colonies, in his lines, put into the mouth of a Pict, about the Roman Empire. If for "Rome," in the following lines, one reads "Britain" and remembers that the political movements, in Asia and Africa, against British rule had begun at much the same time as Kipling went to India, they read almost as a description of the way in which the Empire had been acquired – that mysterious process which J. R. Seeley called in 1881 "a fit of absence of mind"[27] – and the manner in which it was to disintegrate:

> Rome never looks where she treads
> Always her heavy hooves fall
> On our stomachs, our hearts or our heads;
> And Rome never heeds when we bawl.
> Her sentries pass on – that is all
> And we gather behind them in hordes,
> And plot to reconquer the Wall,
> With only our tongues for our swords.[28]

attention to C. S. Lewis's "Kipling's World" in his *They Asked for a Paper* London 1962, especially pp. 90-2. The moral implications of this admirable piece of Kipling criticism are brought out in his essay "The Inner Ring," *op. cit.* pp. 139-49. Professor Lewis is here using Kipling's world in a timeless sense. Kipling's adherence to the "Inner Ring" may, however, be brought into more temporal focus if one examines the manner in which the British community in India drew together in a process which began before the Mutiny, with the speeding up of communications between India and Britain and the breakdown of the East India Company's rule, and increased rapidly after the cleavage of 1858. It was into this "club" atmosphere that Kipling was plunged for seven years after 1882: the effect of this on one who was already constitutionally disposed to the "Inner Ring" approach to life was clearly considerable. The manner in which Robinson and Gallagher discuss the "Official mind" of British Imperialism in *Africa and the Victorians*, suggests that the "Inner Ring" can also be extended into a valid metaphor for the whole process of British overseas expansion at this time.

[27] J. R. Seeley, *The Expansion of England*, London 1883, p. 8.

[28] "A Pict Song," *Puck of Pook's Hill*. What significance is there in the fact that in the *Puck of Pook's Hill* version of this poem the Picts say in verse ii "Leave us alone and you'll see / How we can drag down the Great"; whereas in *Songs from Books* the line reads "How we can drag down the State"?

It was a process which another poet of the time, John Davidson (who like Jack London had much in common with Kipling) called "the same blind force that conquered India at Agincourt 300 years before the event."[29] And of the blindness of the historical process, Kipling had no doubt. Speaking of "Modern Progress," he said that "Forces, Activities, and Movements sprang into being, agitated themselves, coalesced, and, in one political avalanche, overwhelmed a bewildered, and not in the least intending it, England."[30] Would this England find out, before it was too late, the nature of the political, economic and social challenge which the "New Imperialism," to use J. A. Hobson's phrase, presented? Would it rise to greatness or would it let the new opportunities slip between its fingers? Kipling could never be sure. In one breath, he could say of the Boer War, "We have had an Imperial lesson. It may make us an Empire yet!"[31] In another, in his vitriolic poem, "The Islanders," speaking of Britain's "betrayal" of her soldiers in the Boer War, he could denounce working, middle, and upper classes alike for their selfish materialism, and predict a terrible nemesis soon to fall on the whole nation. And perhaps something of this same feeling was at work – at a less polemical level, but more telling because of that – in Kipling's highly symbolical story "They," written in 1904, in which he speaks of England as "the shut island of the North, all the ships of the world bellowing at our perilous gates; and between their outcries ran the piping of bewildered gulls."

In such passages of passionate sincerity Kipling expressed, from his own angle, the sense of impending doom which beset so many of his contemporaries – the feeling that they had reached the end not just of a century, but of an epoch.[32]

There was indeed a moment when Kipling had reflected "the fashionable pessimists."[33] But that was in 1882, while he was still at school and before his travels had started. By the time he was thirty, he had seen all the continents of the world and had en-

[29] J. B. Townsend, *John Davidson: Poet of Armageddon*, New Haven 1961, p. 487.   [30] "Little Foxes," *Actions and Reactions*.
[31] "The Lesson," *The Five Nations*.
[32] See Bernard Bergonzi, *The Early H. G. Wells*, Manchester 1961, Chapter One.   [33] Carrington, *op. cit.*, p. 40.

dured his own *saison en enfer*. From a schoolboy imitator of fashionable decadence, he had become a man who experienced this *fin de siècle* feeling in his bones. Like Arthur Rimbaud, he had felt "la même magie bourgeoise à tous les points où la malle nous déposera."[34] It was a magic that could be either white or black: a magic of technology, building up new cities, linking continents, opening virgin lands; or it could be a magic of destruction, unleashing new and cataclysmic forces. If Kipling never achieved the apocalyptic concentration of Rimbaud's "Soir historique" in his expression of this black magic of the end of an age, perhaps of a world, he came close to it. One thinks of the cryptic but powerful image of the lovers, struck by lightning and turned into statues of charcoal in Central Africa – not far from Conrad's *Heart of Darkness* – in "Mrs Bathurst" which plays on a variety of images of modern technology to produce what, in one way, amounts to a personalised symbol of apocalyptic destruction. Or there is Kipling's vision on the eve of the holocaust of the First World War, watching army manœuvres at Aldershot in 1913, of "the whole pressure of our dead of the Boer War flickering and re-forming as the horizon flickered in the heat."[35]

Another *fin de siècle* symbol which Kipling used with considerable feeling was the crowded, modern city, "the man-stifled town" (as he called it in his poem of 1893, "A Song of the English,") which he contrasted with "the waves and troughs of the plains, where the healing stillness lies."[36] He had always been fascinated by James Thomson's "The City of Dreadful Night" and he used its *motifs* to explore late Victorian decadence in *The Light that Failed*. The equivalent of Thomson's poem in the corpus of Kipling's verse is, in many ways, "The City of Brass," a bitter, apocalyptic denunciation of national degeneration through urban corruption, which, if it lacks the elaboration of Thomson's stanza, has something of the jingle of his rhymes – a brassy ring, in fact, which accords well with the title. And, when Kipling was a young man in India, he used the title of Thomson's poem to describe a walk around Lahore at night, its heat and dirt, its

[34] Arthur Rimbaud, "Soir historique," *Les Illuminations* (various edns), no. XXXII.

[35] *Something of Myself*, Chapter Eight.

[36] "The Settler," *The Five Nations*.

over-crowding and poverty.[37] But he was just as uncomplimentary about London: "half of it is fog and filth, and half is fog and row,"[38] he wrote of the metropolis after he came back from his first visit to India. Elsewhere, some of his writing has an echo of the exploration by Jack London of what the American Revolutionary socialist called *The People of the Abyss*: "This [is] a land where white girls of sixteen, at twelve or fourteen pounds per annum, hauled thirty and forty pounds weight of bath-water at a time up four flights of stairs!"[39] Kipling had, in fact, developed an attitude to the city like that of many of the American "muck-raking" writers of the eighteen-nineties, such as Lincoln Steffens in *The Shame of the Cities*. Indeed, he knew Sam McClure, owner of the famous *McClure's Magazine* which carried many articles by American reforming journalists and published serially his *Captains Courageous*, a story which sang the praises of the wide, open spaces and condemned urban artificiality and corruption. Such pieces show that Kipling's writings provide a British equivalent for that praise of pioneering regions which in Frederick Jackson Turner's "The Significance of the Frontier in American History" of 1893 became a major interpretation of United States history. Just as Turner used the city-frontier dichotomy to mark the end of an epoch in American history, Kipling uses it in a *fin de siècle* context, to explore and define the sickness of his own civilisation.

It may be true that Kipling, like his fellow poet-imperialist, John Davidson, "saw seeds of awakening and growth in the decadence of their time"; and that "both noted that a new order, before it emerges, often expresses itself in the forms of the old."[40] But Davidson never saw the "new order"; he committed suicide in 1909. And Jack London, the "Kipling of the klondyke," who quoted "The Galley Slave" appreciatively in 1915, in his *Mutiny of the "Elsinore"* (a novel of that "natural aristocracy"[41] which like Kipling and the Wells of *A Modern*

---

[37] "The City of Dreadful Night," *Life's Handicap*. Cp. "City of Dreadful Night," his description of Calcutta in *From Sea to Sea*.
[38] Carrington, *op. cit.*, p. 142.
[39] *Something of Myself*, Chapter Four.
[40] Townsend, *op. cit.*, p. 459.
[41] Eric Stokes, *The Political Ideas of English Imperialism*, Oxford 1900,

Utopia he believed would usher in the new age) took his own life the following year. Kipling lived for another twenty years. But the century which had given birth in its old age to his vision oddly combining "decay-of-the-world with anglophile millen-nialism"[42] – to quote Professor Kermode on D. H. Lawrence, with whom Kipling had very much more in common than either of them would have dared to admit – had spawned, on Kipling's death in 1936, a different millennium: Hitler's dream of a Third Reich that would last a thousand years.

Kipling, indeed, has often been accused of being a Fascist. So has Friedrich Nietzsche, with whose outlook on life Kipling's, although he may never have read the German writer, has so much in common – *The Light that Failed*, with its cult of violence and its emphasis on living dangerously, might be called one of the earliest and most readable expressions of Nietzscheanism in English literature. But just as Nietzsche warned against the worship of the State, Kipling, as "MacDonagh's Song" shows, realised that "Holy State . . . endeth in Holy War" and that "Holy People . . . endeth in wholly Slave." Yet if Nietzsche was no proto-Nazi, he has perhaps, unwittingly, a place in the history of ideas that led to Nazism. And it may be the same with Kipling, even though his racialist doctrines were so far removed from Hitler's. His frequent use of the term "Aryan" was, it seems, innocent enough; and his employment at the front of some editions of his books and in the water-mark of the luxurious "Sussex" edition of a swastika was, from his point of view, harmless. But Hitler later put both symbols to very different use. It is an irony which would seem to be a good subject for that "cosmic mirth," which, according to Professor C. A. Bodelsen,[43] was an article of Kipling's faith.

It is difficult to tell how seriously we are meant to take this conception, but if one compares his "cosmic mirth" with that of John Davidson, one sees, perhaps, some of the limitations of

p. 29. London's admiration for Kipling is formally expressed in the moving tribute he wrote when Kipling was believed dead during his serious illness in the United States in 1899: see "These Bones Shall Rise Again" in *Revolution and Other Essays*, London 1910.

[42] *New Statesman* (22 Mar. 1962), p. 423.

[43] Cp. C. A. Bodelsen, "Two Enigmatic Kipling Stories," *Orbis Litterarum*, XVI (1961).

Kipling's imagination. As Dr C. M. Grieve ("Hugh McDiarmid") has pointed out, Davidson hazarded

"the poetical suggestion" that it is the presence of the incommunicable elements – dead gases, ghosts of elements herding with the vapour of dissolution nitrogen – "that maintains the mechanical mixture of the oxygen and the nitrogen of the air: were their ghostly frontier eliminated, the two main members of the atmosphere would unite chemically, forming protoxide of nitrogen, which is laughing gas. Great Pan! How close we are to that rare old fantasy, that the crack of doom will be a universal shout of laughter!"[44]

Kipling was probably incapable of a conceit of this sort. He was a poet of applied rather than pure science. To say that he was obsessed with technology rather than pure science is not to undervalue him. Indeed, such verses as "McAndrew's Hymn" show the magnificent use to which he could put technical imagery. But one cannot imagine him writing such a poem as Davidson's "Snow"[45] in which, for all its anthropomorphism, his use of the new world of crystallography that the microscope had revealed shows the scientific as distinct from the technological imagination at work. Kipling seems to have been incapable of thinking through to their conclusions the implications of the superabundant new techniques of his age. He provides a poetry of process, of means rather than ends.[46]

In a similar way, Kipling's experience of the New Imperialism was quantitative rather than qualitative. He strove to awaken the British people to the opportunities which this seemed to offer: but he never expressed very clearly what those opportunities were. One never finds, for example, the kind of discussion in his work about imperialism which one discovers in John Buchan's early work of 1906, *A Lodge in the Wilderness*. A definition of imperialism is provided here as "the closer organic connection under one Crown of a number of autonomous nations of the same blood, who can spare something of their vitality for the administration of vast tracts inhabited by lower races – a racial aristocracy considered in their relation to other subject peoples, a democracy

---

[44] *John Davidson: A Selection of his Poems*, ed. Maurice Lindsay, London 1961, p. 50.   [45] *Op. cit.*, pp. 207-9.   [46] Cp. Lewis, *op. cit.*, pp. 83-5.

relation to each other."[47] There is no such succinct definition by
Kipling, perhaps because he would not have been able to sub-
scribe easily to the "democracy in relation to each other" idea
about the imperialists. Kipling was highly suspicious of democracy: and yet there is a sense in which democracy – white
democracy – is an essential part of the imperialist process of the
late nineteenth and early twentieth centuries, as the anti-imperialist Olive Schreiner saw when she portrayed the awakening conscience of a private soldier sharer in the early Rhodesian land loot
in *Trooper Peter Halket of Mashonaland*. Kipling, by contrast, was
aware of the divisions and class hatreds within the white group,
as appears in "The Comprehension of Private Copper." And so,
while he could see the Empire growing, almost effortlessly, he
had little idea of its direction. Out of his quantitative appreciation
came nothing akin to General Smuts's *Holism and Evolution*, with
its notion of the creative synthesis of wholes.

If Kipling had an idea of direction, it was spatial rather than
spiritual. However much he strove to "spiritualise" his imperial
ideal, he usually provides little more than a cluster of vague
emotions and aspirations. One has some sympathy with John
Davidson's comment on "Recessional": "a very antique quack
poultice for an uneasy conscience, a pill against an earthquake."[48]
In his approach to Empire Kipling resembled Cecil Rhodes, to
whom he got as close as any man. Rhodes may have had an idea
of a great white nation in South Africa – which Kipling shared,
as his poem "General Joubert" shows – but of the purpose of that
new nation he had no other idea save that of pushing its power
further and further beyond its frontiers. Kipling, of course, dissociated himself from the Boer's "primitive lust for racial
domination"[49] – but they at least knew what they were trekking
into the interior of Africa for. Kipling did not. His prose and
verse provide splendid commentary on Cecil Rhodes and South
Africa, but when he gets beyond the Zambezi, when he ventures
into the interior, he loses himself. East and Central Africa
escaped his imagination – perhaps because Bulawayo was as far
as he got. Sir Harry Johnston once called Nyasaland (before
1907, the British Central Africa Protectorate) "the Cinderella of

[47] John Buchan, *A Lodge in the Wilderness*, London 1906, p. 29.
[48] Townsend, *op. cit.*, p. 487.   [49] *Something of Myself*, Chapter Six.

the Protectorates." Kipling in his Central African tale, "A Deal in Cotton,"[50] plays something of the role of an ugly sister towards this Cinderella, as is plain from his sneer at the beginning about "the Centro-Euro-Africo-Protectorate" and the later reference to the "Sheshaheli" (Swahili, presumably) offering "four pounds of a woman's breast, tattoo marks and all, skewered up in a plantain leaf before breakfast." The exactness of detail, moreover, which he showed about other parts of the world escaped him when he got beyond the Zambezi. The region in the "Heart of Darkness" was a place where you tried to escape from your problems; and Kipling's verisimilitude deserted him there. This is clear from his vague references in "Mrs Bathurst" to Nyasaland which he invariably spells in the old nineteenth-century way as "Nyassa." He shows the same impatience with "that Lake what's 'is name," as one of the characters in the story puts it, as Gladstone did with the pronunciation of Kilimanjaro. Perhaps this is why he could only kill Mrs Bathurst and her lover off when they got near to it. Kipling used none of the fantasy of Rider Haggard about the interior of Africa, except in the manner in which the lovers were killed; but more fantasy might have been the prelude to that genuine exercise of imagination which was needed to cope with these areas which have been, in a very real sense, the touchstone of the New Imperialism. Kipling's quantitative approach could only skirt the problem.

It was very different, however, in his approach to America, which has been generally overlooked by historians of the United States and Anglo-American relations, though not by so distinguished a critic as Mr Edmund Wilson. Kipling had a genuine appreciation of American history. If this sprang largely from three visits to the United States – one of them lasting four years – in the last decade of the nineteenth century, and from an American wife and relations, the ground had been prepared by wide reading of American literature while he was still at school. Kipling was soaked in American humorists – an influence which was strengthened when he interviewed Mark Twain during his first visit to the United States in 1889. He was in America at a time of profound changes: the closing of the frontier; the rise of the big city; the "New Immigration" from Eastern Europe; the

[50] *Actions and Reactions.*

growth of an imperialist spirit which burst the bounds of the
"isolationist" Monroe Doctrine of 1823; savage industrial unrest
such as the Pullman strike of 1894; the spanning of the continent
by faster and faster communications; and, above all, the rise of
American power to challenge the might of the Old World, in
particular, of Britain. He could see as well as Frederick Jackson
Turner that the old America was passing: the "beautiful localised
American atmosphere . . . was already beginning to fade," as he
put it in his posthumous autobiographical fragment, *Something of
Myself*, which contains, in a brief compass, some of his best
writing on the United States; although there are many perceptive
passages struck from the heat of the moment in the letters of
Kipling's American journeys of 1889 and 1892, which were
written for the press and later collected in *From Sea to Sea* and
Letters of Travel 1892-1913. His expression of these profound
changes was sometimes infelicitous, as when he sneered at the
Pullman strikers in the opening lines of his challenging poem,
"An American" (1894), or when he attacked the unsettling effects
of the new immigration in unveiled racialist language. But he
usually saw both sides of the American medal. If he had much of
the Anglo-Saxon racialism of his friend, Theodore Roosevelt, he
could still express wonder at "a people who, having extirpated
the aboriginals of their continent more completely than any
modern race had ever done, honestly believed that they were a
godly little New England community, setting examples to brutal
mankind"[51]; and he was shocked by the conditions and treatment
that awaited the new immigrants, who supplied "the cheap – almost slave-labour, lacking which all wheels would have stopped
. . . they were handled with a callousness that horrified me."[52]
If, again, he was stung by the bitter anti-British feeling in
America and its manipulation for localised interests by American
politicians to such an extent that the savage Anglophobia mani-
fested in the United States during the Venezuela crisis of 1896 compelled him to leave, he still had what he considered to be the
interests of the United States sufficiently at heart to address to
them, during their outburst of expansionist fervour in the Spanish-
American War of 1898, his famous poem, "The White Man's

[51] *Something of Myself*, Chapter Five.
[52] *Ibid.*

Burden." And if he could satirise sharply the aggressive and un-principled side of American capitalism in such a figure as Laughton O. Zigler, he could appreciate that this vigorous new economy could teach the British a few lessons. Kipling, with his doubt of the British ability to rise to the new imperial challenge, must have had some sympathy with Zigler's comment on the British and their Empire, "If you want to realise your assets, you should lease the whole proposition to America for ninety-nine years."[53] On the other side of the medal, moreover, he saw the figure of Harvey Cheyne, the millionaire of *Captains Courageous*. His sketch of Cheyne's rise from rags to riches is a constructive picture, full of sympathy for the suddenly emerged *entrepreneurs* of the United States, and an excellent historical sketch of the new America that was coming out of the old.[54] Above all, in that humour which had been his introduction to the American spirit before he ever visited the United States, Kipling saw the salvation of that country's soul. As he put it, in the mouth of "the American spirit" of his 1894 poem:

> But, through the shift of mood and mood,
> Mine ancient humour saves him whole –
> The cynic devil in his blood
> That bids him mock his hurrying soul.[55]

[53] "The Captive," *Traffics and Discoveries*.
[54] There can be little doubt about America's respect for Kipling and his influence on many of its writers, but the influence of America on Kipling is in some ways as important, and it can manifest itself in unexpected places. He wrote *The Jungle Books*, "with [their] strange ethical concept called the Law of Jungle" (Carrington, *op. cit.*, p. 208), during his four years residence in Vermont. This was a period of what has been called "Social Darwinism" in American thought (Richard Hofstadter, *Social Darwinism in American Thought*, Philadelphia 1945); the period of Theodore Roosevelt, Kipling's friend, and his frequent employment of biological analogies from nature red in tooth and claw to illustrate the social process; and of the conditions in the great cities which led to Upton Sinclair's *The Jungle* in 1906 and the extensive use of this image for the pace of American life and its urban conditions. And Kipling had seen these social conditions for himself. Is it, then, altogether fanciful to suggest that the elements of "Social Darwinism" in the imagery if not the content of *The Jungle Books* and other Kipling writings owed something to his experience of America, its theory as well as its practice?

[55] "An American," *The Seven Seas*.

Perhaps, too, the first verse of the poem which accompanies his story about an American couple who settle in England, "An Habitation Enforced,"[56] may suggest that he saw in America's special relationship with Britain another saving grace:

> I am the land of their fathers,
> In me the virtue stays;
> I will bring back my children
> After certain days.

It is the kind of feeling which provokes all the ambivalence of Anglo-American relations.

To those who know Kipling only by reputation as an Imperialist his sympathy with the immigrant workers of America may seem remarkable; just as for those who know Jack London only by his reputation as an international socialist – or by the fact that he also is one of Russia's favourite writers – his racialism may lead to the raising of an eyebrow. But Kipling, more than London, has suffered from his public image. His imperialism was less far-reaching than that of some of his contemporaries, Henley or Davidson, for example: but he has become the symbol of the imperialist epoch which is now passing so rapidly. He did not, after all, write "Land of Hope and Glory"[57] – though many, if asked to name its author, would have no hesitation in saying "Kipling." If his imperialism suffered from lack of clear conceptualisation – which is, perhaps, why so much of it is expressed in his poetry – later generations have not hesitated to supply it for him. But such conceptualisations have only the effect of over-simplifying the world in which Kipling attained his maturity, and the attitudes which he adopted towards it.

Like all great writers he was both of his world and beyond it. It might be said of him as Walt Whitman (whom Kipling admired) said of himself: "Do I contradict myself? Very well then I contradict myself (I am large, I contain multitudes)." And of all his contradictions, none, perhaps, is greater or more fundamental than the picture of bustling, ever-enlarging Progress – which is given by a superficial reading of his works – and its clash with his underlying, cyclic view of history: "Men and Things come

---

[56] *Actions and Reactions.*
[57] It is by A. C. Benson.

round again, eternal as the seasons."[58] When he visited the Sudan,
a quarter of a century after the savage British campaign against
the Mahdi, he expressed this sentiment with bitter prophetic force.
Speaking of the young Sudanese who were being trained in
British techniques, Kipling proclaimed:

> In due time, they will forget how warily their forefathers
> had to walk in the Mahdi's time to secure even half a bellyful
> ... They will honestly believe that they themselves originally
> created and since then have upheld the easy life into which
> they were bought at so heavy a price. Then the demand will
> go up for "extension of local government", "Soudan for the
> Soudanese", and so on till the whole cycle has to be retrodden.
> It is a hard law but an old one – Rome died learning it, as our
> western civilisation may die – that if you give any man any-
> thing that he had not painfully earned for himself, you in-
> fallibly make him or his descendants your devoted enemies.[59]

This last sentence is a bitter recognition of the inadequacy of
paternalism – a criticism not just of the Sudanese, but of a notion
of Empire he himself had often celebrated. And indeed, if he had
cared to conceptualise briefly the cyclical view of history implicit
in the passage as a whole, he might have reflected with Clifford
Bax, "Age after age [our] tragic empires rise." For a sense of
tragedy co-existed strangely with Kipling's imperialism, con-
tributing often to the complexity and profundity of his vision at
its finest.

[58] *Something of Myself*, Chapter Eight.
[59] "The Riddle of Empire," *Letters of Travel 1892-1913*. This cyclical
interpretation of Britain's role in the Sudan may be contrasted with the
young Winston Churchill's "progressive" interpretation and his tribute to
the Mahdi in *The River War*, London 1899, pp. 18-19, etc.

Alan Sandison

KIPLING: THE ARTIST AND
THE EMPIRE

Tout commence en mystique et finit en politique. – CHARLES PÉGUY

I

"YOU'RE ONE O' the right sort, you are," says Beerbohm's John
Bull to a lantern-jawed Kipling:

"And them little tit-bits o' information what you gives me
about my Hempire – why Alf 'armsworth 'imself couldn't do
it neater, I do believe. Got your banjo with you tonight?
Then empty that there mug and give us a toon."[1]

This cartoon, along with the more familiar one of Kipling
capering over Hampstead Heath on the arm of "Britannia 'is
gurl," and strongly reinforced by Robert Buchanan's abusive
article "The Voice of the Hooligan,"[2] set a remarkably durable
fashion in Kipling criticism. His purpose and achievement, they
suggest, is simply to talk of, and to tell people how to think about,
the illustrious British Empire: to effect in his countrymen the
realisation that they, ahead of all others, have been collectively
placed by the will of the Almighty behind the greatest of his
ploughs. The Imperial Idea, in other words, is to be seen as the
causal inspiration of most, if not all, of his writings.

Since then the position has been modified in some respects,
but whenever the Indian stories come under discussion the
Beerbohm-Buchanan premise comes to the fore in one shape or
another.[3] Yet it is on these earlier stories that I have deliberately

---

[1] "De arte poetica," *Cartoons: "The Second Childhood of John Bull,"* London
1911.   [2] In *The Contemporary Review,* LXXVI (Dec. 1899).
[3] A notable exception is the criticism of Professor Bonamy Dobrée, whose
British Council pamphlet on Kipling is far more suggestive than most full-
scale studies.

chosen to base this essay, because I believe that they tell much more than an uplifting imperial tale: that they can, in fact, bring us nearer than any other category of his fiction to an understanding of his artistic inspiration. Mr W. Y. Tindall has claimed that Kipling's idea of Empire "may be deduced from 'Recessional', 'The White Man's Burden,' and 'Loot' "[4]: I would suggest, on the contrary, that a much more profound insight into the real nature and function of the Imperial Idea in Kipling's works can be obtained from "The Children of the Zodiac," "The Bridge-Builders," "At the End of the Passage," "On the City Wall," and "Without Benefit of Clergy," where we also see more clearly the relation of that idea to his more fundamental concerns, his deeper artistic vision.

Of course no-one would deny that Kipling vigorously beat the imperial drum: nor will anyone seek to contest the fact that a great number of his stories work within an implicit or explicit framework statement reiterating what might be described as the British Imperial Aptitude. Clearly Kipling's artistic inspiration emerges *"en politique."* But to say this as if it were all there is to be said: to see Kipling as "the laureate of Joseph Chamberlain's designs," as Mr Tindall does,[4a] is to see the surface pattern merely – and sometimes not even that. To go further and suggest that Kipling's relationship to the Imperial Idea is thus explained is nonsense. It is, after all, the *"mystique"* from which his expression emerges that must be explained if we would reach a real understanding of the precise nature of that expression: for the two are linked by the closest sequence of cause and effect. Kipling, much more so than one would at first suspect, in talking about political society is talking about self and individual consciousness. Thus even at his most "imperial," for instance in "The Head of the District," he is never being simply political; if we ignore this fact we are closing the door firmly on any hope of understanding what Mr Annan has called "the riddle of Kipling." Not only is Péguy's dictum amply illustrated in Kipling's work, it also represents precisely the essential dualism in which his concern centres and in which his dramatic tension has its roots. To comprehend this

---

[4] W. Y. Tindall, *Forces in Modern British Literature*, New York 1947, p. 65.
[4a] *Ibid.*

is, if not to excuse, certainly to explain his faults and to recognise where his virtues actually lie.

2

Of those of Kipling's stories and character-groupings in which he is frequently seen to be at his most politico-imperial, "The Enlightenments of Pagett, M.P.," in which Kipling sets out to give a reasoned and responsible defence of the Anglo-Indian point of view, comes nearest to political statement of the directly propagandist sort.[5] But although this story is a carefully calculated defence of Anglo-Indian attitudes, to dismiss it with all the disdain of the Western liberal as being no more than this is to perpetuate the injustice of the Beerbohm attack. And even politically it is not so absurd or contemptible as it is frequently assumed to be. Perhaps Kipling never fully realised the part played by democracy and capitalism in the foundation of Empire – in fact he is not in the least interested in first causes – but he was by no means ignorant of capitalism's effects:

"... it is an elementary consideration in governing a country like India, which must be administered for the benefit of the people at large, that the counsels of those who resort to it for the purpose of making money should be judiciously weighed and not allowed to overpower the rest. They are welcome guests here, as a matter of course, but it has been found best to restrain their influence. Thus the rights of plantation labourers, factory operatives, and the like, have been protected, and the capitalist, eager to get on, has not always regarded Government action with favour. It is quite conceivable that under an elective system the commercial communities of the great towns might find means to secure majorities on labour questions and on financial matters."

"They would act at least with intelligence and consideration."

"Intelligence, yes: but as to consideration, who at the present moment most bitterly resents the tender solicitude of

[5] Another story almost comes into this category, but in "One View of the Question" Kipling has created a narrator who is very different from the sober, deliberate Orde: he is, in fact Kipling's "ideal" Pathan warrior, who thus becomes the Free Narrator able to say all those things which the responsible man of common-sense and conscience can not.

Lancashire for the welfare and protection of the Indian factory operative? English and native capitalists running cotton mills and factories. . . . I merely indicate an example of how a powerful commercial interest might hamper a Government intent in the first place on the larger interests of humanity."[6]

That the story as a whole is more than simply political statement we can appreciate if we stand back a little from the process of the argument. What we see then is a man who has deliberately chosen as his field of action and of values the material world; a man who has no time for politics based on abstract theories when millions of people are dying through lack of a planned agriculture, lack of medical treatment, and what Dr Lathrop describes as "an all-round entanglement of physical, social and moral evils and corruptions." In her view the famine- and cholera-ridden people of India "require many things more urgently than votes." And always before the administrators' eyes there is the reminder of the shortness of the present moment and its value:

"Our death rate's five times higher than yours . . . and we work on the refuse of worked-out cities and exhausted civilisations, among the bones of the dead."[7]

Kipling has little time for visionaries who forget about present hells to build future Utopias. Out of the bodies of millions of animalculae Nature may have made the rocks, but, as Rider Haggard remarked in *The Witch's Head*, "the process must have been unpleasant to the living creatures by whose humble means the great strata were reared up." The Rock of God's far-off purpose didn't concern Kipling; there is no clear evidence that he found it anything other than a myth. But the process of the living moment did – all the more so. There was, in his view, little enough time to alleviate the sufferings of the world's brief lives, and none at all to waste experimenting on emaciated bodies with new forms of government, particularly when these forms were based more on metaphysical speculation than on experience, which alone can apprehend the happiness and unhappiness of individuals – the only criterion of government.

---

[6] "The Enlightenments of Pagett, M.P." *The Contemporary Review*, LVIII (Sept. 1890), p. 351.

[7] *Op. cit.*, p. 355.

Naturally, a man [in London] grows to think that there is no one higher than himself, and that the Metropolitan Board of Works made everything. But in India where you really see humanity – raw, brown, naked, humanity – with nothing between it and the blazing sky, and only the used-up, over-handled earth underfoot, the notion somehow dies away, and most folk come back to simpler theories. Life, in India, is not long enough to waste in proving that there is no one in particular at the head of affairs. For this reason. The Deputy is above the Assistant, the Commissioner above the Deputy, the Lieutenant-Governor above the Commissioner, and the Viceroy above all four, under the orders of the Secretary of State, who is responsible to the Empress. If the Empress be not responsible to her Maker – if there is no Maker for her to be responsible to – the entire system of Our administration must be wrong. Which is manifestly impossible.[8]

The sting is in the tail: Kipling is not in the least concerned with metaphysics or an absolute morality, and here he is ironically proving not the system against the principle, but the principle against the system. Whether or not there is a Maker, whether or not there is a morality based on responsibility to Him, there is an Administration with its clear justification in the succouring of India's mass of "raw, brown, naked humanity." In the light of their crying need, First Causes are luxury commodities which can well be done without.

His characterisation has also suffered from a too superficial reading. His notorious "Subalterns," for instance, have again been misconstrued in their superficial as well as in their deeper meaning: far from being the hopelessly idealised *élite* of an imperial *Herrenvolk* that they are often seen to be, these men are in fact drawn from actuality by a peculiarly Stoic mind. For though they may be unreal to us they certainly were not in the nineteenth-century Anglo-Indian scene. This was particularly "the day of subalterns, boys in age, men in character, blessed with the adventurous ardour and audacity of youth"[9]; it was the day of Sir

[8] "The Conversion of Aurelian McGoggin," *Plain Tales from the Hills.*
[9] Maud Diver, "The British Subaltern in India," *Blackwood's Magazine,* CCLVII (June 1945), p. 385.

Henry Lawrence and his "Young Men," through whom he created the basis of sound administrative government in Northern India; it was the day of Lieutenant Eldred Pottinger, "The Hero of Herat," of Lieutenant Proby Cantley, who, totally without experience, designed and built the Ganges canal "on a scale of magnitude hardly conceivable outside India," of Herbert Edwardes who pacified the wild Bannu tribesmen single-handed. If the climax of their exploits occurred prior to the literary advent of Kipling, their traditions and ideals persisted as strongly as ever to the end of the century and beyond. One has only to dip into the mass of autobiographies and descriptive works of the era like the *Memorials of the Life and Letters of Sir Herbert Edwardes* (1886), Winston Churchill's *Story of the Malakand Field Force* (1898), or Sir George Younghusband's *A Soldier's Memories* (1917), to realise how far from unreality Kipling's subalterns really were. Filtered through his own uncompromising vision, their code, their endurance and their objectives became more Roman: for so transmitted, these qualities were the essential ones in Kipling's world if man was to achieve any dignity at all and to survive with any degree of integrity during his battle with life. The story "Only a Subaltern" starts with a quotation from *The Bengal Army Regulations*:

> ... Not only to enforce by command, but to encourage by example the energetic discharge of duty and the steady endurance of the difficulties and privations unseparable from military service.[10]

Duty ... endurance ... difficulties ... privations; attention to the job in hand and fortitude in the face of all which that will bring is what constitutes a man and makes his soul. And to aid and fortify him he has the assistance of his community – in this case the military community – drawing its spiritual sustenance from the same ideals. What is implicit in them is the machinery, not of militarism or anything like it, but of self-consciousness, identity, and moral integrity. Its components are, very largely, the "few simple notions" that we find recommended in Conrad's *Lord Jim*.

Over the years, Kipling's "Other Ranks" have fared better.

[10] "Only a Subaltern," *Wee Willie Winkie*.

Even here, however, accusations of staginess and unreality are still frequent. This is inevitable if, like Robert Graves,[11] we look upon them simply as the adulterous scallywags on whose Imperial doings the sun, with very good reason, is reluctant to set. Again, however, it is actuality refined through what can only be described as a Stoic perception: these men are all that Mulvaney suggests in the summary of his own life in "The Solid Muldoon," but no Kipling character ever wears his heart upon his sleeve, though now and then we may be vouchsafed a glimpse of it. As if he were anxious lest we had failed to appreciate the depths of their consciousness and sensitivity from these brief insights, Kipling reinforces them on a special occasion for each of the "Soldiers Three" in turn: in "The Courting of Dinah Shadd" for Mulvaney, in "On Greenhow Hill" for Learoyd, and in "The Madness of Private Ortheris" for the third member of the group. Of the three, "The Courting of Dinah Shadd" makes clearest the soldiers' appreciation of the public image and the private truth –

> "Good cause the Rig'mint has to know me for the best soldier in ut. Better cause have I to know myself for the worst man.'

– and the awareness which this brings of the loneliness at the core of their individuality:

> When I woke I saw Mulvaney, the night dew gemming his moustache, leaning on his rifle at picket, lonely as Prometheus on his rock, with I know not what vultures tearing at his liver.[12]

At most other times, however, they are found punctiliously observing the rules, living life in full fealty to the God of Things as They Are, although well aware of the depths beneath. They do so, of course, in a manner historically different from that of the Subalterns; while the latter conceal their awareness behind reticence and a gentlemanly nonchalance, the common soldier adopts the front of Barrack-Room Balladry, of garrulousness and belligerence, of scepticism in everything but the chain of command.

As for the "Administrator," he is still seen to have an upper lip

---

[11] Robert Graves, "Rudyard Kipling," *The Common Asphodel*, London 1949.   [12] "The Courting of Dinah Shadd," *Life's Handicap*.

so stiff as to preclude utterly any explanation of his conduct. Yet here again to dismiss him as one more example of Kipling's "Imperial Hero" is to make the old mistake and miss the real significance of his characterisation. What he represents is something which has, innately, little to do with the imperial idea, but a lot to do with Kipling's artistic vision.

Kipling, as I have suggested, had very little interest and no particular faith in the long-term future; the most admirable man in his eyes was he who had learned to live nobly and usefully in the full consciousness of his ultimate destruction. The whole theme of "The Children of the Zodiac" in *Many Inventions* is the progression of Leo and the Girl to this particular awareness.

Early in the story they make the discovery that there is only one world – the world of men – and that no-one is immortal:

> "Every one of those people we met just now will die. . . ."
> "So shall we", said the Girl sleepily. "Lie down again dear."
> Leo could not see that her face was wet with tears.

Then Leo hears his own doom in the words of the Crab, one of the Houses of Death, and achieves his fullest realisation yet of the human situation. Although he would like to "lie down and brood over the words of the Crab," he knows that this would be worse than useless.

> "Well", said the Bull, "what will you do? . . . you cannot pull a plough . . . I can and that prevents me from thinking of the Scorpion."

But Leo can sing, and is exhorted by the Bull to make use of his talent:

> "Help us now," said the Bull. "The tides of the day are running down. My legs are very stiff. Sing if you never sang before."
> "To a mud-spattered villager?" said Leo.
> "He is under the same doom as ourselves. Are you a coward?" said the Bull.

First Leo sang the song of the fearless but soon discovered another much more powerful.

This was a thing he could never have done had he not met the Crab face to face. He remembered facts concerning cultivators, and bullocks, and rice fields that he had not particularly noticed before the interview, and he strung them all together, growing more interested as he sang, and he told the cultivator much more about himself and his work than the cultivator knew. The Bull grunted approval as he toiled down the furrows for the last time that day, and the song ended, leaving the cultivator with a very good opinion of himself in his aching bones.

So Leo becomes the Singer, the Poet, the Writer, or, simply, the Artist, whose role is just such as is described here. Through his efforts man will be helped towards dignity, integrity and self-respect, as well as to the modicum of happiness which he is permitted to achieve.[13]

Unremitting work and sacrifice in the present actuality such as the administrator participated in, was, then, the only meaningful activity. By sharing in it, one not only contributed to the happiness of fellow-humans but also discovered the only means of achieving and sustaining integrity. The harder and more exhausting the task, undiluted by anything which might make it easier or more congenial, the more fully were all one's powers and energies engaged in the struggle; in such conflict with one's environment alone was there the chance to attain even a passing reality.

Thus if in his notorious story "The Head of the District" Kipling can be seen, on one level, as launching perhaps his most savage and bitter attack on the "educated native" who presumed to do a Sahib's job, the second level must, at the same time, be kept in mind. For what Grish Chunder De threatened was to introduce an entirely different code, and one that would utterly profane the Stoic ideal in which Kipling's vision emerged. And if one takes away from man his conflict, his fight against overwhelming odds which clearly was to end in defeat, one does nothing less than deprive him of his salvation: take away man's stoicism and that "Bulkhead 'twixt Despair and the edge of Nothing" will at once disintegrate.

---

[13] In the light of all this it is difficult to accept Mr Edmund Wilson's contention that Kipling "lacked faith in the artist's vocation."

3

It would appear, then, that two levels are to be distinguished in these stories. Let us now examine the deeper level in more detail.

The main character in the Indian stories is not the tired, tough, dedicated administrator nor the resourceful subaltern; the principal role is, in fact, played by India itself.

Looking over the menacing jungle landscape of the Congo, Marlow, in *Heart of Darkness*, had wondered:

> Could we handle that dumb thing or would it handle us? I felt how big, how confoundedly big was the thing that couldn't talk and perhaps was deaf as well.

In Kipling the struggle for mastery is evident in every story which has to deal with the country and nine times out of ten, "great, grey, formless India" wins. Inevitably it comes to represent the forces of persecution ranged against the individual in his struggle to sustain his identity. Physically and morally it overwhelms and crushes. One's own truths and moral definitions blur and diffuse themselves into meaninglessness, just as they did for Forster's Mrs Moore. Mrs Mallowe has, in fact, occasional flashes of Mrs Moore's perception, observing very clearly the moral destructiveness of India where "you can't focus anything".[14]

Faced by a country which can reduce utterly, these beleagured Anglo-Indians band together in pitiful, blind opposition, doomed to ludicrous failure, however much they speak of Smith as a Bengal man, Jones as a Punjabi. Herded together in The Club, in The Station, in Simla, they insist upon their "difference" from the rest of India; but even in the bosom of the Anglo-Indian community they cannot escape the ever-present consciousness of their vulnerability:

> Everybody was there and there was a general closing up of ranks and taking stock of our losses in dead or disabled that had fallen during the past year. It was a very wet night, and I remember that we sang "Auld Lang Syne" with our feet in the Polo Championship Cup and our heads among the stars, and swore that we were all very dear friends.[15]

[14] "The Education of Otis Yeere," *Wee Willie Winkie*.
[15] "The Mark of the Beast," *Life's Handicap*.

This is Forster's famous anthem scene viewed from the inside. But it is in the outposts that India's malignant power is to be seen at its most active in its relentless war against the alien:

> The night-light was trimmed; the shadow of the punkah wavered across the room, and the "flick" of the punkah-towel and the soft whine of the rope through the wall-hole followed it. Then the punkah flagged, almost ceased. The sweat poured from Spurstow's brow. Should he go out and harangue the coolie? It started forward again with a savage jerk, and a pin came out of the towels. When this was replaced, a tom-tom in the coolie lines began to beat with the steady throb of a swollen artery inside some brain-fevered skull.[16]

Even the great British Raj and all its achievements dwindle into insignificance in the face of India's inexorable powers of assimilation. Just how insignificant it really is, "The Bridge-Builders" reveals:

> "They have changed the face of the land which is my land. They have killed and made new towns on my banks," said the Mugger.
> "It is but the shifting of a little dirt. Let the dirt dig in the dirt if it pleases the dirt," answered the Elephant.[17]

But Mrs Mallowe has already come to the same conclusion:

> "We are only little bits of dirt on the hill-sides – here one day and blown down the *khud* the next . . . we have no cohesion."[18]

The Empire, its ideals and works, are by India utterly reduced in time and space:

> "What should their Gods know? They were born yesterday, and those that made them are scarcely yet cold", said the Mugger. "Tomorrow their Gods will die".[19]

And it is of no use saying that because the Bridge – and Findlayson – have survived the fury of Mother Gunga theirs is the last

---

[16] "At the End of the Passage," *Life's Handicap.*
[17] "The Bridge-Builders," *The Day's Work.*
[18] "The Education of Otis Yeere," *Wee Willie Winkie.*
[19] "The Bridge-Builders," *The Day's Work.*

word and the final triumph. Compared to the commentators whose statements are made from above and beyond time, theirs is the most ephemeral of expressions.

The Anglo-Indians' main reaction to this ubiquitous persecution is to assert their own cultural morality more fiercely than ever: to insist on its absolute value and to have no truck with anything which may lie outside it. As a result, most of them fail to get anywhere near an understanding of the people they govern; yet these persecuted aliens are still Imperial aliens who consciously or unconsciously, aggressively or defensively, seek to impose their own cultural ethos upon that of the subject race. Ironically, therefore, Kipling shows us inadequate western morality undermining and destroying the morality and culture of others. "I thought you were my friend," says one of his Pathan characters,

"but you are like all the others – a Sahib. Is a man sad? Give him money, say the Sahibs. Is he dishonoured? Give him money, say the Sahibs. Hath he a wrong upon his head? Give him money, say the Sahibs. Such are the Sahibs, and such art thou – even thou."[20]

A considerable amount of the dramatic tension in Kipling's Indian stories arises from just this collision of the two cultures. There are innumerable examples, but perhaps the best is the case of Wali Dad, since he is most fully conscious of what is happening to people like himself:

"India has gossiped for centuries – always standing in the bazars until the soldiers go by. Therefore – you are here today instead of starving in your own country, and I am not a Muhammedan – I am a Product – a Demnition Product. That also I owe to you and yours: that I cannot make an end to my sentence without quoting from your authors."[21]

While he may be something of a dilettante, Wali Dad is nevertheless equipped with a very clear insight:

[20] "Dray Wara Yow Dee," *Soldiers Three*.
[21] "On the City Wall," *Soldiers Three*.

". . . if you took your place in the world, Wali Dad, and gave up dreaming dreams –"

"I might wear an English coat and trousers. I might be a leading Mohammedan pleader. I might be received even at the Commissioner's tennis-parties where the English stand on one side and the natives on the other, in order to promote social intercourse throughout the Empire."

Is this a source for Mr Forster's Aziz and his famous bridge-party? The remark could certainly have come from Aziz. Because the English could never see the relativity of their own morality they could never reach a sympathetic understanding of the Indian, nor ever grasp the essential, hopeless antagonism of the two cultures.

One of Kipling's best short stories – "Without Benefit of Clergy"[22] – derives its excellence from its intense awareness of, and sympathy with, the human context of this conflict. But it transcends this, for the collision here is observed not so much within the focus of Imperial rule, as is the case in "On the City Wall," as *sub specie aeternitatis*. The brief little tragedy of Holden and Ameera is played out against a background not of marching feet and thudding rifle-butts, but of India's silent, malignant and jealous power which overarches everything and allows none to live save in the grace of its own inexorable law. The duality of meaning in the title itself suggests the compass of the theme. "Without Benefit of Clergy" refers, of course, to the union which is, in conventional terms, illicit, and acknowledges, within the context of antagonistic cultures, the force of the man-made obstacles to happiness and love. But "benefit of clergy" is also a technical phrase meaning originally the exemption which ecclesiastics obtained from criminal process before a secular judge; thus Kipling makes this aspect of his theme clear from the start: there is no exemption – not even for the lovers for all the purity of their emotions.

From the very first words of the story there is an extraordinary sense of helplessness and doom in the face of immensity; and the terrible and inevitable thing is that it is through Ameera, whose love for Holden is no less intense than his for her, that India demonstrates its strength and tyranny. In spite of their love there

[22] *Life's Handicap.*

is a great gulf between them as they both, at heart, know very well, though Holden will not admit it. In their search for a "little name" for their son it is clearly to be seen:

> "Mian Mittu has spoken. He shall be the parrot. When he is ready he will talk mightily and run about. Mian Mittu is The Parrot in thy – in the Mussulman tongue, is it not?"
> "Why put me so far off?" said Ameera fretfully. "Let it be like unto some English name – but not wholly. For he is mine."

Ameera, from the start so conscious of the external strains upon their relationship, had always seen the child as a strengthening of the bond between them, and when he is born she rejoices that there is "a bond and a heel-rope between us now that nothing can break." But she has forgotten the might of the thing she represents and its jealousy. So Toto dies of a fever – "the seasonal autumnal fever" – and presumptuous humanity is beaten down to size.

Throughout the story, with an admirable manipulation of time and space, the relationship between these humans and India evolves: from the intimate opening, close-focused and personal, "But if it be a girl?", we move to the desolate end through a phased depersonalisation showing us first the grey squirrel, now the sole occupant of the bungalow's verandah "as if the house had been untenanted for thirty years instead of three days," and lastly nothing at all:

> "It shall be pulled down and the municipality shall make a road across as they desire from the burning ghat to the city wall, so that no man may say where this house stood."

Time and space have been expanded and man has shrunk to a mere pin-point, and a pin-point which travels across the triumphant mass of India between the City Wall and the Burning Ghat. Here Kipling the artist, is at his purest, and the politician almost entirely absent.

4

The deeper and more significant stratum of Kipling's stories having been examined, it is desirable at this point to consider some of the findings and their implications. Firstly, what sort of being is the Kipling character fundamentally? A man with a burning cause, perhaps, to make the deserts blossom as the rose? A man with the conviction that the world is best ruled by an aristocracy of blood – the bluest and best of which is to be found in British veins? Something of these elements are there but their acknowledgment leaves the surface hardly scratched.

He is, first of all, a man whose vision, far from delighting him with rich and glorious prospects, is bleak and austere. Of his own individuality he is immensely aware and hence of his loneliness.

"I am Kim – Kim – Kim – alone – one person – in the middle of it all."

The burden of sustaining moral integrity is recognised as his alone, and involvement seems to offer the only solution. And the acceptance of involvement means, as the Administrator shows, the unceasing conflict with environment.

This, then, is the real crux of the Anglo-Indian/India relationship, and it is not in the least political. To regard its agonies – so well brought out in "At the End of the Passage" – as a simple description of the triumph of British fortitude under extreme conditions, is to misread completely Kipling's artistic vision. For the conflict is spiritual and tragically inescapable. These Anglo-Indians may writhe and suffer under their relentless persecution, be, like Otis Yeere, "ground up in the wheels of the Administration, losing heart and soul, and mind and strength, in the process,"[23] yet, paradoxically, their existence depends on just this conflict. For these men are less the victims of Empire than of the wider Necessity which has decreed that man shall live forever at the edge of the pit, snatching his identity from the limbo of non-existence which lies at his feet. The conflict between their personal lives and the Empire they serve is only a reflexion of that more fundamental dialectic between self and destructive non-self. And from this permanent state of war there can be no opting out on any terms whatsoever, since only by the closest engagement can even a momentary existence and identity be secured. Only by immersing oneself fully in the world of actuality can one achieve integrity; this had been Stein's advice in *Lord Jim* and the whole point of "The Children of the Zodiac."

[23] "The Education of Otis Yeere," *Wee Willie Winkie*.

Thus the Administrator, as Kipling sees him, has at his core a terrible irony: he who would "administer" and rule this vast mass is himself the victim. Nor could it ever be otherwise. The British work in India was a huge, macabre joke which Kipling and a few – but only a few – of his characters saw. In the light of this, one's primary duty was only superficially to the Queen-Empress: fundamentally, it was to one's own moral integrity.

Such a realisation, such a concern, can only stem from the most lucid clearsightedness. For Kipling as for Conrad there is a crisis of realisation – such as Leo experiences – when man faces his destiny clearly and without illusions. But whereas Conrad projected this in explicit artistic statement through characters like MacWhirr and Mitchell on the one hand and Lord Jim on the other, Kipling leaves it unprojected. The crisis is part of his own experience and though it obviously informs his work it very rarely becomes the immediate subject. And the fact that this is so, that it informs but is seldom fully realised in artistic terms, has an unfortunate effect upon his characterisation. So much of it obviously springs from this crisis, but in the presentation of the individual character all traces are frequently concealed, with the result that the real dynamic of his tension is largely denied him in the moment of his advent; he arrives post-crisis with a well-bred resolve to say nothing about it. Consequently his inevitable courage, fortitude and endurance have too often from the beginning the dead unreality of a *fait accompli*. Kipling seems to shrink nervously from bringing the crisis into the public world of his characterisation, but his awareness of it cannot be suppressed. Adherence to a code, insistence on discipline and the stiff upper lip are in the Kipling hero indications not of shallow-mindedness but of a deep sensitivity which has allowed him to see far into "the wheel and the drift of Things." For to weather the crisis a certain "drill" is demanded: loyalty to a fixed standard of conduct, for instance, and an activist attention to the job in hand, which means, of course, commitment. And commitment in turn means community; though for Kipling, clearly, it is community with a special purpose: society is valued not for the particular morality on which it is based but for the effect it secures – the reassurance of the individual's integrity.

5

Man is alone: this realisation is the core of Kipling's artistic vision:

> . . . that primal instinct of independence which ante-dates the
> social one and makes the young at times a little difficult . . .
> comes from the dumb and dreadful epoch when all that man
> knew was that he was himself, and not another, and therefore
> the loneliest of created beings.[24]

Consciousness of individuality meant simultaneous consciousness
of estrangement – of the

> horror of desolation, abandonment, and realised worthlessness
> which is one of the most real of the hells in which we are com-
> pelled to walk.[25]

And inevitably this led to the antidote being sought in society.

> One of the few advantages that India has over England is a
> great Knowability. After five years' service a man is directly or
> indirectly acquainted with the two or three hundred Civilians
> in his province, all the Messes of ten or twelve Regiments and
> Batteries, and some fifteen hundred other people of the non-
> official caste. In ten years his knowledge should be doubled. . . .[26]

But such reinforcement was not to be had free of charge: it demanded in fact an important sacrifice.

> Not till [man] abandoned his family tree and associated with his
> fellows on the flat, for predatory or homicidal purposes, did he
> sacrifice his personal independence of action or cut into his
> large leisure of brooding abstraction necessary for the discovery
> of his relations to his world. This is the period in our Reverend
> Ancestor's progress through Time that strikes me as im-
> mensely the most interesting and important.[27]

That this should be the period of greatest importance for Kipling
is of the utmost significance, for it is that fundamental moment of
truth when the great conflict between self and society comes into

[24] "Independence," *A Book of Words.*
[25] "Values in Life," *A Book of Words.*
[26] "The Phantom Rickshaw," *Wee Willie Winkie.*
[27] "Independence," *A Book of Words.*

being. The self in isolation is wholly vulnerable to the forces of disintegration as Decoud in Conrad's *Nostromo*, Hummil in "At The End of the Passage," and Dawse in "The Disturber of Traffic" discovered. So the self seeks reassurance of integrity in society and commitment:

> A veil 'twixt us and thee, dread Lord
> A veil 'twixt us and thee
> Lest we should hear too clear, too clear,
> And unto madness see,[28]

But this involves sacrifice, for the creation of society inevitably means, for the individual, a partial surrender of integrity. And here we have the real source of the essential tension in and behind Kipling's writing. Half way between Marx and Sartre he reveals the great human paradox that man can only exist in society which he alone can create out of his own precious store of selfhood: thus every contribution to society is an erosion of the self which it is designed to identify and protect. When society demands too great a contribution it must be resisted for it would mean erosion to the point of complete assimilation; Mulvaney, while admiring the Roman Catholic church, found that it was not one for a weak man "bekaze she takes the body and the sowl av him," and, in a later non-Indian story, "The Mother Hive," the doctrine "we and The Hive are one" is completely rejected. If, on the other hand, too little is given to society, the core of the self is left unprotected and wholly vulnerable.

There is one statement which above all others in his work goes furthest towards explaining "the riddle of Kipling"; at the same time it justifies, in the most succinct terms, the interpretation which has been suggested in the foregoing pages:

> For the eternal question still is whether the profit of any concession that a man makes to his Tribe, against the light that is in him, outweighs or justifies his disregard for that light.[29]

In a way, the Imperial *milieu* of Anglo-India came nearest to offering Kipling the ideal balance. There the present actuality took all one's time, attention and energy, and the friendship and

---

[28] Epigraph to "The Disturber of Traffic," *Many Inventions*.
[29] "Independence," *A Book of Words*.

support of a tightly-knit "knowable" community, though never becoming too intimate nor seeking to break down the barriers of that guarded inner privacy, yet linked individuals in a fortifying alliance against the powers of darkness and disintegration. Not surprisingly after this, Kipling's characters appear to need rather than to love each other:

> The players were not conscious of any special regard for each other. They squabbled whenever they met; but they ardently desired to meet, as men without water desire to drink. They were lonely folk who understood the dread meaning of loneliness.[30]

6

"Society" then, to return to the *politique* of the starting point, is an illusion created by the individual in order to establish, identify and protect the self. It is the product of the conflict between the individual's consciousness of his essential estrangement and the need to preserve his own moral integrity – the conflict from which Kipling's writing evolves.

But Kipling rarely leaves it as a conflict; frequently – too frequently – he imposes a settlement, and it is for this reason, I would suggest, rather than for that advanced by Mr Annan,[31] that "his views and morality have received such harsh treatment." "Il n'y pas de signe dans le monde," Sartre announces, but Kipling, though he more than suspects this truth, firmly resolves that signs there will be, and all the paraphernalia of self reassurance come into being – religion, law, customs, morality, and the rest.

We must, however, be fully aware of this conflict and of where precisely it lies. Mr Annan, for instance, complains that Kipling "hardly ever shows how the social process or social morality affects the individual – how men's characters develop, are corrupted or ennobled"; this shows the dangers which arise when the sociological analogue becomes a method of literary criticism. Kipling does not show us the effect of the social process simply because the conflict for him occurs at a more fundamental level between the individual self and the very concept of society – not

---

[30] "At the End of the Passage," *Life's Handicap*.
[31] See above pp. 120-4.

between the individual and a particularised social morality. The reason why Mr Annan fails to find consciousness of isolation in his work is that he is looking for it in the wrong place. Once Kipling imposes his settlement and affirms man's place in society, the crisis is past, or at any rate papered over. But the isolation of man who has discovered his own essential loneliness remains his preoccupation and emerges in varying guises and strength in, for instance, Hummil, Dawse and Wali Dad: in "Beyond the Pale," "Little Tobrah," "The Children of the Zodiac," and "The Bridge Builders."

"The centre of Kipling's world is society," Mr Annan claims, but this is true, paradoxically, only in so far as it means the individual in society, for Kipling's world remains entirely solipsist. He is not in the least interested in society or morality in themselves, but only in so far as they are essential to the self's existence. From this comes his cynicism and his acceptance of so many of the moral definitions of his caste in despite of his own fuller awareness:

> ... one cannot visit a loafer in the Serai by day. Friends buying horses would not understand it. . . [32]

Even his appreciation of human nature is not, in the last analysis, disinterested. He was too jealous and uncertain of his own soul ever to be magnanimous, and a real, unhampered, outgoing warmth of feeling for humanity is present only sporadically in his work, although his awareness of the human dilemma was, as I have tried to indicate, acute. In "Without Benefit of Clergy" and in *Kim*, for instance, we do, of course, find such warmth, but all too often it is reined and snaffled by his own selfishness. "The Children of the Zodiac" might be taken for an expression of profound feeling and sympathy for struggling humanity, and so it largely is – until the last few lines when Kipling rounds hysterically on those who weaken and let the jungle in:

> After [Leo's] death there sprang up a breed of little mean men, whimpering and flinching and howling because the Houses killed them and theirs, who wished to live forever without

---

[32] "To be Filed for Reference," *Plain Tales from the Hills.*

pain. They did not increase their lives, but they increased their own torments miserably. . . .[33]

And in "Beyond the Pale" his sympathy is likewise flawed by his cynical insistence on the observance of the man-made boundaries to human love.

Professor Trilling discovers a snarl in Kipling's Toryism, but it is to my mind less the snarl of defeated gentility that he suggests than that of the dog in the manger: and his Imperialism is offensive not because it is Imperialism but because it isn't. For Kipling could never be disinterested enough to commit himself to a cause of any self-transcendant objectivity whatsoever. Empire in general and the Indian empire in particular was simply a *Place des Signes*, where the signs could be more easily recognised, where the frontiers of his own personal fear could be more securely guarded and where he himself could find refuge and reassurance in his frontiersmen's ideals. Elsewhere Professor Trilling has written that "ideas, if they are large enough and of a certain kind are not only not hostile to the creative process, as some think, but are virtually inevitable to it."[34] This indicates precisely the inhibiting factor in Kipling: his essential, creative idea is ultimately shrunk by the unrelenting egotism which infuses it, and consequently the Imperial Idea brought in as a vehicle is itself heavily circumscribed, so that it lacks even the largeness it is found possessed of in the works of Buchan. All this makes Kipling a Conservative, but mean-white rather than true-blue.

It was unfortunate, though in the circumstances inevitable, that Kipling chose to enunciate his "eternal question" and to impose his frequent settlements in the context of a political idea – particularly of this political idea. For, in crystallising into a dogma, Imperialism demonstrated its own unreality in the trend of political thinking, and at that very moment Kipling was found to be giving it his whole-hearted support. His guilt was obvious to all – so obvious that it concealed the fact that he was not writing in order to express the Idea of Empire. Given the Idea, he reacted to it in the way any artist would – by finding in it a

[33] "The Children of the Zodiac," *Many Inventions*.

[34] Lionel Trilling, "The Meaning of a Literary Idea," *The Liberal Imagination*, London 1951, p. 293.

means through which to express his own artistic vision. Awareness of man's essential estrangement, illumined with such clarity in the Imperial alien's relationship to his hostile environment, and of his compulsive need to armour himself against the effects of this, is the far from contemptible dynamic which motivates Kipling's work.

I said at the beginning that if we understood the peculiar relevance of Péguy's dictum to an interpretation of Kipling we would be able to explain his faults and to see where his virtues really lay. The flaw which the subsequent analysis suggested is a major one, but it would never be so if it did not spring from a context of major virtue. If his artistic vision is cramped and confined, emerging finally – in the widest sense – *en politique*: if his basic awareness tends repeatedly to disappear in the strong recommendation in which his appreciation of the human situation is nearly always made to terminate: we cannot, nevertheless, deny this awareness its fundamental role as the inspiration of his creativity. It is of the first importance to get the sequence right: *politique*, whether in the wider sense or in the narrower one of a shallow and ephemeral political idea, is neither the measure nor the source of his artistic vision. That was based on something much more vital, much more enduring – an acute awareness of man's essential isolation and an agonised consciousness of the razor edge on which he must balance to sustain his moment of existence.

III. KIPLING'S ART

Andrew Rutherford

OFFICERS AND GENTLEMEN

KIPLING WAS not simply "the prophet of British Imperialism in its expansionist phase":[1] this formula takes no account of many aspects of his art, and ignores important elements even in his poems and stories on "imperial" subjects. Yet it corresponds in part at least to his own conception of his mission as an artist – to the role he chose for himself at an early stage in his career, when he set out "to tell to the English something of the world outside England – not directly but by implication" – a notion which grew bit by bit "into a vast, vague conspectus – Army and Navy Stores List, if you like – of the whole sweep and meaning of things and effort and origins throughout the Empire."[2] This programme was not primarily political – his main interest was in people rather than policies – but it was interpenetrated by political assumptions. And he wished as part of it to celebrate the admirable, even the heroic qualities he had observed in the English overseas – to convey to a public living (as it seemed to him) in ignoble comfort and security some sense of the hardships and dangers willingly endured by their compatriots in the service of Empire.

This aim, particularly as it affected the Army – the force actively engaged in the process of imperial expansion – involved a break with the main tradition of serious prose fiction in the nineteenth century. Heroic endeavour had been traditionally dealt with by epic and romance, but these *genres* were closely associated with particular historical periods and earlier states of society; and whereas the pastoral convention, with its many variants and off-shoots, had a continuing vitality due largely to a

---

[1] The phrase is Orwell's. See above, p. 72.
[2] *Something of Myself*, Chapter Four.

communal awareness (much intensified by the Romantics) of the countryside and country people, epic and romance seemed increasingly irrelevant to life as it was lived in nineteenth-century England.[3] Those obsolescent forms – obsolescent, that is, from the point of view of the contemporary writer – had been largely superseded by the anti-heroic, anti-romantic novel, which dealt characteristically with very different areas of experience. Scott, it is true, had used his unheroic heroes to chart his own reactions to the world of action and adventure to which he was imaginatively drawn; but that world does not figure in the major novelists, who normally display their characters in domestic, social, and professional settings which give little scope for heroism. Thackeray is typical in seeing his place as being with the non-combatants when the gallant –th march out to Waterloo; and his sour reflexions on traditional poetic treatments of war show his awareness of the novel as a *genre* committed not only to different subject-matter, but to a different kind of vision, and a truer sense of values:

> Time out of mind [he writes] strength and courage have been the theme of bards and romances; and from the story of Troy down to today, poetry has always chosen a soldier for a hero. I wonder is it because men are cowards in heart that they admire bravery so much, and place military valour so far beyond every other quality for reward and worship?[4]

His dissatisfaction with such conventional estimates would have been shared by the most important English novelists of his century (except Conrad). Common to all of them is the assumption which Professor Daiches attributes to Scott – the belief that

> heroic action . . . is, in the last analysis, neither heroic nor

[3] See, for example, the doubts Tennyson felt in offering the public his epic fragment, the "Morte D'Arthur" – doubts expressed, self-protectively, through "the poet Everard Hall," who is said to have destroyed all the remainder of his twelve-book epic:

> "Nay, nay," said Hall,
> "Why take the style of those heroic times?
> For nature brings not back the Mastodon,
> Nor we those times. . . ."

(And *The Idylls of the King*, as they afterwards developed, suggest that these early doubts were only too well founded.)

[4] *Vanity Fair*, ed. Saintsbury, The Oxford Thackeray, XI, 372.

useful, and that man's destiny, at least in the modern world, is to find his testing time not amid the sound of trumpets but in the daily struggles and recurring crises of personal and social life.[5]

This general assumption was, however, rooted in local and temporary conditions – in the national security of Victorian England, which can hardly be taken as representative of the human lot. None of these writers had the range, the inclusive vision of a Tolstoy, who could portray the crises and testings of War as well as those of Peace: if soldiers and sailors figure in their works it is only in minor roles; the author's tone in presenting them is often patronising, if not openly satirical; and whole areas of human experience, though treated with full seriousness by Carlyle in his historical and polemical writings, are abandoned by the novelists to a sub-literature extending from the works of Marryat, Lytton, or Kingsley to tales of adventure in the *Boy's Own Paper*.

For Kipling this meant that in celebrating courage and devotion to duty on the imperial frontiers he had to start from scratch, evolving his own methods without any adequate models to assist him. And for us as readers it means that his stories often outrage the expectations which we normally bring to serious prose fiction: the very nature of his subject-matter tends to discredit his art in the eyes of the sophisticated – all the more so since some of his themes recall vividly certain stereotypes of our own boyhood reading. This barrier of stock responses is strengthened by a now general suspicion of the causes in which his soldiers fought and his administrators laboured, also by a generally diffused pacifism – a reaction from the horrors of two world wars and the prospect of a third. Thus Conrad's assertion of the value of courage, endurance, devotion to duty, is more readily accepted by the modern reader since these qualities are shown by his sailors in the course of struggles with the impersonal ocean, not with foreign foes or natives who must be shot or bayoneted for the Empire's good.[6] (Though there is also the extreme case of those

[5] David Daiches, *Literary Essays*, Edinburgh 1956, p. 88.

[6] In Kipling's heroes too, of course, these qualities can often manifest themselves in less morally ambiguous activities – in the famine relief of "William the Conqueror," for example, which commands our whole-hearted admiration.

readers who are driven by their own neuroses to repudiate "the manly virtues" with a sneer, no matter in what context they occur.)

Such literary, moral, and political assumptions underlie the modern reluctance to come to terms with Kipling's art, to explore its actual complexities, and to work towards a genuinely critical assessment of his strength and weakness as a writer in this new heroic vein.

"A Conference of the Powers" (1890)[7] forms a useful starting point for such an inquiry. Kipling as narrator acts here as mediator between the world of action and Empire, represented by three subalterns on leave from India, and the "civilised" world of London, represented by the novelist Eustace Cleever. The opposition thus established is less crude than the contrasts he was sometimes tempted to draw between these worlds. The subalterns are not the low-browed extroverts he often holds up for our admiration – they have at least read Cleever's book, and enjoyed it in their unsophisticated way. While he, in spite of some "pundit caste" affectations of speech, is presented to us as no despicable aesthete, but a great novelist, whose greatness (often insisted on) lies in his deep understanding of the English countryside and people. His knowledge does not extend, however, to the English overseas:

> He could not altogether understand the boys, who hung upon his words so reverently. The line of the chinstrap, that still showed white and untanned on cheekbone and jaw, the steadfast young eyes puckered at the corners of the lids with much staring through red-hot sunshine, the slow, untroubled breathing, and the curious, crisp, curt speech seemed to puzzle him equally. He could create men and women, and send them to the uttermost ends of the earth, to help delight and comfort; he knew every mood of the fields, and could interpret them to the cities, and he knew the hearts of many in city and country, but he had hardly, in forty years, come into contact with the thing which is called a Subaltern of the Line.

This description, with its pervasive tendency to over-writing, generates a certain uneasiness in the reader – an uneasiness which is at its most acute (for me at any rate) over the phrase "steadfast young eyes": their steadfastness would hardly be apparent on a

---

[7] *Many Inventions.*

social occasion like this (any more than "slow untroubled breath-
ing" would be a matter for remark), and one realises that Kipling
is infiltrating a term of quasi-moral praise into what purports to be
simple description of "the boys" as they first appear to Cleever.
Hence the passage suggests an emotional commitment which the
author is not prepared to acknowledge openly – which indeed he
seeks to conceal by his pretence of anthropological detachment
in the phrase "*the thing which is called* a Subaltern of the Line."

He goes on to show excellent qualities in Cleever as well as in
the subalterns, but whereas they already know the novelist's
work and admire it, he must be taught to know and admire theirs.
This is achieved largely by means of the Infant's story of war in
Upper Burma, which opens Cleever's eyes to conditions of life
outside the sheltered world in which he moves:

> "The dacoits were having a first-class time, y'know – filling
> women up with kerosine and setting 'em alight, and burning
> villages, and crucifying people."
> The wonder in Eustace Cleever's eyes deepened. He could
> not quite realise that the cross still existed in any form.
> "Have you ever seen a crucifixion?" said he.
> "Of course not. 'Shouldn't have allowed it if I had; but
> I've seen the corpses. . . ."

This passage, like the story as a whole, points to a major difference between the preoccupations of Kipling's age and of our own.
Our recurrent political nightmares are of tyranny – the horrors
of Fascist or Communist police-states, or of repressive colonialist
regimes, whereas Kipling was more aware of the horrors of lawless anarchy, such as were forced again on our unwilling attention
by events in the Congo. The wanton violence which raged beyond
the frontiers of the Empire was to him an emotional and moral
justification for extending those frontiers; though in "A Conference of the Powers" he is less concerned with justifying the
annexation of Burma than with displaying the qualities of the men
engaged, as he sees it, in bringing law and order to the wretched
villagers of the Shan States.

His account of the process involves no sentimental idealising
of the British, no simple antithesis between black (or brown) and
white. We hear of the C.O. – " '*Pukka* Bounderby; more Bounder

than *pukka*' " – and his fussy incompetence; the Infant's fellow
subaltern – overbearing and too prone to fever; the private
soldiers, who enjoyed the fun of dacoit-hunting, but expected to
live on fresh meat and full rations as though they were in barracks.
As a contrast we have the Burmese mounted police with whom
he then worked: " 'nippy little devils, keen as mustard'," though
they told their wives too much and all his plans got known, till
he learned to give false marching orders over-night, and take the
men to a different village in the morning. There was also his
friend Hicksey of the Police – " 'the best man that ever stepped
on earth; a first-class man' " – praise which draws its strength
from the Infant's usual habit of understatement, and from the
contrast with all the other Englishmen mentioned, including the
Civil Officer (" '. . . he was awf'ly clever . . . but I don't think he
was quite steady enough for dacoit-hunting' "). The climax of
his story is the capture of Boh Na-ghee – an episode in which
violence and farce intermingle; and the Boh himself turns out to
be a sportsman in spite of his villainies, a good loser who begs
only to be hanged on the spot instead of sent for trial:

> " 'If I'm sent to Rangoon,' said he, 'they'll keep me in jail all
> my life, and that is a death every time the sun gets up or the
> wind blows.' But we had to send him to Rangoon, and, of
> course, he was let off down there, and given penal servitude for
> life."

Up to this point in the story Kipling's own role has been largely
that of *compère*, introducing the subalterns, but letting them reveal
themselves (almost unconsciously) in conversation and monologue, while he intervened occasionally to interpret some piece of
army slang. Now, however, he feels impelled to point the moral,
and if we sensed his thumb in the scale in his earlier description
of the boys, its pressure is unmistakable in the conclusion.
Cleever, whose admiration for them is by now unbounded, spends
the whole evening delighting in their company – they, for their
part, consider him " 'as good a man as they make' " – and when
he leaves Kipling asks him his opinion of things generally:

> He replied with [a] quotation, to the effect that though singing
> was a remarkably fine performance, I was to be quite sure that

few lips would be moved to song if they could find a sufficiency of kissing.

Whereby I understood that Eustace Cleever, decorator and colourman in words, was blaspheming his own Art, and would be sorry for this in the morning.

Earlier in the story Kipling had himself drawn an antithesis between action and expression: " 'How can he speak?' " he had said of the Infant. " 'He's done the work. The two don't go together.' " And the implication is that an author (even of stories like this) is inferior to a man of action – those who can, do; those who can't, write. Now that Cleever has come to the same conclusion, however, Kipling rebukes him for blaspheming his own art – yet even while delivering the rebuke he seems to endorse the blasphemy. Cleever's art is dignified with a capital A (which might have been ironical were it not for the earlier unequivocal praise), but subtly devalued by the description of him as "decorator and colourman in words." The artistry which this phrase suggests is something very different from the greatness as a novelist previously attributed to Cleever, so that Kipling seems to be evading the question he himself has posed, about the relative value of great art and heroic action: he evades it by cooking the experiment, and diminishing the allegedly great art (with its insights into human nature) to a mere aesthete's preoccupation with beauties of language. The phrase also discounts Cleever's deep knowledge of the English countryside, and shows Kipling avoiding serious consideration of his own implied question "What should they know of England who only England know?" – a question which as far as this story is concerned remains merely rhetorical. (And indeed, although Cleever shows a certain generosity of spirit and a readiness to have his ideas enlarged, his knowledge of England is not *shown* to extend beyond the coteries of London.) Hence we feel that Kipling does not really fulfil the expectations he arouses: it is as if he were unwilling to explore fully and freely the case he has presented – as if, too, he did not trust his artistic vision to correspond at all points to his intention, so that he intervenes himself to make sure that the tale comes out at the "right" conclusion.

This artistic dishonesty is the more regrettable since the story, apart from these unfortunate manipulations, is undoubtedly successful in its minor way. Its success lies in his presentation of the subalterns – in his virtuosic use of their speech with all its slang, colloquialisms, banalities, and *clichés*, to reveal their characters and the nature of their experiences. And in this we see one of Kipling's characteristic strengths. He had a remarkable faculty of observation, which had been sharpened, he thought, like Fra Lippo Lippi's by the hardships and sufferings of his child-hood; and an extraordinary ability to profit from other people's observation – to get as vivid a picture of a scene from someone else's account as he could have got at first-hand. Nor was it simply a matter of getting the gist of what anyone told him: he was also fascinated by the manner of the telling, and his ear for speech habits and variations was as remarkable as his gift for visual observation. He realised that the best way "to think in another man's skin"[8] was through a study of the other's use of language; and he therefore regarded men's conversation as one of the best clues to their character.

> They were direct of speech among each other [he wrote of the middle-aged politicians he met in Australia], and talked a political slang new to me. One learned, as one always does, more from what they said to each other or took for granted in their talk, than one could have got at from a hundred questions.[9]

In his fiction Kipling aimed at dialogue and monologue which would be equally revealing without ceasing to be authentic. And at best this was not just a matter of regional dialect or trade jargon (which could fairly easily be faked), but of catching the very idioms and rhythms proper to a character's modes of thought as well as speech. To take only one example; when the Boh was pleading to be hanged, " 'If I'm sent to Rangoon,' said he, 'they'll keep me in jail all my life, *and that is a death every time the sun gets up or the wind blows.*' " This phrase strikes a poetic-philosophic note quite alien to the Infant's own slangy colloquial discourse. Whether or not it is true to what a Burmese dacoit might have said, it *sounds* convincing, and establishes him as a definite per-sonality expressing itself in idioms and speech-rhythms quite

[8] *Something of Myself*, Chapter Eight.
[9] *Op. cit.*, Chapter Four.

distinct from the Infant's or the narrator's; so that we glimpse through this request itself and the manner in which it is made a world of feeling and experience as remote from the Infant's as the Infant's was from Eustace Cleever's.

The subalterns' own use of language, however, which gives the tale its documentary and imaginative validity, also betrays their limitations. In the Infant's references to kerosene and crucifixions there is no attempt at recreating the atrocities imaginatively, yet paradoxically we do apprehend them through the deliberately inadequate medium of the subaltern's discourse; and his very curtness – the discrepancy between the horrors themselves and his casual, matter-of-fact statements – helps to establish Kipling's ideal of men who express themselves characteristically in deeds rather than words. But this is a technique which brings diminishing returns. Casual references to horrors may lead *us* to take them casually; or if our moral sensibility remains unblunted, we shall find ourselves condemning the speaker for his imperception or brutality. And this is indeed a recurrent problem in Kipling's presentation of soldier-heroes: in too many of his portraits we see an abandonment of the centuries-old European attempt to combine courage and military skill with culture, intelligence, and sensitivity. Not that he can himself be blamed for the failure of what one might call the Spenserian synthesis, for this was an historical as well as a literary phenomenon. The specialisation of functions in nineteenth-century English society had already led to the growth of a professional officer caste which had little contact with or interest in the world of letters; so that in portraying men like the Infant and bestowing on them the crude *patois* of a minor public school, Kipling was not inventing a type, but recording facts as he had observed them. In presenting such men for our admiration, however, he seems at best unaware of their limitations, while at worst he glories in them. Thus his praise of courage is too often associated with a denigration of intelligence: there was for him a significant correlation between the Civil Officer's cleverness and his cowardice, between his moral sensitivity and his weakness of character; just as in a later story, "The Honours of War," one of the main counts against an unpleasant and unpopular subaltern was the fact that he talked too much and had a university degree. This aggressive anti-intellectualism was no doubt Kipling's response to contemporary provocations: conscious of the lack of sympathy with which most intellectuals viewed the men and values he admired, he carried the war into the enemies' camp – the more eagerly since he was deeply committed emotionally to the defence of his officer and administrator heroes. Quite apart from their unquestionable virtues, these were the men by whom he had first been accepted into manhood; more important, these had been the boys among whom he first found friendship – and comradeship against adult oppression after the isolated suffering of his childhood. Hence he could never view them with the detachment which Waugh brings to his admired Halberdiers, and which Kipling himself brought to other races, other classes, Other Ranks. Sentimentality such as he lavished on Bobby Wicks is rare – it is usually precluded by a sharper awareness of social realities; but he does tend to accord such men his undiscriminating admiration, while sometimes his prejudices lead him to play up their least attractive features as if these were merits. Hence Dunsterville, for example, emerges from his own *Reminiscences* as a much more intelligent and humane personality than Stalky does in Kipling's fiction.[10]

Indeed the last chapter of *Stalky & Co.* (1899) exemplifies the dangers for Kipling of over-emphasis shading into propagandist over-statement. Here the same Infant, some years older, has resigned from the service, having inherited a baronetcy and an estate; and he is entertaining a group of his old school-mates, most of them on leave from India. From their talk we learn of another notable frontier action – North-West Frontier this time; and there is what seems at first sight the same kind of army jargon, slang, colloquialisms, the same kind of authentic detail in the narrative: yet here the whole effect is curiously off-key.

For one thing, the action described seems unnaturally neat. In the Infant's expedition courage and planning had combined convincingly with elements of cowardice, muddle, and good luck. Here everything is much simpler: the Politicals have landed the

---

[10] It is, for example, impossible to imagine Kipling's Stalky making friends with an Hungarian musician, however aristocratic, and persuading him to spend a winter as his guest in the Mess at Lahore. Yet Dunsterville played host in just this way to the consumptive Sigismund de Justh. (L. C. Dunsterville, *Stalky's Reminiscences*, London 1929, pp. 110-12.)

troops in a mess – Stalky proceeds to extricate them by means of his superb fieldcraft and tactical sense, his heroism, and his un-rivalled knowledge of the native mind. There is nothing im-possible in what he does, but our sense of its improbability is in-creased by the fact that this adventure does not stand alone – it is the culmination of a series every item of which has shown com-parable triumphs stemming from comparable qualities in the hero. This recurrent pattern has been explained by Edmund Wilson as "an hysterical outpouring of emotions kept over from school-days," revenge-fantasies replacing the realities of schoolboy experi-ence, but it is also a result of Kipling's heavily didactic intentions. *Stalky & Co.* developed from his "idea of beginning some tracts or parables on the education of the young," and in 1935 he still felt that in its finished state it was "a truly valuable collection of tracts"[11] – presumably because it demonstrated the continuity of school and adult experience, and showed so clearly the qualities he thought most worth developing in boys and men. Yet the very tract-like nature of these tales – the remorselessly recurring pattern of "stalkiness" bringing its own reward – strains our credulity, especially when in this last episode the praise of the hero becomes too unanimous and hyperbolic: " 'Stalky is the great man of his Century' " – " 'Stalky *is* a Sikh' " – " 'Don't you remember how Rutton Singh grabbed his boots and grovelled in the snow, and how our men shouted?' " Even the saturnine M'Turk is described as "swelling with pride" at having seen Stalky more recently than the others – almost as if he were a disciple favoured with the last glimpse of his departing deity. This particular inflation is symptomatic: whereas the Infant in the earlier story had been a first-rate subaltern, Stalky is now spoken of as a kind of superman, almost a demi-god. And even when Kipling-Beetle denies his uniqueness – " 'India's full of Stalkies – Cheltenham and Haileybury and Marlborough chaps – that we don't know anything about' " – the effect is not to de-tract from this mythical quality but to enhance it, by suggesting that Stalky is less an individual portrait than a symbolic figure – the very embodiment of the British officer-ideal as Kipling con-ceived it.

This tendency to convert actuality to myth accounts for much

[11] *Something of Myself*, Chapter Five.

that I find distasteful in the book – its local faults in tone as well as the structuring of the narrative as a whole. There is a curiously hectic note in passages like

> Luckily the baize doors of the bachelors' wing fitted tight, for we dressed promiscuously in the corridor or in each other's rooms, talking, calling, shouting, and anon waltzing by pairs to songs of Dick Four's own devising.

However "authentic" this may have been as a description of the behaviour of ex-public-schoolboys, the last detail, coloured as it is by the oddly challenging "promiscuously," has for us overtones of abnormality which were certainly no part of Kipling's intention, but which result from his over-insistence on the cult of self-sufficient masculinity. (One might compare the incident of M'Turk's reaching forward absently to twitch the narrator's dress-tie into position – a completely innocent action, but one so described as to suggest that friendship is being offered here as a substitute for *wifely* intimacy.) Our embarrassment is not, however, simply embarrassment at the behaviour portrayed, for Kipling's style on such occasions generates an acute discomfort of its own: when, for example, he tells how Dick Four at the climax of his story had to wait until "the roaring, the shouting, the laughter, and, I think, the tears, had subsided." Here it is clearer that Kipling is not writing realistically so much as working his material up to give us the *quintessence* of reunions and the emotions they evoke. The trouble is that he works it up to a point where it seems not only offensive in itself but at variance with the realistic mode in which most of the narrative is cast: we doubt very much whether men of this type would in fact have wept on such an occasion – Kipling's own doubt is suggested by the coyness of "I think, the tears" – and this discrepancy between reality and myth is a root cause of our discomfort.[12]

The same process of working up affects the language of the

---

[12] This is, indeed, a recurrent fault in Kipling: one might compare the psychological implausibility in "A Matter of Fact" when a mythically conceived England is shown impinging on a realistically presented American journalist: "I heard Keller gasp as the influence of the land closed about him, cowing him as they say Newmarket Heath cows a young horse unused to open courses." (*Many Inventions*.)

characters themselves. Indeed a sophisticated Philistinism, a deliberate brutality of speech, is one of the most unpleasant features of *Stalky & Co.*[13] The Infant's references to death and violence in the earlier story had been genuinely laconic in a boyish way – matter-of-fact, without any trace of self-conscious Hemingwayan toughness. But such toughness, with its disturbing suggestions of connoisseurship in violence, is exactly what repels us in remarks like Dick Four's

> "One of our men, a young fellow from Dera Ismail . . . jumped down, blubbing like a child. He'd been hit smack in the middle of the hand. Never saw a man yet who could stand a hit in the hand without weepin' bitterly. It tickles up all the nerves."

The Infant's understatements, again, had been part of the genuine speech habits of a semi-articulate subaltern: in *Stalky & Co.* understatement becomes part of the mystique of British heroism, and is therefore overemphasised, sometimes to the point of caricature. ("'Adequate chap. Infernally adequate,' said Tertius, pulling his moustache and staring into the fire"; and his utterance is obviously meant to have the force of many superlatives.)

In passing from "A Conference of the Powers" to *Stalky*, then, we see how genuine experiences and observations can be crudened and distorted by their conversion (or partial conversion) into myth or fable – a process all too frequent in Kipling's art. He tends often to discredit his original perceptions, which may have had a real validity of their own, by an over-emphasis manifesting itself in both the style and structuring of his stories, and provoking us to incredulity, irritation, or disgust. (The closest parallel that comes to mind is the Lawrence of "St Mawr" or "The Virgin and the Gipsy.") And a related weakness in his narrative technique is his tendency to intervene as ineptly and disastrously as Thackeray at his worst, with comments – sententious, brutal, sentimen-

[13] In *Something of Myself* Kipling defends the book against the charge of brutality by asserting its truth to the facts of school life. (Cp. Noel Annan, p. 123, above.) But this is to blur the distinction between sociological observation and gleeful acceptance of such facts; nor does Kipling seem to see the moral and political implications of making such a school the paradigm of Empire.

tal, or facetious – that antagonise the reader by their vulgarity of tone as much as by their content.

The myth-making tendency of his mind, however, operates to very different effect in *The Jungle Books* (1894, 1895), and *Puck of Pook's Hill* (1906). These have an imaginative potency and a profundity of unstated meaning which set them apart from his mere elaborated anecdotes (and "A Conference of the Powers" is not much more than this); yet they differ from his more obvious parables or allegorical stories (like "A Walking Delegate" or "The Ship that Found Herself") in that their significance is not exhausted by a simple transposition of the narrative into conceptual terms. Their success is due largely to a happier blending of the myth-making with the realistic impulses in Kipling's imagination – also to his abstracting his plots from the contemporary circumstances and contemporary pressures which were often responsible for the distortions and excesses I have noted.

Parnesius' tale (like *Puck of Pook's Hill* as a whole) emerges from Kipling's sense of his country's history and traditions. It refers also to circumstances of his own day: the parallel between the Great Wall and the North-West Frontier has often been remarked on – so has the resemblance between the Winged Hats and the Prussian menace. But the story is more than the imaginative recreation of an historical event, and more than an allegory of contemporary problems: it is Kipling's supreme presentation of one of the major themes that fired his imagination – the defence of civilisation against savagery by men whose chosen duty it is to spend themselves in such a cause. The notion had cropped up in "A Conference of the Powers" when we were told that it was the Army "whose toils enabled [Eustace Cleever] to enjoy his many-sided life in peace"; but the absence of a European threat and the remoteness of the imperial frontiers in that story kept us from taking the claim very seriously. What did make an impact was the picture of the Infant, servant of an expanding empire, dealing with violence outside the pale (or just within it), and bringing the *pax britannica* to areas where it had never before reigned. The underlying assumptions are optimistic: progress is demonstrably taking place, and the values of law and order are confidently asserted, even though Kipling is more interested in the process of pacification and the heroic action this involves, than in the ends to which that action is directed. This bias is intensified in *Stalky & Co.*, where the ultimate aims of heroic activity have receded still further into the background. We are never told why deeper penetration into Afghanistan should be thought desirable, or why we should despise the Viceroy for discountenancing it. The answers could be found in contemporary political disputes, but they are not embodied in Kipling's fiction; and it begins to looks as if he approves of empire-building not for the sake of empire so much as for the qualities which it develops in the empire-builders: frontier soldiering seems so admirable as a way of life that it becomes virtually an end in itself. Soon after the publication of *Stalky & Co.*, however, the Boer War jolted Kipling into a sharper awareness of military and imperial realities. Along with the revelation of incompetence at so many levels throughout the Army, came a sudden realisation of the hostility of the major European powers, and from now on Kipling's thoughts turned more and more to problems of defence. In bitter polemical verses like "The Islanders" and "The Dykes," in impassioned pamphleteering like "The Parable of Boy Jones" or "The Army of a Dream," he warned Britain of the need to prepare for Armageddon, to make ready to defend herself against dangers of invasion and defeat which she had not had to face since the overthrow of Napoleon. This gave a more pessimistic turn to his own imaginings. He could still write a confident tale of the expanding Empire in "A Deal in Cotton" (1907), where the suppression of the slave-trade, the establishment of peace, and the development of the country's natural resources all serve to justify the efforts, the heroic endurance, of the soldier-administrators.[14]

---

[14] We do not doubt that the Sheshaheli will be better off growing cotton under Strickland junior than cannibalising and being hacked to pieces by Ibn Makarrah's young men. Kipling's Law and Order are unquestionable values when asserted in such contexts, and the Progress the tale celebrates is real. Yet it is oddly qualified by the kinship young Strickland feels with the Arab slaver (which closely resembles the earlier kinship between the Infant and Boh Na-ghee). The friendship of two such strong men, such "Great Ones," obscures the moral antitheses which the tale assumes; it also emerges as more important than anything pertaining to the lesser beings for whom the *pax britannica* is nominally being secured. Kipling was not the first writer to find epic values more inspiring than those of pastoral, but he found it peculiarly difficult to evolve a synthesis appropriate to his imperial theme.

But in Parnesius' story the tide is flowing the other way: the Roman Empire (prototype and symbolic equivalent of the British) is declining, contracting – the old province of Valentia is lost irrecoverably, and the tribes beyond the pale now constitute a threat to peace and order within the Empire itself. Only the Wall and its custodians stand between civilisation and the anarchy that would destroy it. This makes for a grimmer heroism than Stalky's or the Infant's: the weight of responsibility, the greatness of the issues, and the fierceness of the fighting soon banish the notion (tenable in mere frontier scuffles) of war as a game. And the tale is more deeply satisfying than those of the Indian frontier – partly because heroism always seems greater when the odds are unfavourable – partly because the situations symbolically presented are closer to our own experience in the twentieth century – but also because the distancing of these events in time has had a purifying effect on Kipling's vision. This hero has a finer fuller humanity than his nineteenth-century equivalents, and the values which he represents are asserted with new tact, new subtlety, and an imaginative power that has no trace of propagandist zeal.

Parnesius at the beginning of his story is an Infant of those days, and when he sets out on his long march north he comes up against difficulties very like those the Infant had met with in Burma:

"Their very first day out, my men complained of our water-ground British corn. They said it wasn't so filling as the rough stuff that is ground in the Roman ox-mills. However, they had to fetch and eat it. . . . [But they] looked at the flour in their helmets as though it had been a nest of adders."[15]

Although Kipling is intensely aware here of the parallels between past and present – of the similarity of the tests young officers have had to face throughout the centuries, he does not try to bring this out by making Parnesius speak like the Infant. (That would have had a disastrously anachronistic effect.) Instead he

---

[15] Cp. " 'I was grubbing on fowls and boiled corn, but my Tommies wanted their pound of fresh meat, and their half-ounce of this, and their two ounces of t'other thing, and they used to come to me and badger me for plug-tobacco when we were four days in jungle. . . . They wanted all the luxuries of the season, confound 'em.' " ("A Conference of the Powers.")

gives us, simultaneously, a sense of the difference of the past, partly by means of vividly imagined detail – that touch, for example, about the men bringing flour from the mill in their helmets – and partly by the manner of Parnesius' speech. In phrases like "the rough stuff that is ground" or "as though it had been a nest of adders," the slight but unmistakable formality of syntax and rhythm superimposed on his easy colloquial speech sets him off from the contemporary; and the cumulative effect of such details is to suggest convincingly the Roman dignity and higher intelligence which differentiate him from Kipling's nineteenth-century subalterns.

Miss Tompkins, however, draws our attention to still further stylistic variations in Parnesius' tale:

> When he describes his home in Vectis he uses language entirely familiar to the children who question him, but, as he moves into the longer laps of unbroken narrative, the rhythm strengthens, and the language, without ceasing to be entirely speakable – we never question the authenticity of the narrating voice – acquires a precision and an order which is strictly outside colloquial usage. "Red-hot in summer, freezing in winter, is that big, purple heather country of broken stone." At the height of the story, when the Winged Hats bring the Emperor's letter to the Captains of the Wall, they show Parnesius "a dark stain on the outer roll that my heavy heart perceived was the valiant blood of Maximus," and the deliberate, dragging cadence, the stately artifice of the words, commend themselves to the hearer as what the event requires.[16]

Clearly, this goes beyond establishing the narrator's personality, period, and race: it amounts to a richer orchestration of the whole story. And that richer orchestration is called for by the story's richer meaning, which requires in the narrator a more flexible and eloquent mode of speech than Kipling's British officers could ever attain to. They had all, like Major Cottar of "The Brushwood Boy," been taught "not . . . to dwell on [their] emotions, but rather to keep in hard condition" – to keep their pores open and their mouths shut – with the result that they are incapable of expressing intense emotions such as love or grief, which render

[16] J. M. S. Tompkins, *The Art of Rudyard Kipling*, pp. 72-3.

them tongue-tied or maudlin. The sentimentalities of "The Brushwood Boy" are an embarrassing attempt to give a new dimension
of uninhibited private emotion to what is essentially a public type;
at the opposite extreme, but equally embarrassing, are the clipped,
restrained love-passages of "William the Conqueror." In "The
Head of the District," on the other hand, the dying Yardley-
Orde speaks movingly and without inhibitions of his wife and
district, yet this is an exceptional case, where approaching death
has loosened the taboos of his class and service.[17] Generally, therefore, such men make good heroes (in a limited sense) but very
inadequate narrators.

This is one aspect of a wider problem involved in treating the
life of action: men who excel in it are often unaware of the values
which the author perceives in them – their own consciousness is
not adequate for rendering his sense of what they are. To bestow
his own consciousness on one of them, as Conrad did on Marlow,
is to evade rather than solve the problem: more to the point is
the virtuosic narrative technique by which he brings us to a full
appreciation of the qualities of the inarticulate MacWhirr.
Kipling, writing as omniscient narrator, can make us similarly
aware of heroism in his Scotts, Ordes, Tallantires; but he was
drawn characteristically to the use of fictional narrators, who speak
either directly to Kipling himself or to other auditors within the
tale. This may be regarded as a journalistic technique (of securing
copy through interviews or conversation) which has been con-
verted to the purposes of art. It was certainly a device which by
its demands for dramatic propriety in speech often helped him to
a surer stylistic control than he could guarantee when writing in
his own person.[18] And in *Puck of Pook's Hill* this device is central.
Kipling himself does not share the children's experiences –
significantly, their father is kept firmly in the background – so
that they and we are spared his knowing interpretative comments.

[17] Taboos which Kipling often shares: see, for example, his repeated
attempts in his autobiography and elsewhere to depersonalise an intensely
personal relationship by substituting the definite article for the possessive
pronoun in phrases like "the Mother" and "the Father."

[18] Although at times – in certain of the Mulvaney stories, for example, not
to mention some notorious Barrack-Room Ballads – an ostensibly anthropological approach enabled him to indulge vicariously his taste for sentimentality
and violence.

When some comments *are* required to modify the *naïveté* of Dan and Una's reactions, these are provided pungently and economically by Puck, while Kipling preserves his role of impersonal narrator, leaving the main burden of the story to his fictional creations. A Roman centurion was the obvious choice for the narrator-hero of this episode, dealing as it does with service on another, more ancient imperial frontier; but in order to bring out the full significance of his story Kipling had to bestow on him a more adequate consciousness – one capable of apprehending and communicating deeper truths and a wider range of emotions than the Infant or Stalky could ever discern or experience. Yet he did not make the mistake of letting Parnesius perceive too much – of making him a mere mouthpiece for the author. This hero can render his own experiences superbly, but he has the limitations of vision inherent in any genuinely fictional narrator; and Puck's comments, the framing narrative, and the intervening poems all help to create new perspectives of which he is unaware, but which form an important part of Kipling's meaning.

The story opens with Una making ready to meet Lars Porsena's invading army, and chanting verses from "Horatius" – whose defence of the bridge foreshadows (though in childishly "heroic" terms) the theme of Parnesius' tale. The high-pitched rhetoric of her defiance is soon deflated, however; and the explanations when Parnesius reveals himself are in familiar friendly vein, so that we pass quickly from the melodramatic to the domestic. (Any relapse into heroics is precluded by Parnesius' own modesty and sureness of tone, reinforced by Puck's friendly mockery – "Let the hero tell his own tale" – and the ready irony Puck brings to any touch of excess in the narration.) In response to Una's questions Parnesius now describes his childhood in Vectis, and this evocation, uninhibited by any cult of the inarticulate, does more than sketch in his own background. The picture of happy family life, the warm affection, the glimpses of society beyond the island – the expedition to Aquae Sulis, the sister married to a magistrate in the west – and the brother now settled on the estate – all these domestic details, with their suggestions of simple, peaceful, happy lives give warm reality to the elusive concept of civilisation, and make the defence of the Wall meaningful in human terms.

This is all the more important in view of the political uncer-

tainties of Parnesius' world. Born and bred in Britain, he resents
the arrogance of the Roman-born, and though his father reminds
him that their duty is to the Empire, this can no longer command
unquestioning allegiance: it is already showing signs of disintegration, several Provinces have tried to set up Emperors of their
own, while the present ruler, Gratian, is said to have "turned
himself into a raw-beef-eating Scythian." This awareness of
decadence at the heart of the Empire is expressed still more strongly
by Parnesius' father; and although his son listens with a young
man's impatience – touches like this give the tale its full fictional
vitality – he accepts the conclusion that Britain may yet be saved,
in spite of Rome's corruption – that Rome's northern frontier
must be guarded, therefore, as a national frontier, whatever the
condition of Rome herself.

The issue is still further complicated, however, by the intervention of Maximus, a figure at once beneficent and sinister,
through whom Kipling suggests the ambiguous nature of power
and the inhumanity that lies at the heart of imperial greatness.
Parnesius has just quelled an incipient mutiny in the draft he is
conducting to the Wall:

> "Then, quietly as a cloud, Maximus rode out of the fern (my
> Father behind him), and reined up across the road. He wore
> the Purple, as though he were already Emperor; his leggings
> were of white buckskin laced with gold.
>
> "My men dropped like – like partridges.
>
> "He said nothing for some time, only looked, with his eyes
> puckered. Then he crooked his forefinger, and my men
> walked – crawled, I mean – to one side.
>
> " 'Stand in the sun, children,' he said, and they formed up
> on the hard road.
>
> " 'What would you have done," he said to me, 'if I had not
> been here?'
>
> " 'I should have killed that man,' I answered.
>
> " 'Kill him now,' he said. 'He will not move a limb.'
>
> " 'No,' I said, 'You've taken my men out of my command.
> I should only be your butcher if I killed him now. . . .' "

The episode is of profound importance. "Don't think yourself
Emperor of Britain already," the mutineer had shouted at

Parnesius, and the insult showed how disorder in the draft mirrored disorder in the Empire as a whole. In his new garb Maximus might seem to embody this spirit of rebellion, yet his personal authority is so great that we feel he has simply assumed the role for which he is best fitted. It is not the imperial purple that quells the soldiers, but the sense of Maximus' own latent power, communicated by the dramatic quietness of his approach, and the way his threats manifest themselves only in an economy of gesture and deceptive mildness of speech. We realise that this is a man born to rule, and that although he is himself a rebel he is likely to suppress disorders in the Empire as readily and as ruthlessly as in this draft of legionaries. For ruthlessness is what he will employ if necessary – hence his command to kill the offending soldier. And Parnesius' refusal to obey such an order, even when it comes from his commander-in-chief, marks the essential differences between them. Parnesius exemplifies the soldier's code, but it is far removed from that of Nazi Germany or the centurions of Lartéguy: for him a sense of basic human decency over-rules strict military (or political) obligations, and he emerges from the test with increased stature in our eyes. But success to us is failure in the eyes of Maximus:

". . . Maximus frowned. 'You'll never be an Emperor,' he said. 'Not even a General will you be.'

" I was silent, but my Father seemed pleased.

" 'I came here to see the last of you,' he said.

" 'You have seen it,' said Maximus. 'I shall never need your son any more. He will live and he will die an officer of a Legion – and he might have been Prefect of one of my Provinces. . . .' "

For Kipling supreme power involved inhumanity – or at least a complete detachment from humanity in the making of decisions. But his whole-hearted admiration was reserved for the subordinate commanders (like Sir Richard or Parnesius), deeply involved with their fellow men, and defining their sense of duty in terms of a fully personal integrity. Yet Maximus has great potentialities for good: paradoxically, his cold-blooded self-seeking ambition might well be the motive force which would restore the Empire's greatness. "It is always one man's work," he mutters later in the story, establishing a parallel as well as a contrast between his battles in Gaul and Parnesius' duties on the frontier. But finally the insatiable egotistic nature of his ambition brings him to the ruin Parnesius' father had foretold; and although the deep loyalty he inspires in the young men is never devalued, we see more clearly than they do the inhumanity involved in his kind of greatness. "Only a life?" he exclaimed, when Pertinax asked for justice against his uncle: "I thought it would be money or an office. Certainly you shall have him." Clearly, there is a kind of poetic justice, tacitly endorsed by the author, in his now dying (however bravely) the death he had meted out so ruthlessly to others.

Ironically, the Captains who had held the Wall while Maximus gambled and lost have now to defend it knowing that even if they succeed they may meet the same fate at the hands of the victorious Emperor. But the uncertainty that this breeds for the future – the uncertainty indeed that it breeds about political values in the present – serves only to emphasise, to isolate in even greater clarity, the soldier's code, the soldier's virtues of courage, endurance, loyalty, friendship, honour, sense of duty.

> " 'It concerns us to defend the Wall, no matter what Emperor dies, or makes die,' I said.
> " 'That is worthy of your brother the philosopher,' said Pertinax. 'Myself I am without hope, so I do not say solemn and stupid things!' "

Pertinax's jesting tone contrasts, as it often does, with Parnesius' solemnity, but his testing irony finds no weakness here – indeed, it is itself discredited as it plays against Parnesius' statement without undermining it; and the two men now unite in a stoical acceptance of their professional military ethic.

The success with which this is presented derives from Kipling's full imaginative awareness of the actual complexities of soldiering in any age, as opposed to the heroic simplicities he often inclined to. Thus he is simultaneously conscious of the Wall's symbolic value and of the squalid realities of garrison life: Parnesius passes directly from his magnificent description of the Wall itself to an account of the vicious and corrupting town that lies behind it. There is also the shock of realising that this great defensive line is manned by troops and officers of doubtful quality – of finding, too, even here on the frontier, a cynical disregard of duty which recalls the decadence of Rome herself. "Oh, you'll soon outgrow that sort of nonsense," Parnesius is told when he refuses to accept a drink before handing over his men; and he sees all round him signs of professional disintegration. Kipling's rejection here of the facile City/Frontier opposition is symptomatic of the story's strength: so is the vividness with which the hero's bitter loneliness and disillusion are conveyed to us, though they are beyond the children's comprehension. The whole narrative, indeed, carries conviction by its refusal to oversimplify, morally, politically, or psychologically. Rutilianus, the old general commanding the garrison, is an easy-going glutton, but Kipling shows genuine insight (and avoids the temptation to caricature) by making him fight bravely when the fighting comes. The futility of his heather-burning policy is clear to Parnesius: this in itself is nothing unusual, since Kipling's officers can nearly always see the faults of their superiors; yet here the perception has its roots in an understanding of the Picts which enables Parnesius to see the Empire itself from the point of view of those outside it – to look at the Wall, as it were, from the other side. Thus Maximus asks him, when they meet again, whether he could hold and govern the old province of Valentia:

> " 'No,' I said. 'You cannot remake that Province. The Picts have been free too long.'
>
> " 'Leave them their village councils, and let them furnish their own soldiers,' he said. 'You, I am sure, would hold the reins very lightly.'
>
> " 'Even then, no,' I said. 'At least not now. They have been too oppressed by us to trust anything with a Roman name for years and years.' "

Parnesius is no anti-imperialist – he remains throughout a Roman centurion: "You little painted beast!" were the first words we heard him utter – "I'll teach you to sling your masters." But his kindly, if paternalistic, concern for the Picts' welfare, and still more, this ability to see things from their point of view, humanise his imperialism and keep it from ever becoming oppressive or expansionist. He will fight the Picts and the Winged Hats only if they attack the Wall which it is his duty to defend, and his relationship with Amal shows his respect for Rome's enemies as human beings in their own right. The last episode, moreover, which deals with the actual fighting, is far removed from the light-hearted boy-scoutery of Stalky and the Infant. This tale is told in a different part of Far Wood

> sadder and darker than the Volaterrae end because of an old marlpit full of black water, where weepy, hairy moss hangs round the stumps of the willows and alders. But the birds come to perch on the dead branches, and Hobden says that the bitter willow-water is a sort of medicine for sick animals.

To impose a strictly allegorical interpretation here would be to falsify, but the sadness and darkness of this setting clearly foreshadow the nature of the tale itself. And while the last sentence suggests that Kipling finds redeeming qualities in the bitterness of war, the paradox is fully acknowledged on this symbolic level – just as in the literal narrative there is no attempt to minimise the bitterness of the experiences which made Parnesius seem old before his time.[19] The emphasis throughout is neither on adventures nor on violence, but on the psychological effects of war and command – the burden of responsibility, the strain, the sense of unreality, the sheer exhaustion – all the pressures which by testing bring out the full value of men's courage and preserved integrity.

Paradoxically, these redeeming qualities which shine out from the darkness of Parnesius' tale are set in a context which seems at first sight to reduce them to insignificance. "Trouble not . . . Rome's arm is long," says the ambassador from Theodosius, whose fresh legions re-establish the crumbling frontier, while behind it the Empire is unified under this new Emperor as it might have been under Maximus. Yet *we* know that this success could only be temporary – that Rome was in fact doomed and the Wall's days numbered. Nor is this just a matter of historical hindsight, for the point is made fictionally by the structuring of the book, as well as by details in the tales themselves. Before we ever meet Parnesius we have the whole life-cycle of Sir Richard

---

[19] It is a measure of the tale's success – of the "economy of implication" which Kipling aimed at – that the intensity of the fictional experience lived through makes it easy for us to accept this change in the hero's appearance.

(who is himself remote from us in time) as he passes from youth, love, and adventure to old age and loneliness. To be then transported still further back through the centuries to Parnesius' world gives us a poignant sense of transience. For his world, we know, is soon to pass away: he himself can still speak of Rome as "Eternal," yet the very language of his Empire is now "dead" – it has become the "beastly Latin" of a schoolboy's imposition, references to which frame the first instalment of his tale. This is itself preceded by a poem which makes the point explicitly, in a quasi-Elizabethan lyric mode:

> Cities and Thrones and Powers,
>   Stand in Time's eye,
> Almost as long as flowers,
>   Which daily die. . . .

And the same theme is later transposed into the sombre cadences of a medieval hymn, as Puck chants the "Cur mundus militat sub vana gloria" of Jacopone da Todi. This, coming where it does in the story, seems to pass judgment not only on the ambitions of Maximus ("Quo Caesar abiit celsus imperio?"), but on most human activities, including Parnesius' self-dedication to service on the Wall. Indeed the phonetic similarity of "militat" and "military" draws soldiering unmistakably into the category of "vana gloria." And the futility of heroic endeavour is suggested again by the "Pict Song" at the close of his tale, in which the mutability theme is restated in political terms, foretelling the fall of Rome and of the Wall Parnesius had successfully defended.

This recognition of time's destructive power gives an added resonance to the tale. It also plays against the optimistic theory of history implied by Puck's "Weland gave the Sword! The Sword gave the Treasure, and the Treasure gave the Law." Modern England is certainly seen as heir to the whole of her own past, but the deliberate dislocation of chronology in the arrangement of the stories seems to deny any simple pattern of progress, as does this sense of the impermanence of human achievement. Yet each age does leave something to posterity, even if the contributors are long forgotten. Parnesius, it might be said, leaves nothing but an example, yet his defence of the Wall is as satisfying and praiseworthy an achievement in its way as Hal o' the Draft's rebuilding of St Barnabas'. The heroic qualities which were acknowledged in his own day by a well-earned Triumph are celebrated again in Kipling's story, and epitomised (with much less subtlety) in the hymn to Mithras which precedes the Winged Hats episode. This poem confines itself to the limited time-span of a single day: Morning, Noontide, Sunset, and Midnight symbolise the crises of a soldier's life, and (less immediately) phases of human life itself, which can be imaged in its brevity in terms of a day. Yet the hymn – and the story – assert not the futility and evanescence, but the *value* of an individual life well-lived, well-spent in service. For Kipling's awareness of the mutability inherent in a wider time-scale does not lead him to a nihilistic denial of significance to human endeavour. In "The White Man's Burden" he foresees that the only reward for imperial effort will be

> The blame of those ye better,
> The hate of those ye guard,

that in the long run "Sloth and heathen Folly" will "bring all your hope to nought." Yet this does not detract in the slightest from the immediate duty (as he sees it) of self-sacrifice and labour: the work must be undertaken for the good that can be done now, even if it ultimately comes to ruin. Similarly, Findlayson's achievement in "The Bridge-builders" is dwarfed by the temporal perspectives in which it is placed: when many centuries have passed it *will* seem like the shifting of a little dirt; yet when the vision ends the bridge still stands against the flood, and we rejoice in the great qualities that went to its creation. Kipling's sombre secular vision of change and decay saves him on such occasions from his own tendency to brash progressive optimism, but it never leads him to despair. The dark background serves rather as a foil to his conception of human greatness, as he shows men like Parnesius doing their duty regardless of encroaching muta- bility and death. Their achievements are none the less because they must ultimately perish: this is simply the condition of life on earth, and Kipling recognises the existence of no other. Yet that condition can be transcended – not through religion but through art, for the celebration of such men and their works by the artist-creator is itself a triumph – the only possible triumph – over Time the destroyer.

Mark Kinkead-Weekes

VISION IN KIPLING'S NOVELS

"AS A novelist Kipling . . ." – no, one cannot usefully begin that way. Kipling resists generalisation: he always had "two separate sides" to his head and sometimes more, and his work is radically inconsistent and unequal. Though the verbal artistry can be said to mature, the man and his vision cannot. To the very end, in every collection and at every stage, the good Kipling lies beside the bad, and the novels are a typical cross-section. *The Light that Failed* shows him at his most brutal and adolescent, with dark streaks of violence and sadism, and a bitter contempt for women and their love. Yet the Kipling who finished it in August 1890 revealed very different attitudes in "On Greenhow Hill" in September and "The Courting of Dinah Shadd" in March. And if *Captains Courageous* is the product of a clear and controlled, if limited, vision, and *Kim* in its wisdom and humanity the living contradiction of nine-tenths of the charges ever levelled against its author, we still cannot speak usefully of development or maturity, for much of the worst is still to come. What we need is some idea of the factors that make one kind of imaginative vision so remarkably different from another.

What strikes us about *The Light that Failed*, indeed, is not so much the blindness of its hero as the blindness of its author. The brutality is the product of an atrophy of imagination, but this in turn seems to be the result of private pressures revealed with extraordinary nakedness. In the scene where Dick Heldar terrorises the cardiac publisher who has tried to exploit him there is no mistaking the caressing tone. He talks at the man, treats him as an object; he is felt, handled, walked around, pawed like a hearthrug, finally spoken of as a "thing"; but the thing is "soft all over –

like a woman," and there is a vibrantly physical element in the fondling, the hand run down the plump body, the pawing, the tracing forefinger, which makes the insult operate in more than one way. Above all there is suspense. The threat of violence hangs in the purring voice and the insultingly caressing hand, and that is precisely the satisfaction. At the end of the chapter Dick wishes he had hit the man, but neither he nor his author would have enjoyed it as much. Now Kipling knows about his hero's self-centredness in this passage, and how his aggressiveness is the product of his childhood, but that is all and it is not enough. He has ceased to imagine the publisher as a human being, and he seems to have no idea what kind of satisfaction he is offering himself or his readers. He has ceased to *see*. And the reason is glaringly obvious in his private experience. What the scene in fact is for, is to express what the diminutive Kipling would have liked to do to the publishers who had pirated his stories.[1] It has the lip-smacking, the abrogation of responsibility, of the day-dream revenge fantasy.

We need however to make certain distinctions about "brutality." The charge is often brought against Kipling far too simply: one must distinguish between a "brutal" subject or situation treated objectively, and a brutal attitude or satisfaction felt towards it. It is sentimental to confuse the two or object to the first; but the charge against the second is one of imaginative and artistic, as well as moral, failure. Three related passages may illustrate the point. The first is probably the finest in the book, the description of the attack of three thousand Sudanese, "naked humanity, mad with rage," on the square of British soldiers.

[1] The fierceness of his feelings can be gauged from "The Rhyme of the Three Captains," published in December 1890 after the climax of the *Harper's Weekly* piracy. The robbed trader speaks:

"Had I guns (as I had goods) to work my Christian harm,
I had run him up from his quarter-deck to trade with his own yard-arm;
I had nailed his ears to my capstan-head, and ripped them off with a saw,
And soused them in the bilgewater, and served them to him raw . . .
I had stripped his hide for my hammock-side, and tasselled his beard in the mesh,
And spitted his crew on the live bamboo that grows through the gangrened flesh. . . ."

Carrington, in his biography, suggests an origin for the publisher scene in Kipling's rescue of Phil Burne-Jones from a disreputable syndicate.

The camel-guns shelled them as they passed, and opened for an instant lanes through their midst, most like those quick-closing vistas in a Kentish hop-garden seen when the train races by at full speed; and the infantry fire, held till the opportune moment, dropped them in close-packed hundreds. No civilised troops in the world could have endured the hell through which they came, the living leaping high to avoid the dying who clutched at their heels, the wounded cursing and staggering forward, till they fell – a torrent black as the sliding water above a mill-dam – full on the right flank of the square. Then the line of the dusty troops and the faint blue desert sky overhead went out in rolling smoke, and the little stones on the heated ground and the tinder-dry clumps of scrub became matters of surpassing interest, for men measured their agonised retreat and recovery by these things, counting mechanically and hewing their way back to chosen pebble and branch. . . . Their business was to destroy what lay in front of them, to bayonet in the back those who passed over them, and, dying, to drag down the slayer till he could be knocked on the head by some avenging gun-butt. . . .

When thirty or forty yelling and hacking men burst through, the journalists and the doctor become involved.

Dick was conscious that somebody had cut him violently across his helmet, that he had fired his revolver into a black, foam-flecked face which forthwith ceased to bear any resemblance to a face, and that Torpenhow had gone down under an Arab whom he had tried to "collar low", and was turning over and over with his captive, feeling for the man's eyes. . . . The representative of the Central Southern Syndicate had shaken himself clear of his enemy, and rose, wiping his thumb on his trousers. The Arab, both hands to his forehead, screamed aloud, then snatched up his spear and rushed at Torpenhow, who was panting under shelter of Dick's revolver. Dick fired twice, and the man dropped limply. His upturned face lacked one eye. . . .

This is surely masterly, and there is no sense calling the passage brutal. It has the stark realism that Kipling gives Dick Heldar's

paintings of men in action, and he is clearly behind his hero's
scorn of the "art-manager of that abandoned paper" who "said
that his subscribers wouldn't like it. It was brutal and coarse and
violent, – man being naturally gentle when he's fighting for his
life." The first part, particularly, is beautifully controlled; no-
where more securely than at those moments when natural
images of perfect accuracy mark the appallingly unnatural perspective of the action. The involvement of the non-combatants,
including the doctor, simply shows what happens in the middle
of a square: Kipling only needs to point briefly to the "unen-
durable tension," the need to do something and, when the square
breaks, to the random and instinctive nature of behaviour. Even
the eye-gouging by an unarmed man is no different in itself from
the bayoneting in the back and the clubbing with gun-butts.
Man is not naturally gentle when he is fighting for his life;
Kipling aims at, and achieves, a clear sense of what happens
when maddened men meet in battle.

Yet the eye-gouging *is* different. "Captive" and "feeling"
suggest a wavering of control, they are too deliberate, leisurely,
sensual; and there is something wrong about "the representative
of the Central Southern Syndicate" and the wiping of the thumb
– wrong not with the horror of the detail itself but in one's sense
that it is being somehow dwelt upon and enjoyed. Torpenhow
sets out to maim and is apparently satisfied when he has succeeded
– the gesture is of a man dusting his hands off – and this is oddly
associated with the reference to his status. What does his civilian
position matter at a moment like this? The answer is of course
that it does matter – to Kipling. Once again he has become personally involved; in a totally objective passage the writing has
suddenly become subjective. He insists on showing that his
newspaperman is as tough as, even tougher than, the soldiers;
supremely a man of action capable of dishing the roughest stuff
out with his bare hands and rising (not scrambling to his feet) to
wipe off the dirt. The real brutality comes not from the incident,
shocking though it is, but from the way that it is chosen and
dwelt upon to serve a private need of Kipling's own.

On two later occasions the novel refers back to this scene and
in both the brutality still partly incipient here becomes explicit
and unmistakable. "D'you remember that nigger you gouged in

the square? Pity you didn't keep the odd eye. It would have been useful. Any letters for me?" In a novel about blindness, at a moment when the hero has just learned in his own experience what blindness means, this is almost incredible. Yet the intention is not to criticise Dick's total lack of imagination, which is the mark of brutality. It is true that the attitude is not as simple as it looks. The letters he asks after so casually are Maisie's, and the mode is stiff upper-lip and schoolboy irony. The letters do matter, and so does the eye – to Dick. But such irony cannot excuse what we are offered, and there is no sign that Kipling understands how the brave jest relates to the blindness of self-pity, and the incapacity to imagine or care about the "nigger."

The clearest exposure comes, however, in that very unpleasant Chapter Eight where the "go-fever" battles in Dick's blood against the love of Maisie. He longs to "taste the old hot, unregenerate life again . . . to hear the crackle of musketry, and see the smoke roll outward, thin and thicken again till the shining black faces came through, and in that hell every man was strictly responsible for his own head, and his alone, *and struck with an unfettered arm*" [my italics]. "Hell" now means something quite different from its use in the original passage; its human significance is not only emptied out, it actually becomes something to long for and enjoy because it brings freedom to be unregenerate, to shake off human responsibility and human vision, to express one's inner violence unfettered by any control. The "shining black faces" again become simply objects. So, in the last chapter, shooting at human beings becomes an avidly desirable experience. "Dick stretched himself on the floor, wild with delight at the sounds and the smells. 'God is very good – I never thought I'd hear this again. Give 'em hell, men. Oh, give 'em hell!' he cried." And, when it is over: "It was a lark, though. I only wish it had lasted twice as long. How superb it must have looked from outside!" "It palls after the first few nights" the subaltern replies. Yet this twinge of criticism is not enough either; there is no real awareness of how much more than boredom might be involved in that kind of blindness.

Clearly then the atrophy of imaginative vision comes from a partial intensity, some glare or stare, that expresses a private need or inner pressure of Kipling's. It is because Dick becomes in the publisher scene so intense a vehicle for Kipling's hatred that he can no longer see the publisher as a human being. It is because Kipling is so driven to assert the toughness of the journalist as man of action, and the desirability of the life of action, that Arabs, niggers, shining black faces, become emptied of human reality and exist merely as objects to satisfy an inner violence. Moreover the intensity of this partial vision is responsible not only for the novel's badness, but also for a curious kind of power. It isn't bad with the badness of the merely second-rate and dull, or the wholly unimaginative; it has a kind of compulsion that can make scenes and situations memorable long after other bad – and much better – books have been forgotten. While the total vision atrophies, the partial, subjective, mesmeric stare often dwells lovingly on the details that satisfy its needs and makes them live, and the emotional temperature rises. A fine adolescent anarchism falls into memorably explicit posturings.

There are three kinds of light in the novel, but it is only too easy to see how they relate to Kipling's private experience in 1890. There is the transfiguring light that falls on the mud-puddle in childhood with Maisie, though her hair blinds and stings Dick's eyes, and his bullet sings out to an empty sea. This is the light of Love, and it fails. There is also the light into which Dick turns Binat's head, the light from without and within the human eye by which one paints, the light of Art, and it fails too. There is, finally, the desert light falling across the bloody spear after the battle. Dick associates this in delirium with his experience with Maisie, but the novel not only separates Love and the Trail (the life of action and danger), but opposes them. At last, when Love and Art have failed, it is to a dawn attack in the desert that Dick returns, to find merciful release in a man's arms as a bullet finds its mark. All this is clearly a highly charged dramatisation of certain private agonies and dilemmas. Like his hero, Kipling had returned to London to experience a spell of poverty followed by immense success, but he had also been "checked by a woman who admitted all the success and did not immediately care for him." His sister had recalled how Kipling's face worked as he told her not only of his break with Caroline Taylor but also of his chance meeting with Flo Garrard and the return of all his old feelings; hopelessly, for she was "naturally cold, and she wanted to live her own life and paint her very ineffective little pictures."[2] His letters to Henley in 1890 are full of hostility to women and marriage,[3] and there was a consequent tendency to exalt the strength and loyalty of male friendship, and the joys of the life of action, against the cosy restrictions of domesticity. Dick Heldar directly reflects many of his author's feelings in 1890 – the biting contempt for the publishing world, the coteries of artists and critics at best cloistered and at worst epicene, for ever talking about "Art and the state of their souls," the stifling suburbia, the philistine reading-public half bloodthirsty, and half prissy and sentimental. Kipling felt himself a man of the world who had seen something of action and the stirring life of the frontiers, and even without the pressure to assert these things against women – and men – who presumed to find him wanting, his relations with the literary world and the reading public alone would do something to account for the contempt for the "stay-at-home" that streaks his novel. As Charles Carrington suggests, the way Kipling first published it, with a perfunctory sentimental ending, is surely directly related to Dick's present to his public and critics of what they really wanted in the painting of "His Last Shot." Yet behind Kipling's enormous confidence, not to say arrogance, about his talent, there remained a secret fear. Over and over again the reception of his work had been soured by prophecies and warnings about writing himself out; and this is the explanation of the theme of blindness: the possibility that the light by which he created might fail. All his life Kipling maintained, as Dick does, that his best work came from a daemon outside his control. The fear that genius might dry up and leave him only talent, the painter's hand without the painter's eye, was therefore painfully real.

These then are some of the things the novel is about. This doesn't get us very far, however, for the unpleasantness and immaturity come not from the private pressures themselves, but from the way they are succumbed to and orchestrated.

It is true that the book is partly a painful struggle towards a better perspective. Dick is obviously meant to change as we watch him. His success is revealed to him as worthless beside the hope of love. His childish pique against the world, his aggres-

[2] Carrington, *op. cit.*, pp. 157-8.   [3] *Op. cit.*, pp. 171-2.

sive drive to wrest from it what it owes him, is symbolically re-
nounced when he throws Maisie's threepenny bit into the Thames.
But Maisie hasn't had success, and her whole life is centred on her
determination to get it. In arguing with her Dick begins to for-
mulate a theory of art which contains implicit self-criticism.
Good work doesn't belong to the artist, it is a gift from outside;
and the moment one tries deliberately to achieve success one loses
everything. It cannot be achieved by sacrificing other people,
"you must sacrifice yourself, and live under orders, and never
think for yourself, and never have real satisfaction in your work
except just at the beginning, when you're reaching out after a
notion. . . . That's the law, and you take it or refuse it as you
please."

Dick, the exploiter of the sufferings and degradation of others,
has to learn what it is like to be material for someone else's work,
his arrogant ego meets its match, and he begins to learn to serve.
Only, his idol is worthless. Maisie distrusts "over-sea emotion,"[4]
fears and is disgusted by even the tiny modicum of sex that
Kipling allows into the novel. The fact that her pictures lack
conviction, do not have to be painted, reveals the essential
pettiness of her egotism. In her meditation at Vitry-sur-Marne,
where a dry and dusty rose ironically takes the place of the
nodding sea-poppy at Fort Keeling, she gets near to grasping her
need of Dick; but when his need of her is finally apparent, she has
nothing to offer, is incapable of service, sacrifice, love.

It is apparent then that Kipling does see some of the implications of Dick's arrogance and selfishness, and means him (in
contrast to Maisie) to develop a more adult outlook. It even
appears, in the affair of the red-haired girl, that there might be
some awareness of Dick's inability to recognise the human
realities of other people. Unfortunately all this is vitiated by
Kipling's involvement with his hero. The criticism operates in a
very restricted area, and Kipling is far too often self-justifyingly,
self-pityingly, self-indulgently *with* Dick Heldar. There is a pun-
gency and enjoyment in the lashings of the semi-detacheds, the

---

[4] This reveals, both ludicrously and pathetically, Kipling's translation
of his private hurt into big angry generalisations. The association of love
with the "clumsy and coarse-built" in the Embankment scene is also revealing.

British public, the epicene cosiness of the art-world, that betray
his own voice. The few protests Torpenhow is given neither
penetrate to the real trouble – the blindness to human complexity
inherent in the simplifications and posturings – nor consequently
disturb the satisfaction these offer. If there are possibilities with
the red-haired girl they are never realised. She tends to act almost
entirely as a contrast with Maisie, not as a criticism of Dick. And
when finally Dick suffers, Kipling never seems to see that the
opposite of arrogance is not humiliation but humility and the
opposite of selfishness not abasement but charity – the ability to
feel for all conditions of men and women. Dick's real pride is
untouched, as his angry rejection of pity shows. He remains an
adolescent, smarting.

The quality of the love the novel proffers is also significant.
Kipling's presentation of Dick's doglike devotion and exag-
gerated protectiveness shows an awareness that such attitudes are
comic as well as pathetic, but Dick is also ludicrous in ways his
author doesn't realise. It is not only Maisie whose attitude to sex
is prissy. In his relationship with her Dick behaves with exag-
gerated delicacy. Outside it, the sex-posturings – " 'You have to
supply me with men-servants and maid-servants,' – here he
smacked his lips" – or the affair with the "sort of Negroid-
Jewess-Cuban" – are unmistakably adolescent. Maisie hardly
exists as a *woman* for Dick, let alone for us, and we have to take
her fascination wholly on trust. What he does respond to is
either the waif or, tellingly, the boy-girl.[5] The effects of this are
increased by Kipling's satirical involvement, his need to canalise
his bitterness about Flo Garrard. In *Manon Lescaut*, of which he
said his novel was a "sort of inverted, metagrobolised phantas-
magoria," there is already the problem of making us respond to
the obsession without losing all pity and respect for the hero; but
where Kipling's bitterness is busy emptying out of Maisie the
little vitality and attractiveness she had to start with, the problem
is insoluble.

One can see what Kipling was trying to do in evolving his
theory of art, and respect his attempt to come to grips with the

[5] "It isn't a pretty tale, but you're so like a man that I forget when I'm
talking to you." Compare the treatment of the heroine in "William the
Conqueror," *The Day's Work*.

self-centredness and human failure that marked his abortive love. Yet there remain silliness, sentimentality, over-dramatisation, callowness: continual failures in vision and insight. The trouble really starts, however, when he feels compelled to *generalise* about women, and to assert, against the smart of his defeat by them, the superiority of male love and the male life of action. There are annunciations of a defiantly male ethic: "Orgies are healthy . . . but when it comes to women making eyes I'm not so certain," or, "She'll spoil his hand. She'll waste his time, and she'll marry him, and ruin his work for ever. He'll be a respectable married man before we can stop him, and – he'll never go on the long trail again." Now Torpenhow is a "clucker" on this topic, but there is an explicit endorsement of his "austere love" from Kipling himself.[6] We may smile at Torpenhow for fussing when there is nothing to be done, but we are not meant to be smiling at the love and concern themselves.

In that most significant eighth chapter,[7] male friendship and the life of action are directly opposed to the love of Maisie and the hope of marriage. A series of songs brings the conflict more and more into the open. The stately "Farewell and adieu to you, Spanish Ladies," with its unstately ranting and roaring chorus, gives way to a song celebrating, at the end of a man's life as in his prime, the slipping of the cable, the farewell to the lady-wife, the longing for the otherland, the boon companion, the nutbrown maid. The last song, "The Sea is a wicked old woman," asserts

[6] "Torpenhow came into the studio at dusk, and looked at Dick with his eyes full of the austere love that springs up between men who have tugged at the same oar together and are yoked by custom and use and the intimacies of toil. This is a good love, and, since it allows, and even encourages strife, recrimination, and the most brutal sincerity, does not die, but increases, and is proof against any absence and evil conduct."

[7] Both a "happy-ending" and a "sad-ending" version were deposited in the Library of Congress for copyright purposes in Nov. 1890, before the former appeared as the first edition of the novel in *Lippincott's Monthly Magazine* for Jan. 1891. Significantly however neither contained this chapter, which appeared only in the First Macmillan Edition in March, in which "Mother o' Mine" also made its first appearance. See James Stewart, *Rudyard Kipling, a Bibliographical Catalogue*, Toronto 1959, pp. 81-7. Kipling roundly stated "This is the story of *The Light that Failed* as it was originally conceived by the Writer." He may have felt, with justification, that the chapter gave too much away to appear earlier.

that the go-fever is more powerful than any woman; it leads straight into the memory of Dick's finest hour, and that passage about the "old hot, unregenerate life." Dick found his greatest happiness and fulfilment on a rattletrap cargo boat between Lima and Auckland, making love to the Negro-Jewess-Cuban with the ever-present fear of drowning or the jealous captain's knife in his back, and painting his greatest picture on the ship's side. It is an illustration of two lines from Poe's "Annabel Lee," but there is no Annabel Lee in the picture. What has caught Kipling's imagination is the idea of *sea*-devils and *sea*-angels fighting over a soul; what both picture and passage proclaim is the fatal fascination for good or bad of the Wicked Old Woman, and the hopelessness against her drawing power of any enduring passion for the Ladies of the world. The "Sea" encompasses the thrills of danger, and sex, and violence. The "sort of Negroid-Jewess-Cuban; with morals to match" is an extraordinarily explicit sex-fantasy; an apotheosis of the lure for the adolescent imagination of exotic, half-repulsive, half-daemonic, totally uninhibited sex experience with a *combination* of the races supposed to excel at the sports of the dark gods. And to it are added the *frissons* of danger and forbidden fruit: "Just three colours . . . and the sea outside and unlimited lovemaking inside, and the fear of death atop of everything else, O Lord!"

The demands of *Manon* "metagrobolised" insist that the obsessed Dick should remain, against all Kipling's rhymes and reasons, constant to his worthless lady in spite of the pull of the Sea. Yet the sub-plot of Bessie Broke continues to assert against women the Male-world and the Trail. Torpenhow's weakening is seen as pitiable, and Dick's rescue of him from the "futile little Jezebel" as wholly admirable, not for moral or religious reasons, but as a return from temptation to a finer manhood. Indeed, it is because she tries to tempt Torpenhow with domesticity that she is "immoral," not because of her waif's plea to be his mistress until "Miss Right comes along." When Torpenhow returns from his short Trail "to regain tone," he is able to treat Bessie as a man should: that is, listen to her passionate pleading, pick her up, kiss her, and put her down outside the door with a recommendation not to be a little fool. But Kipling is not content with this; he has to give the rejected woman a scene at the keyhole in which she watches the strong men walking together, hand on shoulder, and knows herself finally locked out.

Bessie's destruction of the Melancolia is hardly surprising in the light of Dick's refusal to recognise her as a human being, but the criticism is all of the "vicious little housemaid's folly," and Dick's one "mistake" is the same as Torpenhow's: having anything to do with women, and putting himself in their power to hurt and damage. At this important moment for Kipling, as at several others, only a religious reference will do – "He saved others, himself he cannot save."

Against this, and Maisie's worthlessness, the male love is shown at its deepest at the time of Dick's blindness. What is most interesting about it, moreover, is Kipling's determination to give it physical expression.

> He made as if to leap from the bed, but Torpenhow's arms were round him, and Torpenhow's chin was on his shoulder, and his breath was squeezed out of him. . . . The grip could draw no closer. Both men were breathing heavily. Dick threw his head from side to side and groaned.

Now Kipling knew about homosexuality, and his insistence a moment later on Torpenhow's "large and hairy paw" is a clear, if misconceived, attempt to clear his picture of any taint. All the same the physical emphasis is extraordinarily explicit – he *wants* his two strong men to wrestle their trouble together, and the wrestling is climactic, with a panting conclusion, dropping through the dark, sleep, and a final tender kiss. Kipling is making this male love a substitute and haven, and the very overtness of his worry over homosexuality shows the pressure that insists on risking it. One can now see why Dick must die in Torpenhow's arms in a conclusion which re-orchestrates this scene. Explicitly in the closing chapters it is women and the domestic world that Dick is shaking off, to return spruced, trim, and restored to self-respect, to the Trail. The only woman allowed now is Madame Binat, and she is explicitly a mother-figure. Her function is to dress out the broken boy, and arrange for him to find his release "as near the old life as might be" in the arms of the "very strong *man*, Kwasind."[8]

[8] My italics. Kipling identifies himself with Dick in writing the novel, but

What would one do if both one's hopes of love and one's life-work failed? While Dick can still paint, indeed, deliberately using the last of his sight, he produces the symbolic attitude of the Melancolia. He begins to paint it in pique with Maisie but comes to realise that this is wrong; what it must do is "laugh right out of the canvas, and every man and woman that ever had a sorrow of their own shall – what is it the poem says? – Understand the speech and feel a stir Of fellowship in all disastrous fight." Under the pressure of Kipling's emotions, however, the picture is more than this. As he describes it – the woman who had known all the sorrow in the world and was laughing at it, full-lipped, hollow-eyed, insolent, and with "a sort of murderous, viperine suggestion in the poise of the head" – the picture is as over-dramatised and self-indulgent as the book it symbolises. It strikes an attitude false not only to the hurt and smarting reality the novel reveals, but false in itself. It is again the unmistakably school-boyish "I don't care!" Only by caring a great deal more clear-sightedly for all the human factors involved could something more mature have emerged.

But the Melancolia can only be painted while the artist's light lasts, and the attitude it enables Kipling to strike cannot meet his horror of what it would be like to be able to write no longer. He will not have Dick turn to any hope of the ordinary life of limited human beings, or any hope of a life with women. Only the Trail remains, and if one is so maimed as to be unable finally to live it, there is only the hope of meeting death like a "man." The twin urges of self-dramatisation and self-pity can be satisfied with nothing less than Dick's last ride to death. It does not occur to Kipling to wonder whether Dick's death-wish really is different from the suicide he rejects as cowardly; whether true courage might not demand some attempt to win back to ordinary human modes of being, undramatic perhaps, but not easy to regain in the midst of suffering. In the face of all this – the ugly flirtings with violence, the blindnesses, the enormous self-pity – the con-tinual assertion of divine design is peculiarly repellent. God is

we cannot simply equate Dick with Kipling. "Mother o' Mine" expressed his faith that *he* would have been saved by his mother's love; yet the relation-ship of the dedication with the novel remains ironic. The poem may well have been written later.

good when he allows Dick to re-experience the shooting of the unimpressionable Fuzzy in the open, Christ is called upon to witness the irony of Dick's inability to rescue himself from women, St Antony to image Torpenhow's testing by Bessie, and the escaping Israelites to hymn Dick's last desert escape. The world is a cruel shambles into which helpless animals are driven, and "the good things spoil one's eye." But God, though terrible, is just. He gives Dick sleep, and a last vicarious taste of violence, he guides him through the desert, and, the presumption is strong, he vouchsafes the crowning mercy. " 'What luck!' . . . said Dick. " 'It's *just before the battle, mother*! Oh, God has been most good to me!' " Blinkered subjectivity could hardly go further.

Yet – one repeats – it is not a matter of discussing "views" so much as the failure to focus which causes them. There is an attempt to contain Dick within a broader vision, but *that* is the light that fails most disastrously. Kipling cannot finally see beyond his own private agonies and violences; this means that he is less and less able to achieve any real focus at all.

By contrast, the first characteristic of *Captains Courageous* is its utter objectivity. It is written by another Kipling who was fascinated by facts and processes of all kinds for their own sakes, and who claimed that the "shop" of professional men was the highest kind of conversation. Subtitled *A Story of the Grand Banks*, it is at first sight just that – a brilliant documentary of the cod-fishing fleet in the last quarter of the century. With Dr Conland, who had fished the Banks and gave him the idea, he spent about a fortnight in Gloucester and Boston, and absorbed everything he could with the mastery of technical detail he justly prided himself upon, and with the good journalist's insistence on seeing for himself exactly how things get done.[9] He clearly lost himself – the *cliché* becomes meaningful – in the delight of learning a whole professional way of life quite alien to him, and that is still the primary pleasure of his book. Perhaps it seems no more than sharply-focused journalism, vivid, nervous documentary: but Kipling is a master here, and it would be an impoverished

---

[9] See *Something of Myself*, Chapter Five. The delight in reality for its own sake, and in seeing exactly for oneself, is very clear: "Also, by pure luck, I had sight of the first sickening uprush and vomit of irridescent coal-dusted water into the hold of a ship, a crippled iron hulk, sinking at her moorings."

imagination and curiosity which failed to respond. The book indeed begins by plucking a would-be "superior" pair of eyes from a stern-rail high above sea-level and bringing them down to the dories, to the little *We're Here*, smack up against a reality objectively "there." It suggests that the proper response is not to patronise or condescend to this real world, but to learn to respect it and find out how it works. "We're here," the old chant runs, "because we're here, because we're here, because we're here." Reality is its own justification and needs no other. But one has sometimes to be made to see it, and this may need the purging of bad blood and the shedding of fancy clothes; false senses of superiority and false ideas of reality.

It is pointless to complain that the conversion of Harvey happens too easily, or that Kipling is suggesting that the way to deal with delinquents is to punch them on the nose and set them to work. He isn't so much concerned with Harvey, and certainly not in a psychological or "character" sense. Harvey is primarily there as a pair of ignorant eyes which gradually enact the process of seeing that Kipling expects from his readers. In the boy's consciousness or motivation he has no interest, and there are no "characters" of that kind. The *personae* are defined by their professional skills, and secondarily by their eccentricities; it is a book about fishing, not a story of "personality"; its hero is not Harvey but the *We're Here* and her sisters, and the Captains Courageous who sail them.

Yet it is more than first-class journalistic documentary, and one soon realises that more than technology is being conveyed. We begin to see beyond what men do and how, to what men stand for, mirrored in the way they act. The fishermen's world is revealed as a world of value. Yet there is no preaching, everything is concrete, and one only gradually realises how one's eyes have been sharpened. We start on board thousands of tons of metal steaming at speed through a fishing-fleet in a fog, with voices asking how far they have reached and what speed they are making. Harvey's "You can hear the fish-boats squawking all around us. Say, wouldn't it be great if we ran down one" marks an adolescent limit of blindness and irresponsibility. But we need to notice that the Chief Engineer is not much better: "We've shaved three dories an' near skelped the boom off a Frenchman since noon, an'

that's close sailing you may say." Now Kipling is partial to
Chief Engineers, and this one is obviously neither a fool nor a
monster. Yet we must feel that there is something wrong, long
before we come to the great passage that tells us what it is.
Kipling reverses the situation. Harvey on the *We're Here* at four
in the morning, in swirling fog, finds himself

> hammering literally for the dear life on a bell smaller than the
> steward's breakfast bell, while somewhere close at hand a
> thirty-foot steel stem was storming along at twenty miles an
> hour! . . . Then Harvey felt that he was near a moving body,
> and found himself looking up and up at the wet edge of a
> cliff-like bow, leaping, it seemed, directly over the schooner.
> A jaunty little feather of water curled in front of it, and as it
> lifted it showed a long ladder of Roman numerals – XV.XVI.
> XVII.XVIII. and so forth – on a salmon-coloured, gleaming
> side. It tilted forward and downward with a heart-stilling
> 'Ssssooo'; the ladder disappeared; a line of brass-rimmed port-
> holes flashed past; a jet of steam puffed in Harvey's helplessly
> uplifted hands; a spout of hot water roared along the rail of the
> *We're Here*, and the little schooner staggered and shook in a
> rush of screw-torn water, as a liner's stern vanished in the fog.
> Harvey got ready to faint or be sick, or both, when he heard a
> crack like a trunk thrown on a sidewalk, and, all small in his
> ear, a faraway telephone-like voice drawling: "Heave to!
> You've sunk us!"

A man has lost a $9000 boat that is his livelihood, his summer's
work, his crew of at least four, and, but for a near miracle, his
only son, in "thirty counted seconds." Kipling doesn't need to
explain what is wrong: the explanation is there if we look, in
Harvey's memories of his cherry-red blazer, the staterooms dry and
upholstered, each with its bath, the gilt-edged bill of fare; there
also in the towering bow and the Roman numerals of displacement, the jaunty feather, the steam and hot water. All this
coalesces in that last extraordinary touch where, almost deafened
by the steamer, we hear the splitting of a ship as no more than the
noise of a trunk dropped on the pavement, and the cry of agony
is so distanced that it "drawls" like a "telephone" voice. Progress
and technology have obscured reality, and with it, responsibility.

The wildness and danger of the sea are hidden from those on the steamer by its size and luxury, its imitation of the cosy comforts of the shore. The real terror actually happening "down there" is dwarfed; becomes tiny, domesticated, unrealisable. Because "don't know" leads to "don't care," the officers of such ships are implicated as well as the passengers. The law permits a certain speed, permits liners to storm along their straight mechanic paths, issuing their mechanised warnings to tiny craft which depend on men and the natural forces of wind and wave.

Once we have known life on the *We're Here*, however, we see that this is not good enough. Where the steamer crashes along "there or thereabouts," Disko Troop feels his way with consummate skill from berth to berth, knowing exactly where he is, just what the depth of water under him will turn out to be, what is going to happen to the weather, exactly where he is going and what he is doing. The steamer is blind, but Disko can see; and Kipling's fascination with his professionalism enables him, and us, to see too. "Disko, ye kape your spare eyes under the keel." But it is not magic; it is experience, fine professional skill, and hard and careful thinking. The feel of wind on his cheek, the quality of sludge or shell on the lead, the lessons of a lifetime watching fish, wind, and water, provide the material for his "jedgements" – but a deep professional integrity, responsibility, and pride make him take the utmost pains to ensure that these are never "mistaken." He silently communicates this kind of professionalism to the whole crew, and the *We're Heres* – (*i.e., here*, not "there or thereabouts") – have no time for ships and skippers who lose their way, get out of control, or simply don't care. Each of the crew proper has skill and knowledge that have become instinctive, but the point is that this makes them responsible and independent, never a danger to themselves or to others. Danger is serious: they will take great risks to save life, even Abishai, whom they despise and detest, but they will permit no empty bravado or unnecessary risks. They are a team in which each member is an individual but none an individualist. Their professionalism encourages competition, but its sense of integrity is a firm protection against sharp practice. With this goes a strong sense of justice – even, comically, for Skipper Ireson long since dead – this is the other quality of the "jedgements" of "the justest man in the fleet." Finally, the presence of Penn bears witness to their compassion; the way the realities and dangers of the sea have opened their eyes to human suffering and frailty and made them care. Responsibility, integrity, justice, compassion, humanity – these things are not preached, but made concrete in everything the *We're Heres* do and say. The little ship becomes an image of human life and value. Close to wind and water, knowing the realities, the beauties, the terrors at first hand, and humanised by them, the fishermen pit their skill and courage against the elements. The accuracy and unsentimentality of Kipling's vision is, moreover, guaranteed by the way he needs the shore as well as the ship for his full perspective. We have at the end to know what the sea, and those fish-balls on every American table, *cost* – in the gravity of Mrs Troop; the fact that a hundred men a year are drowned from Gloucester alone; the realisation of this in terms of lost love, the black widows on Memorial Day, the interminable list of the names of the dead. We have only to think now of Chapter Eight of *The Light that Failed* to mark the world of difference. By being caught up with his Massachusetts fisherfolk, learning to see and image values clearly in documenting their way of life, Kipling achieves a vision that makes its own critical comment on the cult of violence and danger, the cheap sneers about the love and loyalty of women, the posturings about maledom and action of the earlier work. This sea and these human beings are real and valuable; learning to see them sharpens one's own vision.

So when we are confronted by the Cheynes – ostensibly the one case of mistaken judgment in Disko – we are using new eyes, and they give us a clear focus on the irresponsibility, the slack sense of what is real and important, of the millionaire and his neurotic wife. It is not the plush comforts of the *Constance* that are finally impressive as the Cheynes speed from coast to coast, nor even the power and wealth that make this possible. What finally catches the imagination is once again the professionalism and skill of the human beings in the "naked necessity of the combination," who hurl the giant locomotives across mountain and desert, and clip records not through competitive instinct, but because of their pride in their work and their sense of human need and pity. They convert Cheyne's world of telegrams into reality, and they make his entourage, and the "illustrious magnates" who climb aboard to talk business, unmistakably smaller than their own valuation. Part of Kipling is, to the end, wide-eyed at the glamour and the power, just as part of him is unfortunately a-tremble with sentiment over the suffering mother: yet the final focus is perfectly sharp. He knows that the Cheynes must be found wanting, not only by contrast with the *We're Heres*, but even with the inhabitants of the Gloucester boarding-house, and he makes Cheyne confess it. In his heart now the millionaire hates the *Constance*, the "distressful palace of all the luxuries"; and, when it is gone, he tries to recapture the fascination for realities, and for how things get done, that he had when he was making his way. As he succeeds, he regains not only vitality and self-respect but also the respect of others, for "Men can 'most always tell when a man has handled things for himself, and then they treat him as one of themselves." Millionairedom, deals made through telephones and telegrams, "power," and "empire" and other abstractions *unrealise*. Respect is reserved for people who know, do, and build real things, and become real human beings responsible to other human beings – like sons. For the first time Cheyne and Harvey can communicate and come to terms, and it is the doing of the *We're Here*. For the first time Cheyne can tell the story of his life, which is the story of the new burgeoning America and by implication the new Africa and Empire too. Yet there is a control very often absent in Kipling: "through the mad shift of things . . . moved Harvey Cheyne, alert and quiet, seeking his own ends, and, so he said, the glory and advancement of his country." That quiet irony is the mark of what the book has done. For Cheyne's story is "like watching a locomotive storm-ing across country in the dark" – the steamer, not the *We're Here* – and, although Kipling respects the way he has "crawled round, through, or under mountains and ravines, dragging a string-and-hoop-iron railroad after him," he never gives Cheyne the respect that belongs to the note of humanity and responsi-bility in Disko Troop. Nor should we remember the end of the tale too simply in terms of the "master/man" reversal between Harvey and Dan, for Dan smiles the smile of a brother, not an employee, and the last words are not about the shipping-line, but about the *We're Here* and her skipper, and what is owed to them.

There are of course areas of consciousness and social complexity where to see with the vision of *Captains Courageous* would be not to see enough. Yet within its limits the vision is clean and sure; what is seen is fully realised and the response to it firmly controlled. Value emerges concretely from the objective concern with the facts of the fishermen's life.

Kim also starts from a fresh and delighted response to a real world, but the fascination is heightened by the immeasurably richer variety of India. The eye is caught by a whole kaleidoscope of race, caste, custom, and creed, all seen with a warm affection that is almost unique in Kipling. Such a vision involves, as in *Captains Courageous*, the deliberate exclusion of attitudes of superiority, but it does so in a more challenging and significant way because objectivity now demands not merely social, but religious and racial tolerance. The epigraphs to the first three chapters appeal for this, but the Little Friend of All the World bodies it forth.

Our first glimpse of him on Zam-Zammah is emblematic. He is playing with the son of a Mohammedan sweetseller and the son of a half-millionaire Hindu with the "perfect equality" he has with all the boys of the bazaar, and what he says of race and creed carries no more sting than his chant about the pastrycook and the *ghi*. They are playing at supremacy, on the old gun that has been the first prize of grown-up war and conquest. But it is only a game, and the irony about Kim deserving to be on top because he is a member of the master race points to the difference between game and reality. Not that there is anything sentimental here. The urge to assert one's supremacy, to insult one's rivals and kick them off whatever "castle" is at issue, is deeply ingrained in every human being. That is why all children everywhere play this game and chant this kind of chant. But here the reality of the urge is taken up into the humour of the game. The Punjabi policeman, the low-caste water-carrier, the Museum carpenter, all "grinned tolerantly" and "so did everybody in sight." It is the characteristic response to Kim the boy, and the first response Kipling wants towards the novel as a whole. Embodying his author's most humane and affectionate vision, the Little Friend of All the World moves through India's range of caste, race, and creed all condemning and judging one another, making no such

judgment, fascinated by all forms of humanity, offering universal
friendship with no apparent awareness that it is anything unusual.
We cannot say that this is just because he is a child. The other
two children, confronted with the Lama, react immediately with
the prejudices of their parents. If Kim is different, it is because
he has no parents and so has no built-in reactions; the bazaar
has been his nursery, and the whole population of Lahore has
brought him up. The effect of that background, moreover, is to
create an oddly adult consciousness within a child. There is
comedy in the contrast: but, for all the residual childishness, it
is clear that Kim's tolerance cannot be put down to "innocence."
Kipling is unfortunately inclined to overdo and romanticise the
nature of his "experience"; Kim's junior version of "the Great
Game" – his stealthy commissions on the housetops – involves
danger, intrigue, and worldly knowledge of a sort, but it hardly
supports the claim that "he had known all evil since he could
speak." Indeed, the world is strangely disinfected as it passes
through Kim's eyes. Nevertheless, he does have experience of
many kinds of intrigue and dishonesty, and is wholly capable of
looking after himself in an adult way. The keen gaze and in-
exhaustible interest indeed are not so much the eyes and interest
of a child as those of the young Kipling on his late-night expedi-
tions into the old walled city.

From the beginning, however, Kim also embodies the urge to
attain a deeper kind of vision, the urge not merely to see and
know from the outside, but to *become* the "other." Kim's more-
than-chameleon ability to change, not only his clothes, but his
voice and mannerisms, his whole identity, represents something
different from Harvey's accidental experience of a strange world,
something far more creative and imaginative in Kipling: not
merely the observer's sharp eye, but the dramatist's longing to
get into the skin of many "others." Kim is an expression of what
Keats called "negative capability." Where *Captains Courageous* is
objective in contrast with the overheated subjectivity of *The Light
that Failed*, *Kim* moves beyond objectivity into drama: the ability
to become many very different kinds of human being, and see
with many very different eyes. This means that *Kim* is the most
complex of all Kipling's accounts of reality, and potentially the
finest, since it was over-simplification that caused most of his

blindness. Yet complexity is not valuable in itself. What really sets Kim off from almost all Kipling's other work and makes it his masterpiece is the quality of its inner questioning. If self-projection into other and conflicting points of view is carried far enough, it can result in a loss of confidence in the self; a questioning not only of values but of identity. This could not happen to Dick Heldar or Harvey Cheyne, but the fact that it happens to Kim on three crucial occasions shows the depth of the probing that is going on.

From the start, Kim moves between the opposed worlds of Mahbub Ali and the Tibetan Lama. At first it is Mahbub Ali who seems to draw him towards manhood. The bustling energy and colour of the Kashmir Serai is a man's world, and to thread one's way through it demands self-possession, courage and resourcefulness. Here the Lama seems helpless and out-of-place. Mahbub Ali connects the worldliness of the man-child and the junior Game with the real thing; he reveals an enlargement of certain of the Kim capabilities, particularly the "stalkiness" that Kipling so admires. He is the master strategist, player of secret hands, seizer of chances, expert in a world of spying, power struggles, and feuds. When he sends Kim off with the "white stallion's pedigree," it is a kind of initiation, though Kipling is hardly serious yet. Nevertheless when Kim copes with ticket-seller and courtesan, spies on Creighton, plays the prophet in the village, and outwits the crooked priest, he is already playing the Game where victory goes to the stalkiest; and we become aware of certain adult perspectives behind our amusement at his resourcefulness, though they have yet to come into focus. The Lama, on the other hand, first interests us as he interests Kim, as a collector's item, a curiosity, touching in his naïve piety and sincerity, but irrelevant to the world we live in. He belongs to an otherworld – the strange Greco-Buddhist sculptures in the Wonder House, the Lamassery of the Painted Rocks, the beautiful meaningless life-history of the Buddha – that is the more attractive as it has less apparently to do with the real world beyond the turnstile of the Museum where he is revered as a museum-piece should be. Perhaps the Curator of Images reminds us of the need for humility; and certainly the Lama's serene faith, arcane knowledge, and truth give him dignity; but the dominant attitude to-

wards him remains one of patronage or protectiveness. As soon
as he is outside the Museum, he becomes a child, with a child's
simplicity and a child's rapid emotions. Much of the humour of
the first chapters springs from the sight of the little man-child
piloting the old child-man through the shoals of life in the outside world; and though the humour is gentle and loving, it does
initially carry the suggestion that the Lama is something less than
a full and responsible adult. His goodness tends to be diminished
when it is so hedged about with amusement, as it is when he hails
the Amritsar courtesan as a nun. His complete truthfulness, far
from criticising the deceptiveness and stalkiness of Mahbub and
Kim, seems at this stage sympathetic, even good, but much in
need of being shushed and smiled at, like a child in the presence
of grown-ups.

Very soon, however, we begin to realise his peculiar stature.
Unlike Kim, he judges men's failings crisply, but quite without
animus and in complete charity. And, whereas Kim does not
care about caste, the idea cannot exist for the Lama. He does not
say "Pride is wrong"; he says "There is no pride among such as
follow the Middle Way." Even a vicious cobra is seen as a fellow-
creature on the Wheel of Life, and there is absolutely no fear or
hatred. "The coiled thing hissed and half opened its hood. 'May
thy release come soon, brother!' the Lama continued placidly."
There is again no sentimentality. The poison and danger are as
real to the Lama as to us: but, whereas E. M. Forster felt he had
to protect a similar attitude with whimsy in the episode of Professor Godbole and the wasp, Kipling puts it simply, even drably,
and the effect is curiously impressive. "Placidly" is uniquely right.
The moment is wholly undramatic and lacking in grandeur because there is no possibility of any violent reaction. There is no
talk of the Sanctity of Life; only an *absence*, an impossibility of
violence even directed against "evil." Perhaps the Lama is often
too naïve to recognise evil, but it makes no difference when he
does.

What of times like the Mutiny, however, when only the sword
of the soldier can save the innocent and helpless from the sword?
The Ressaldar speaks for the Kipling who knew and feared the
possibility of anarchy on the Frontiers and within them, when he
retorts that "if evil men were not now and then slain it would not

be a good world for weaponless dreamers." Yet it is not a
question of merely showing up the dreamer either, for the Lama's
questioning of the ultimate value of a soldier's life and death is
not easily answered. The good achieved by the Ressaldars is valid
in itself, but is it enough to validate a whole human life and death?
In its third chapter *Kim* is already involved with questions of deep
significance to Kipling, and it is the Lama who is posing them.

On the other hand, there are elements in the Lama's Buddhism
that are very unsympathetic to Western eyes. Since the world is
all the domain of Maya, illusion, the sage must separate himself
as far as possible and be completely apart. Over and over again,
Buddhist texts[10] stress that this means non-involvement in friendship and love, whether for companions, or parents, or wife and
children. So the Lama tells the Ressaldar "that marriage and
bearing were darkeners of the true light, stumbling blocks upon
the Way." It may be "good to be kind to babes," but it is not
good to become involved in any way at all. So even the little
episode of the toddler and the rosary is suspect, and the relationship with Kim is full of danger. The tension increases in the
brilliant section on the Grand Trunk Road, which is one of the
finest in the book. Kipling is fascinated and absorbed in the
uniqueness of each of the races, castes, and types as this "River of
Life" flows past, vividly aware of the richness of colour, and light,
and texture, and smells, and sounds, and language. Kim mediates
his delight and ours: "this was life as he would have it – bustling
and shouting . . . and new sights at every turn of the approving
eye."[11] The Maharanee, too, is a woman of the world, totally
absorbed in its sensations and its goings-on. The Lama, however,
strides through it all with eyes downcast in meditation, seeing and
hearing nothing, withdrawn. When he does look up it is with

[10] See particularly the poem "The Rhinoceros" from the ancient Pali
Sutta Nipata, also "The Buddha's Law among the Birds," both in Edward
Conze, *Buddhist Scriptures*, Penguin Classics.

[11] George Moore said of the description of evening that Kipling "seems
to have followed it about like a detective employed in a divorce case." Wit
blurs the perception – it is precisely the sharp focus on each of a series of
particular details that is the whole aim of the style. The uniqueness of each
apprehension, whether of human beings or sense impression, is exactly what
is implied by "every *turn* of the approving eye," or ear, or nose. The sharp
differentiation of the Kim vision is set off against the indifference of the Lama.

pity for all on the Wheel, and whereas to Kim life is wonderful, to the Lama it is always "a great and terrible world." Yet there is never any doubt of his growing love for Kim, or of his loving nature. On the River of Life he is affected by Kim's joy and the old lady's respect; he is still withdrawn, but he is happy. And, paradoxically, each tendency to fail as a Lama raises him in our eyes as a man.

His self-condemnation in the Rev. Bennett's tent is all the more agonised. It is a mark, moreover, of Kipling's success in creating this very strange mind that we should respond not only to the pain of human parting which is half the tragedy, but also to the desolation of self-reproach by the canons of an alien creed. In fact, Father Victor and the Rev. Bennett show us how much of our Westernised vision we have already been enabled to leave behind. The response of anger and contempt for the Anglican chaplain is strong. We really resent the eyes that look at the Lama "with the triple-ringed uninterest of the creed that lumps nine-tenths of the world under the title of 'heathen'," and see him as a "*fakir*," the boy as his "dupe" and the Search as "gross blasphemy." It is important however to realise that Kipling's anger is not only, or even mainly, anti-clerical. It is unmistakably *anti-racialist*. For Bennett treats Kim quite differently as soon as he knows he is white. He is certain that only white men know what to do with white boys, and unaware, not only that yellow men may be wholly proper companions, but that they have human feelings. And even although Father Victor has much more humanity, and more insight, he, too, is found wanting His tag "Powers of Darkness below!" explains why he talks to a Buddhist about Kismet, and equates the begging bowl with vagrancy: he, too, has never been interested enough to sort the heathen out. Wise in the confessional, he can perceive the human suffering of the Lama and even half-perceive the spirituality behind Kim's ludicrous Eurasian-lingo account of the Search. Nevertheless, seeing all this where Bennett is arrogantly blind, Father Victor still assumes as a matter of course that only white men are fit to educate white boys; though it is perfectly clear to us that the Lama represents a higher human order than the two priests, let alone the regiment, and clear that even Father Victor has no idea what he wants to educate the boy to be. Whatever

Kipling may have felt or thought elsewhere in his work, at this moment he finds this racial thinking repulsive, and so do we; and again the Lama is the reason. As the end of the novel's first movement takes Kim from him, he has already decisively altered our sensibilities.

Nevertheless, long before Kim speeds south with Colonel Creighton to the sahibs' school, puzzled for the first time about his own identity, the presence in him of another nature has been marked by a title different from the Little Friend of All the World. It is heard only sporadically while Kim is with the Lama, but it begins to dominate more and more after the Lama has gone. The "Friend of the Stars" seems *destined* to the red and angry sign of war, the Game of power and "dreadful secrets," excitement, adventure, danger. The part of Kim (and, of course, of Kipling) that the Lama does not satisfy now gets its head as he passes into the very different mentorship of Colonel Creighton, Mahbub Ali, the Healer of Sick Pearls, and the Babu, and his training for the Great Game begins.

Much of the novel's gentle, mellow tone vanishes, but there is a new narrative energy and excitement, and it becomes more like an adventure story. What is perhaps most significant, however, is to establish what happens to the qualities of the Little Friend of All the World. There has always been a contrast with the Lama's direct truthfulness. Now Creighton and Mahbub use double-talk even where there can hardly be any need: but this appeals to something in both Kim and his creator, and the old admiration of stalkiness comes flooding back. Creighton is "a man after his own heart – a tortuous and indirect person playing a hidden game." Nothing now is ever what it seems, all speech must be scanned for the hidden trap, everything has a hidden purpose, and Kim is always being tested – hence the narrative suspense. Now "tolerance" preached in such a context is bound to sound different. Creighton warns Kim that although he is a sahib he must never "contemn the black men." The reason, however, is that this leads to the worst of sins, *ignorance*; and Mahbub's proverb about only the hound of Mazanderan being able to catch the jackal of Mazanderan explains the valuation. Ignorance gets you killed, knowledge makes the successful spy. Not only the Lama's refusal to acknowledge the reality of distinctions among men has gone here, but also his essentially loving heart. Kim does not need to be told that Creighton has no feeling for him but is using him, as he uses all men.

Creighton's vocations are significant too. Where Kim longs to get under the skin, to the heart, of "this great and beautiful land" and all its inhabitants, Creighton is officially an ethnologist, unofficially a spy. He trains Kim to be a surveyor. Confronted by a city, Kim's instinct would be to plunge into its human heart, Creighton wants a map and a report on the nature and attitudes of the ruler for strategic use. Where he is not bleakly utilitarian he is coldly scientific. The Babu shows similar characteristics. It is he who teaches Kim to use a rosary for secret surveying, not for comforting children or for meditation. While he can see that there are "marks to be gained" by knowing French, Latin, the *Excursion*, *Lear*, *Julius Caesar*, and "the eminent authors, Burke and Hare," he has no idea that these could convey anything valuable about the natural world, or power, or the good and evil of the human heart.[12] What he, too, sees as really important in Kim's education is to learn to *measure*, for "by merely marching over a country with a compass and a level and a straight eye," a boy could "carry away a picture of that country which might be sold for large sums in coined silver." The contrast with the Lama is unmistakable. Though he only says two things about education, one transmitted through a bazaar writer's English, the note of human responsibility sounds clear: "Education is greatest blessing if of best sorts. Otherwise no earthly use"; and "You take him from me and you cannot say what you will make him . . . it is not a small thing to make a child." He pays for Kim at St Xavier's under the impression that he is being educated to become like the Keeper of Images, a fellow priest of kindness and courtesy and the human spirit, a fellow scribe with whom one can exchange the spectacles that aid vision and the writing materials that record it. If Kim is to become a "scribe," this

[12] The implicit criticism may be measured against the endorsement of William's preference for "men who do things" and her contempt for the "poetical" teacher of the *Excursion*, to whom she "explained that she didn't understand poetry very much; it made her head ache." Kipling's "views" change with the angle of his vision. In that story of famine-relief he is wholly taken up with action.

means the Lama's picture-writing of the Wheel or the Keeper's books – writing humanised, spiritual, beautiful – not the drawing of maps and the writing of espionage reports, or the transcribing of treasonable accounts stolen from traitors. Father Victor worries about "takin' a heathen's money to give a child a Christian education"; but when Creighton answers that the Lama "said explicitly what he wanted," the critical irony is doubled.

We should also notice the remarkably consistent attitudes to religion. All Kim's new mentors reduce religion to theory or ceremony on the one hand, and utilitarian practice on the other. The ethnologist Babu examining the Lama about devil-worship merges into the nervous observer of Huneefa and the inventor of the practical flummery of the Sons of the Charm. Mahbub dry-washes when he has time, and propitiates the Sons of Eblis although he is a free-thinker, for "when one can get blind-sides of a woman, a stallion, or a devil, why go round to invite a kick?" Lurgan is much edified by discussing metaphysics with "long-coated theatrical natives"; he also teaches Kim to recite the Koran just like a Mullah, and writes parchment charms, "elaborate pentagrams crowned with the names of devils." Interesting theory or ceremony, utilitarian practice or knowledge – what these eyes cannot see is the human relevance of religion, its sense of good and evil, its belief in the reality of the spirit. We have only to compare the Lama's contempt of "devildom, charms and idolatry" (his drawing of the Wheel against Lurgan's parchment and Huneefa's spells); and his insistence on the Law (charity, courtesy, humility) and on the Search (for freedom from illusion and sin), to get the sharpness of the contrast.

Finally, the Kim-qualities of observation and mimesis are developed by the Healer of Sick Pearls, but again their value changes in their new context. The Jewel Game is fascinating, and produces a genuine kind of mental power and accuracy: but what the little Hindu produces is nevertheless a quantitative catalogue which empties out all life and beauty. Lurgan never communicates any understanding of the beauty or meaning of the things in his shop. Kim is of course, better on people than on things: but here, too, there is a subtle alteration. What he has to learn is to analyse, not just a man's character, but "his real errand"; not the observation of people for their own sakes, but to catch them out by superior stalkiness in the cynical certainty that each has something to hide. This is not the vision of the Little Friend of All the World. And when Kim finally comes into his own as a chameleon, the praise the Babu gives is for a "most extraordinary and effeecient performance." Lurgan teaches technique. Its object is not human understanding, but secrecy and power. Behind his arts of observation and disguise lies a darker one, hypnosis, whereby a man can "make any one do anything he wants." Lurgan sees human personality as essentially an *instrument*, of power.

The Game-fascination is given its head, then, and the battles of wits, and courage, and resourcefulness, appeal to our imaginations as they appealed to Kipling. Yet whatever he may have intended originally, this world cannot hold or satisfy. The creating of the Lama has decisively altered the vision of the book, and even when he is off-stage we see what is before us more sharply and critically because we have known him. Indeed, our sense of *loss* finds an exact image at those two moments before the ironically named Gates of Learning when Kim leaps from the sahibs' carriage, or over the sahibs' wall, to rejoin for a little the Lama's world of moral law and love, and take him to his heart "in the presence of the proud-stomached city." There is another acid test in one's imaginative memory. Ask oneself who among the mentors of the Game has real stature? The answer, I think, is bound to be Mahbub Ali, and it is because of his movement away from the Pathan who told himself that even if "the boy came to harm, the paper would incriminate nobody," and whose opening words were always "God's curse on all unbelievers." For there grows between Kim and Mahbub a human relationship of love and trust where stalkiness is abjured and news is told for love not money; and where the proud Moslem begins to move towards the Lama's tolerance, to stop himself with an effort from using his instinctive curse on the "other," and to respect through all his jealousy the old man himself, and the quality of Kim's feeling for him. Behind the gift of clothes and pistol is a new language of "father" and "son"; and with Mahbub as with the Lama, Kim is never a sahib, or if so, only in jest.

For Kim, however, the conflict between the two worlds is neither understood nor resolved – indeed, the self-questioning and loss of identity is far more acute as the train takes him once more from one world to the other. At first, being with the Lama again seems to bring about an instantaneous change, Kim begins the healing of the sick child in pretence and pride as well as humanity, but the effect of the Lama's "loving old soul" and simple trust is to shame and transfigure.

> "To heal the sick is to acquire merit; but first one gets knowledge. That was wisely done, O Friend of all the World."
> "I was made wise by thee, Holy One," said Kim, forgetting the little play just ended; forgetting St. Xavier's; forgetting his white blood; forgetting even the Great Game as he stooped, Mohammedan-fashion, to touch his master's feet in the dust of the Jain temple.

Kim may be muddled, but the Moslem gesture to the Buddhist Lama in the Jain temple is significant, and it is no accident that the Lama lodges with the Jains. For they are the most all-embracing of sects, and they sweep the ground before them to avoid killing anything, for they reverence all forms of life. The Lama too, as the Babu had discovered, "is not a dam particular" – he knows that the Excellent One is beyond all religious forms, and at the very first he had told Kim that he worshipped not a God but a Way and a Law. We are back with the loving vision that acknowledges no real distinctions among men, sees them all as travelling to the feet of the One, and deals with them in truth, goodness, humility, and mutual reverence. So when Kim directs the Jat's thanks away from himself to the gods of the Jains, he may seem to repeat the stalkiness of the Friend of the Stars in the village of the unscrupulous priest, but the whole significance is different. As they set off together, all things are unified for the Lama; his Search assured as the inevitable reward of faith and love. "It is sufficient. We are together, and all things are as they were – Friend of All the World – Friend of the Stars – my *chela*!"

Kim is still partly acting, however, and when the Great Game tumbles into the carriage with the Mahratta, the epigraph to the chapter suggests that he may be born to *that* kind of part. Certainly he responds no less instantaneously, and the challenge of action and danger appeals to him in a deep and innate way. Again, it is one thing to be a *chela* in a temple, but another on the road, the River of Life. Through all the serenity of the wanderings around Saharunpore we are always aware of the contrast between Kim's role and his behaviour; aware, too, of the ease with which he is distracted from the Lama's exposition of the Wheel by the fascination of the men and women on it as they bustle past him. Soon he is risking, and receiving, a sharp rebuke for arguing against the Lama's distrust of action on the grounds that he is a sahib, and it is unbefitting a sahib to refrain from action. When there arrives a physician who "heals," not to acquire merit, but to acquire disguise; who thinks straight speaking "so veree disconcerting of the Europeans" (always with the Babu we are reminded of distinctions, racial, social, even "departmental"); and who thinks that the Search can be *combined* with the Great Game – Kim sees no reason to object.

The first two movements involve us in the worlds of the Lama and the Game separately; the third will bring out unmistakably the depth of their essential conflict. It is worth pointing out at once, however, that the conflict is put in *absolute* terms. Calling the Indian Secret Service the Great Game – not, of course, Kipling's invention – is one of those tiresome defensive ironies, which is not in the least intended to diminish its seriousness; and in Kipling's time the threat from Russia to the Indian Frontiers was very real. Yet the more one realises this, the more one is also forced to realise how unpolitical Kipling's treatment is. He makes little attempt to make us take the Russo-British conflict seriously; his "We/They" opposition is the most naïve possible, straight out of any schoolboy spy story, and begs every important question.[13] This is not, however, as simply damning as it seems, for the angle of Kipling's vision is actually such that differentiation would be marginal. The real opposition is between the Lama and *both* sides of the Game. The climax of the novel is set in a natural perspective which dwarfs Us as well as Them,

[13] The Babu's "stalky" denunciation of a system which gives the Indian a white man's education without his prospects certainly raises a burning question, but equally certainly isn't intended to. Kipling's eye is also far from sharply focused on what he is doing when he illustrates the fact that They "do not know how to deal with the native," not only by their blow at the Babu's wrist, but also by their inviting him to eat and drink with them. We get a sudden glimpse of the racialist attitudes the Lama enables Kipling to transcend. Otherwise the struggle is at best a matter of *realpolitik*.

and We are as implicated in the blow which fells the Lama as They who actually strike it.

Questions of perspective are vital as the novel reaches its climactic scene.

> At last they entered a world within a world – a valley of leagues where the high hills were fashioned of the mere rubble and refuse from off the knees of the mountains. Here one day's march carried them no farther, it seemed, than a dreamer's clogged pace bears him in a nightmare. . . .
>
> "Surely the Gods live here!" said Kim, beaten down by the silence and the appalling sweep and dispersal of the cloud-shadows after rain. "This is no place for men!"

Kipling makes the Himalayas serve the same function Forster wanted from his Marabar Caves; they make manifest a vision of the world as inhuman, incredible, unintelligible, utterly dwarfing man. Yet to the Lama it is the mountains that are ultimately illusion. As he instructs Kim in his vision of a deeper reality there is re-enacted "the birth of a religion – the first teacher and the first disciple"; and instead of looking down on tiny dwarfs, we come with the "Russians" and the Babu *up* a steep spur to watch "bareheaded in the wash of the afternoon sunlight low across the gold-coloured grass." It is a moment of deep beauty, if unwashed, and also of great reverence, if unintentional. Yet the strangers respond to it from other perspectives still. The Frenchman sees the beauty and reverence, but only as picturesque – to be sketched rather than questioned. The Russian is the more, not the less, sensitive. What he feels is spiritual authority, but he reacts to the implication of his own inadequacy in pride and passion, seeing the Lama's eyes as "insolent" because he senses what their verdict on him would be, and insisting on making *his* mark, as against the religion of the extinction of self. When the Lama speaks, in Hindi so that all can understand, nobody listens. They are blind to him and his meaning; they can see only a "picture" to sketch, another picture on a "dirty piece of paper" and an "unclean old man" haggling. Kipling now knows, moreover, that blindness, the failure of human imagination, leads to brutality of attitude and behaviour; and that failure to care about and respect human beings results in a world of power and violence. So we get the brutal assault on the old man, and one brutality releasing another: strangling, kicking in the genitals, a head battered against a rock, stoning, shooting, lynching only just averted. The "picture of the birth of a religion" becomes a picture of blind hatred and bloodlust in which even the Lama is momentarily tempted to revenge.

It is the surest sign of the new vision of *Kim* that the creator of Dick Heldar and the publisher should now be able to make us know on our pulses, and understand, how brutal and brutalising the blow at the Lama is. Yet if one's first reaction is at all like Kim's – anger and horror so intense as to demand a violent satisfaction – the Lama has not been seen or understood. His greatest suffering is not caused by the blow, but by the huge effort to rid himself of the violence it taps in him. Even as a response to unquestionable evil, the very existence of violence in the soul is wholly evil and can only beget more evil. The cobra scene has been re-orchestrated in a far more difficult context. Kipling is not dewy-eyed about it: there is an exaggeration in the Lama's remorse that is meant to raise half a smile; and his attitude is saved from the charge of empty idealism only by the emotional and physical cost of attaining it, which nearly amounts to his life. Yet the Lama has real authority now, paid for in effort and suffering; and though we can see why Kim feels his values are "too high," there can be no shrugging them off. Yet if we do take this seriously – as we surely must – then it is not only the "Russians" who stand condemned. There is a clear correspondence between Their attitudes and Ours. Our Players of the Game also convert the Lama's truth into "interesting" theory, and his holiness into the "curious"; they, too, subject human beings to their purposes, and fail in human vision, affection, and respect. The Game *itself* is a Hobbesian war of all on all, which may start as a battle of wits but must end in violence – for its laws are kill or be killed, strike or be struck, take or have taken from you. If They are responsible for the death of E23, We create the pool of blood on the railway line. While the "Russians" are sketching, the Babu is playing the Game with Kim; and we ought to be able to measure what is involved in his delight at the outcome. " 'Thee outrage was accidental, but onlee me could have worked it – ah – for all it was dam'-well worth. Consider the moral effect upon these ignorant peoples!' "

Kim really becomes a *chela* in the agonising escape from the Hills, and begins to deserve the comparison with Ananda, living the role he has acted so long. There is no longer any conflict; he angrily rejects the least reference to his sahib-hood, and, if once he could rid himself of the documents, "the Great Game might play itself for all he then cared." The only realities left are those the game denies – love, and the responsibility of love. The Lama fills his whole horizon. Again, however, there is no sentimentality; what Kipling wishes to bring home to the imagination is the tremendous cost of such dedication. Kim wears himself out to the point of collapse, but he is always chokingly aware of the failure to love and care enough. "I have – I have . . . *Hai mai!* But I love thee . . . and it is all too late . . . I was a child . . . Oh, why was I not a man?" Given the exhaustion and hysteria (and the Lama's gentle affection restores perspective), there yet speaks in this a new maturity, the coming of age of the Little Friend. At the Maharanee's, too, the whole emphasis is on tending others, as the old lady's loving care pulls Kim back to life, and the Lama grows strong again.

In this world the Babu can only be an intrusion; his attitude to the Lama and his notes for the Royal Society a stupidity; his readiness to commit a "dacoity" – the word is deliberately loaded – on the Maharanee's home a matter for Kim's "black disapproval." He remains a great "character," full of imaginative vitality, but there can be no doubt of the disabling criticism that has been directed at the Game through him.[14] Even Mahbub Ali (who has been consorting with the Lama "no end") sees this on their last encounter. The scene is suffused with the Pathan's humorous response to the Lama's unwordly simplicity; but a new affection and respect shine through. Mahbub Ali has entered a different world; and though he will continue the Game and expect Kim to do so too, it could hardly be played in the same way.

We should need very strong evidence, however, to support the

---

[14] The Babu does of course rescue the Lama from drowning – which could be emblematic of the need for protection that justifies Secret Services and Armies. The curious fact remains however that after the Ressaldar passage Kipling never makes such a case in *Kim*.

idea that Kim could return to the Game, against the whole current
of the book's disabling criticism – and there is no such evidence.
We must not mistake the last direction of the novel's imaginative
exploration; for the remaining conflicts of Kim and the Lama
are essentially complementary, and the issue leaves them finally
united. When Kim staggers from his sickroom with the last and
worst loss of his sense of his own identity, it is because as *chela*
he has been involved not only with the old man's loving soul,
but also with his Buddhist ideology. It is because of an essentially inhuman strain that he

> felt, though he could not put it into words, that his soul was
> out of gear with its surroundings . . . the parrots shrieked at
> him, the noises of the populated house behind . . . hit on dead
> ears. "I am Kim. I am Kim. And what is Kim?" His soul
> repeated it again and again. He did not want to cry . . . but of
> a sudden easy, stupid tears trickled down his nose, and with an
> almost audible click he felt the wheels of his being lock up
> anew on the world without. Things that rode meaningless on
> the eyeball an instant before slid into proper proportion. Roads
> were meant to be walked upon, houses to be lived in, cattle to
> be driven, fields to be tilled, and men and women to be talked
> to. They were all real and true – solidly planted upon the feet
> – clay of his clay, neither more nor less.

So his restoration is completed full-length on the earth, drawing
strength from it. As the "gear" imagery makes clear, this is commitment not to the Game, with which we are no longer concerned,
but, at a far more fundamental level, to the Wheel of earthly and
human life, against the view which holds that all these things are
illusion, and one must keep oneself apart from them. Yet this
means no final conflict with the Lama, because in the end the
Lama rejects apartness too. At the moment of achieving the final
extinction of his humanity within the world-soul, he turns back
"with strivings and yearnings and retchings and agonies not to be
told." At the very last moment, love and human relationship are
more important than Nirvana for oneself, and the images Kipling
uses are all creative, active, fructifying. "As the egg from the fish,
as the fish from the water, as the water from the cloud, as the
cloud from the thick air; so put forth, so leaped out, so drew

away, so fumed up the Soul of the Teshoo Lama from the Great
Soul." It is only then that he sees the River which can cleanse
him from a sin still with him; and when one has reached this
point, any old river will do. The "sin" can only be the element of
selfishness in the search for the perfection of self by turning away
from others. It is by giving up self-perfection – "I pushed aside
world upon world for thy sake" – that he finds it. Greater love
hath no man than this, than that he lay down his after-life for his
friend. The eyes that lock home on the Wheel and the eyes that
look down on the Beloved and the River still see on very different
levels, but they share the same kind of human commitment. The
reconciliation can be put in an image, and Kipling's father does
so, with exact sensitivity, in the last and finest of his illustrations
of the book. In the foreground Kim half-reclines on the earth,
but our eyes move past and through him to the Lama who confronts us in the classic attitude of meditation. But the tree that
arches over him is not the Buddha's Bodhi Tree, and the Wheel
of the bullock-cart is between him and it. Behind it again, distanced, but still part of the same world because he has begun to
share its loving vision, is Mahbub Ali. The Lama's head is in
the centre of the Wheel: he defines its hub, it gives him a kind of
halo. Perhaps at this moment we might remember that the
Miracle of the Arrow was performed by a Buddha not "apart,"
indeed, in the act of proving himself strong enough to love.

Once again it must be said that limitations remain. Kipling
took refuge too easily in his theory of daemonic creation when
he told his father that the novel stopped by itself, as a thing complete. For he doesn't finally face up to the problem of what Kim
is to become in the world; the problem of working out the reconciliation of the book's deepest values with involvement in
society – or, indeed, with the protection of society. Oddly for
Kipling, one can see that the Game is given less than justice because there is no powerful enough experience of evil. Kim's eyes
do disinfect the world, and we get the notation of evil without its
stench. The blow of course has deep symbolic significance, and
it does raise the problem of how the world's evil is to be met, but
without more agonised experience of the sort of thing the
Ressaldar has known, the Little Friend and his Lama are not
perhaps sufficiently tested. On a more technical level one also

notices a tendency to abstraction in the final movement. Faced with a man of inaction and inner life like the Lama, Kipling's ability to render value concretely in terms of action cannot fully operate, and he hasn't the ability to convey the experience of inner conflict. Consequently he has to resort to direct exposition on several occasions, so that a quotation can sound like a sermon, and the critic who wishes to discuss it can seem to indulge in straight moral debate. Even at the great final *cruces* one experiences narrative and image rather than inner drama.

Nevertheless *Kim* as a whole is a triumph of exploratory vision. The blindness of *The Light that Failed* is replaced by a far deeper, truer focus. Only in one respect, the attitude to women, does myopia remain, and it is marginal.[15] *Kim* is the answer to nine-tenths of the charges levelled against Kipling and the refutation of most of the generalisations about him. Yet it is not the result of a change in his personality or his thought, and it is by no means permanent. It is the product of a peculiar tension between different ways of seeing: the affectionate fascination with the kaleidoscope of external reality for its own sake; the negative capability getting under the skin of attitudes different from one another and one's own; and finally, a product of this last, but at its most intense and creative, the triumphant achievement of an anti-self so powerful that it became a touchstone for everything else – the creation of the Lama. This involved imagining a point of view and a personality almost at the furthest possible remove from Kipling himself; yet it is explored so lovingly that it could

[15] Lispeth has thematic relevance: she makes manifest the warping effect of failure in love, and tolerance, and truth. Her betrayal at Kotgarh mission – the story appears in *Plain Tales from the Hills* – has embittered her whole life, and the bitterness spurts out in "Thy Gods are lies; thy words are lies; thy words are lies. There are no Gods under all the heavens." Yet she is redeemed by an act of selfless charity.

The trouble is that Kipling insists on grafting onto this another flirtation with exotic sex experience, and then draws back with unpleasantly prissy condescension. He has oddly, because so irrelevantly, touched once or twice on Kim's sexual attractiveness, and several times preached the old doctrine of the nuisance of women. On the one hand, the irrelevance shows how marginal the fault is; on the other, the fact that he is driven to put it all in, in spite of its irrelevance, points to the persistence of the old pressures, and marks by contrast the degree to which he transcended the other elements of *The Light that Failed*.

J. H. Fenwick

SOLDIERS THREE

IN MOST serious criticism of Kipling's work the soldier stories have been either ignored, as of minor importance, or praised superficially for their authenticity and vivid reportage, while their literary worth as closely integrated, fully achieved works of art has gone largely unrecognised.

This is not altogether surprising, for from this point of view the earliest tales in which Mulvaney, Ortheris, and Learoyd figure[1] are almost negligible, and the crudity of their appeal has tended to discredit the later more complex achievements. Yet even in these early stories we can see not only Kipling's mastery of the device of multiple narration, but the beginnings of his progress towards the technical and emotional subtleties of *Soldiers Three*. "The Madness of Private Ortheris," for example, shows significant changes in the narrator's relationship with the three men, and in his attitude to military life in general. From being a writer who buys their stories with drinks and claims them (rather over-insistently) as friends, he has become a humble listener aware of his own ignorance, his lack of experience or real understanding. In spite of the fact that it is the narrator, with his superior education and position, who succeeds in bringing Ortheris to his senses when he wants to desert, it is with Mulvaney that the other finds real communion. The emphasis is on the narrator's position as an outsider – his emotional involvement, but also his feeling of helplessness both as a man of action and a

---

[1] "The Three Musketeers," "The Taking of Lungtungpen," "The Daughter of the Regiment," "The Madness of Private Ortheris," *Plain Tales from the Hills* (1888). The first three of these stories had been published in *The Civil and Military Gazette* in the course of 1887.

moralist, and his awareness of the whole military condition as one involving problems that *cannot* be resolved. This informed and deeply-concerned frustration leads directly into the deeper tones and emotional complexities of the second collection.

There is also an important technical advance, clearer in *Plain Tales* as a whole than in the soldier stories taken by themselves. While engaged in writing these "plain" tales Kipling seems to have become increasingly aware of his own uniquely allusive and heavily textured style, and one result is that the later written stories make much fuller, more deliberate artistic use of the containing social scene. They exploit the fact that this is a collection with a single and coherent setting, so that individual stories gain from the atmosphere created elsewhere. Within the stories, too, one part begins to comment upon and affect the impact of the other. In "The Daughter of the Regiment," for instance, the sadness of the central episode is modified by the gaiety of the frame, so that the total effect is one of slightly comic, yet poignant triumph in the face of conditions of life in India. Such advances are all-important to the more intricate achievements of *Soldiers Three*.

With a smaller and even more coherent society, that of the private soldier, Kipling makes increasing use of the environment he treats. At no point does one find him suggesting that there is an answer to the problems raised by the conflict of this society and the individual. Instead, his acceptance of the military situation as an insoluble pervades the whole collection with sadness and a sense of strain, focused in the personal commitments of the narrator and his three friends, and intensified by the larger insolubles of aging, sickness, and death which form a permanent background to the action. This results in the collection as a whole presenting a more unified appearance than *Plain Tales*, so that the stories may be appreciated singly, yet are never completely detachable from their context. And Kipling's interest in this whole society, this way of life, as well as in his individual characters, is reflected in the very framework of the book – in the pattern created by the arrangement of the stories.[2] "The God from the

---

[2] This arrangement – or rather rearrangement – of the stories is presumably deliberate. The dates of their original publication are as follows: "The God from the Machine" (7 Jan. 1888), "The Big Drunk Draf'" (24

Machine" views military society and sees the corruption at bottom, but it is told from a distance: Mulvaney's involvement is negligible and the story itself slight. "Private Learoyd's Story" is even slighter, though it tells more of the condition of the three and of private soldiers in general. "The Big Drunk Draf'" is a *pièce à thèse*, dealing comprehensively with its subject, and examining military and personal problems with light-hearted clarity. "The Solid Muldoon" returns one to moral problems in a military setting, and though the corruption is less apparent than in "The God from the Machine," the sadness underlying the story is deeper. "With the Main Guard" treats the harshness of conditions in army life with an intensity of concern that is overwhelming. "In the Matter of a Private" takes this same theme and transforms it into a thesis story, weakened only by the rhetorical introduction and conclusion, which are much less effective than a narrative frame would have been. The growing violences, hatreds and harshnesses, the underlying sadness of the whole collection, find their finest expression in the last story, "Black Jack." And one's final impression is that through this sequence of stories Kipling has approached the military condition first lightly, then with pity and horror, and that the examination has been complete, scrupulous, and intense.

This examination is carried out with great tact – owing to the relationship between the narrator and the three – and with great narrative skill in the handling of the three themselves as spokesmen. At the end of *Plain Tales*, as has been said, the narrator was seen in a new and humble position, and this is developed throughout *Soldiers Three*. His social standing is peculiar. He is involved with the private soldiers, but is not one with them. Nor is he a full member of the ruling class, a representative of Authority. There is present always a strongly-felt class difference, and the narrator is forced to hide his intimacy with the three from the officers with whom he associates, but there is no evidence that he has an intimacy of any sort with that stronger class. His position

Mar. 1888), "In the Matter of a Private" (14 Apr. 1888), "The Solid Muldoon" (9 Jun. 1888), "Private Learoyd's Story" (14 Jul. 1888), "With the Main Guard" (4 Aug. 1888). All were printed in *The Week's News*, the magazine supplement to the Allahabad *Pioneer*. "Black Jack" was published for the first time in the collection (1888).

as a journalist seems to put him in the state of being able to communicate with all classes, without being wholly accepted by any of them. He is committed to the group as individuals, as a gang, and as a society representing the larger one containing it. He comprehends their difficulties and their code. Yet his understanding does not give him any rights. This awareness of the barrier between himself and them gives dignity and delicacy to the whole situation. The relationship with Mulvaney is the crucial example of this. There is a fine balancing of strengths between them. Mulvaney always perceives and accepts any subterfuge the narrator attempts: "You know you can do anythin' wid me whin I'm talkin'!" he exclaims in "Black Jack." The narrator also recognises Mulvaney's superior strength, experience, and wisdom, and regards the stories told to him as of extreme value. But circumstances, and occasionally education or insight, place the narrator in the superior position. It is a difficult and tactful relationship of mutual respect. Though the outsider position sometimes leads Kipling into sentimental idealisation – of Mulvaney, for example, as a "grizzled, tender, and very wise Ulysses"[3] – it usually has a beneficent effect by enforcing an emotional and moral restraint. He is inhibited from any comment, even on tales of fraud, dog-stealing, and seduction; and instead of his speaking (as he often does elsewhere) as a representative of Authority, we find him accepting, humorously and compassionately, the imperfectibility of man; while those stories which do have a basic moral theme gain in tact and power from the difficulty the narrator finds in making any overt moral statement at all.

In the stories in *Plain Tales* Kipling had shown immediate technical mastery of the device of divided narration, and this is further developed in *Soldiers Three*. Mulvaney quickly takes on the position of narrator-in-chief – partly because he is given the most complex character and range of experience, partly because his voice is more adaptable to the demands of narrative. Ortheris's essential quality is anti-sentimentality: he acts as a corrective to the romanticism which Mulvaney often brings, and the harsh quality of his voice makes him useful as an interrupter.[4] Learoyd

[3] "Private Learoyd's Story."
[4] It is less suitable for sustained narrative or commentary. When a long

is a static figure, bringing to this study of the soldier dignity and a shrewd simplicity, but in this collection he is largely silent. His character demands this, and his voice rhythms are in any case too slow for easy intermingling. Mulvaney, however, is at the centre of interest throughout, and the romantic-sensational elements in his character are counteracted by a more acute moral awareness, where he is concerned, on the narrator's part. This comes from the fact that he skates more dangerously on the border of immorality than do Ortheris or Learoyd. Moreover, he is the clearest example of the strain between individual and society. There is a highly strung tension between his social and anti-social tendencies. He treads a narrow path between preservation of others and destruction of himself, for those strengths which stem from his virility and make him a leader and support to others, also lead him into drunkenness, to the verge of adultery and mutiny.[5] He is thus the ideal figure to express the curious balance the collection preserves between individual and general interest, between the personal and the sociological.

As a group the three men have a similar function. They form a sort of miniature society within the larger one. All three, taken together, may be said to represent the lower reaches of military life, and their national variety and assortment of characteristics reinforce this impression. Yet by their independence as a group, and by its anarchic, recalcitrant individuality, they form a sort of free-wheeling irritant which explores the bounds of its restraining discipline. Each individual adds something to the group's essential stability, correcting those faults in the others which might tend to weaken the group or the military ethic, yet each has his own vice or vices, which bring him into conflict with this ethic; and the precarious balance thus achieved is immensely fruit-ful in the sort of exploration which Kipling's own ambiguous atti-tude leads him to carry out. While serving to reveal their society in this way, the three also facilitate a wide range of reference, bind-ing story to story, leading outside the collection to a background of suppressed material, and causing one narrative detail to com-

speech is essential, in "The Madness of Private Ortheris," his mode of utterance changes and he speaks (we are told) in an unusual, slow, "cadenced" voice.

[5] See "The Solid Muldoon" and "Black Jack."

ment on another. This depth of background is reflected in the structuring of the stories, one set of facts being placed against another so as to bring out the interrelation of different circumstances and problems.

"Black Jack" is the clearest example of the way in which Kipling can, by interweaving two tales or incidents, call on all the resources of this society which he has recreated. It is also the best example of the complex unity, both moral and aesthetic, that he can achieve by this sort of equipoise – by the elaborate structure of cross-references, parallels and contrasts between the frame and the central narrative.

Three main strands run through this work. The first is the problem of revenge. The second is the loneliness of moral action. The third is the poignancy of the effects of time. The last two themes give emotional depth to the work, but both act through the first theme and are expressed within it.

This first theme, the problem of revenge, is what drives the story on, the narrative pivot, but it is not presented as primarily a moral problem at all. It is felt as an emotional one, and the moral aspect is ignored. Action is judged by result alone, and so what the story does is to explore the actions performed from the desire for revenge in terms of their consequences. In the frame, Ortheris, Learoyd, and the narrator are all concerned with the basic problem which besets Mulvaney. He has an emotional need to be revenged on Mullins, the young sergeant who has wronged and humiliated him, and yet logic and necessity, as all recognise, dictate that he should not seek vengeance at all. All advise resignation, but resignation is not at that point felt to be an emotionally satisfactory solution. The *motif* recurs in the central narrative, where Vulmea seeks revenge on O'Hara, and Mulvaney rejects his mode of action: Mulvaney is left alone and in danger, with the problem "Fwhat will I do?" And later O'Hara muses on the same problem: how shall he revenge himself on those who attempted to murder him? " '*Now* fwhat will I do?' sez O'Hara." The driving force which urges the reader on from frame to story and out again is thus not simply what will happen next, but how will Mulvaney behave? There is no lack of narrative excitement, but it is not the excitement which comes from one event hurrying directly into another. Instead each event is scrupulously examined: the narrative is almost leisurely, and the detail holds the story almost static without destroying its excitement. This sort of slow, carefully-examined narrative, unusual in a short story, is to become one of Kipling's greatest strengths, and at this point in his development gains enormously from the social interest the whole collection has aroused.

The urge to find a solution to the need for emotional satisfaction is felt by the reader as much as by Mulvaney himself, and this is due to a great extent to the unusual relationship "Black Jack" has with the rest of the collection. It is the last story in the anthology, and the last written.[6] Its frame both comments upon the story it contains, and links the whole work strongly with the rest of the book, giving to *Soldiers Three* what seems to be a deliberate conclusion. Many *motifs* from earlier works – the mental agony of "The Madness of Private Ortheris," the money-scraping of "Private Learoyd's Story," the adultery of "The Solid Muldoon," are here represented. Moreover, the beginning and ending bring the three as a group firmly into the forefront of the attention, and they are seen finally from a distance, merging into the social framework of which the colonel's barouche reminds one. This conclusion, while thus putting them at a distance, none the less celebrates the group's continuing existence and vitality. But as well as giving a fitting ending to the collection "Black Jack" gains a great deal from the preceding stories. There is a sense of shock, even outrage, in the discovery of Mulvaney's humiliation, for the other tales have made it clear that Mulvaney is vulnerable, but they have also made clear his great strengths and his stature as a good man and a leader. This is the first time that the society's potential for harm has been fulfilled. The stability known from the other stories is rocked, and Mulvaney is seen humiliated and morally naked. So recognising the depths of the humiliation, the reader also appreciates the need for compensation.

In addition, with the evidence of the other tales already given, the reader knows that Mulvaney's character prohibits him from taking the revenge his instincts demand, and we are thus involved in his frustration and his search for some other compensating action, a search which only his reminiscences can satisfy. In the

[6] At least this seems the logical conclusion from the fact that it is the only one of the tales not previously published.

central story is given a picture of a younger Mulvaney who cannot be so humiliated, and to whom no insoluble emotional problem is set. It is a response to the need of the frame.

It is strange that in a story which is to some extent a celebration of the group of three, one of the predominating effects should be of loneliness, but in fact this is intensified by the group action of the opening. The outsider *motif* has never been stronger. The narrator is left outside the group of three as Ortheris and Learoyd attempt to bring Mulvaney back to normality. Mulvaney does not at first recognise him, and Mulvaney himself needs to be "walked off," and brought out of his angry isolation:

> " 'E ain't fit to be spoke to those times – nor 'e ain't fit to leave alone neither."

Within the story, too, Mulvaney is both emotionally and morally isolated. He is at war with the rest of his barrack-room, and his closest friend is only "by way av bein' a frind av mine." These isolations are clear to see. What really makes the loneliness felt and all pervasive through the narrative is the way in which comparisons are continually made between different men's courses of action. This is found within the frame, within the central narrative, and in continual correspondences between the two. These comparisons are not only, or even primarily, moral comparisons. They are rather examples of the gulf which separates one man from the next. Ortheris and Learoyd have differing attitudes to the ethics of money-finding. The differences between Mulvaney and Vulmea, Mulvaney and O'Hara are stressed, and while these are indeed moral differences they seem in a sense inevitable. Each meaningful action is taken alone – by Mulvaney, Vulmea, and O'Hara. They are all isolated figures, and yet they seem to have little real moral choice. They are trapped in their own characters, as O'Hara unwittingly points out when Mulvaney attempts some sort of moral advice and communion:

> "Do you go your way, Privit Mulvaney, an' I will go mine."

This sense of the inevitability of moral choice is probably what accounts for the way in which revenge is never inspected as a moral idea. One feels which courses of action are preferable;

there is a definite understanding of the futility of vengeance; but these come from the emotional effects of every action, not from their abstract moral value. There is only one achieved revenge in the whole work, set apart in time from both frame and centre. The whole central narrative is played against the knowledge of it:

"Rafferty shot him [O'Hara] for fooling with his wife."

There is something automatic about this circle of action: cause has given rise to predictable effect. But there is no feeling that that was a satisfactory course of action for Rafferty. (One might compare the futility of the revenge shooting in the frame of "Love o' Women.") Simply, three people have been destroyed. It is by denying effect to cause, as Mulvaney and O'Hara do, that some sort of meaningful action is created. What triumph is possible lies there, in such inaction as theirs.

Yet there was no triumph in Mulvaney's inaction in the introduction, and it is here that the story gains its wry poignancy. The effects of time are double-edged, and one of the most important comparisons in the work is the comparison between the older Mulvaney and the young one. There is a curious *impasse* in the tale as a whole, expressed through this comparison and the circle of other comparisons surrounding it. The story began with a search for emotional satisfaction, which Mulvaney found in the picture of his action in youth. Yet the balance between the two figures, the old and the young, is carefully equal, even slightly in favour of the older man. The young Mulvaney is brash and arrogant, and his placidity under the attack of O'Hara comes from the security he draws from his own pride and as yet unfrustrated ambition:

"I wud not mind duckin' him in the Artillery troughs if ut was not that I'm thryin' for my shtripes."

Self-disillusion has brought greater wisdom to the older man:

"I had not learned to hould my liquor wid comfort in thim days. 'Tis little betther I am now."

Yet this young man, inferior in wisdom and further from the reader in sympathy, has been proved superior in action to his wiser older self:

" 'Twas for less than that the Tyrone wud ha' sent O'Hara to hell, instid av lettin' him go by his own choosin', whin Rafferty shot him," retorted Mulvaney.

"And who stopped the Tyrone from doing it?" I asked.

"That ould fool who's sorry he didn't stick the pig Mullins."

This loss is stressed by other comparisons within the work. Mulvaney, young, is carefully shown to be a better man than O'Hara, though sharing some of his vices. But O'Hara is also shown to be a better man than Mullins, not only in his virtues, but even in his vices themselves – for the two, like Mulvaney's, seem inseparable. Yet the despicable Mullins has defeated the older Mulvaney, where the respectworthy O'Hara could not defeat the younger one. Time has brought a loss as great as any gain, and the only real satisfaction is that defeat is not completely a defeat when met with the dignity the three bring to it. They return to barrack life without regret at the end.

This narrative of isolated moral action, set in a framework of decay, contains a great many references to damnation, which add to the sense of fear and tension throughout the story. Each man goes his own way inexorably, and yet each man is doomed to a judgment:

"An', in the ind, as I said, O'Hara met his death from Rafferty for foolin' wid his wife. He wint his own way too well – Eyah, too well! Shtraight to that affair, widout turnin' to the right or to the lef', he wint, an' may the Lord have mercy on his soul."

This echoes Ortheris's warning to Mulvaney before the central narrative began, and in doing so ties O'Hara and Mulvaney even closer together. There is a sense of moral jeopardy, in spite of the story's lack of moral statement. Mulvaney has not escaped defeat, as O'Hara has done, but he has escaped moral collapse. The emotional effect of the ending is ambiguous – optimistic, but also singularly wry.

"Black Jack" is the last story where there is a real and successful balance between the problems of the individual and that of military society as a whole. After Kipling leaves India the soldiers continue to appear,[7] but one can mark the way in which the old

[7] "The Incarnation of Krishna Mulvaney" (Dec. 1889), "The Courting of

frame formula is becoming anachronistic, often effective in itself, but seldom serving an exploratory or analytic purpose. Kipling is once again looking for a satisfactory approach to his medium, and in this period of transition complete success has the air of being a fluke.

In both failures and successes, however, one can see two major changes deeply affecting the soldier stories. The first relates to Kipling's attitude to group phenomena, and to military society in particular. His love of expertise, the Science which the group can impart, swells in importance and becomes dangerous. For instance, although the introduction to "The Courting of Dinah Shadd" is really well suited to the mood of the central tale, it is so closely detailed and lacking in relevant action that the whole piece seems ill-balanced: unless one shares Kipling's interest in the details of a military exercise one cannot be wholly satisfied with the story's effect.

There is also a loss of tact, the disastrous effect of which can be seen in "His Private Honour." Within the rules of the code by which this story lives, the narrator, as a civilian, is unbearably presumptuous in his outspokenness, and overweening even in drawing attention to his feelings on a matter which should not concern him: the narrator's basic limitations have been forgotten. There is also in some of these stories an increasing tendency to rhetorical persuasion, such as had figured in "In the Matter of a Private." The rhetoric is sometimes crude, sometimes effective, but its very existence shows that Kipling's aim is no longer strictly fictional – that it verges at times on the propagandist.

These changes in the treatment of the group show that Kipling's attitude has become too idiosyncratic for the three to be suitable mouthpieces any longer. Just as disruptive in effect is the increasing complexity of the material with which Kipling is dealing. The old frameworks cannot completely hold it, and Mulvaney cannot do it justice. The three, in spite of the subtlety with which they are used, are scarcely designed for great character-develop-

Dinah Shadd" (Mar. 1890), "On Greenhow Hill" (Sep. 1890), *Life's Handicap*, 1891; "My Lord the Elephant" (Dec. 1892), "His Private Honour" (Oct. 1891), "Love o' Women," *Many Inventions*, 1893; "Garm – A Hostage" (Dec. 1899), *Actions and Reactions*, 1909. The dates given in brackets are those of the stories' first publication.

ment. They are figures who first of all elicit a stock response, and for Kipling's original purposes these are all that is required. "The Courting of Dinah Shadd" takes the revelation of Mulvaney's character as far as it will go, though its bitter ambiguities are not fully explored, whereas "Love o' Women" fails in its centre because both Mulvaney and Kipling are unequal to it. There are notorious faults of detail in this story, but the basic trouble is that Kipling does not fully recognise the complexity of what he is handling. Larry Tighe is scarcely drawn at all. Kipling relies on the kinship-difference link with Mulvaney which was so successful in "Black Jack," but the tale is too involved for this comparatively simple technique. Instead of pursuing the difficulties of neurosis which his frame and subject suggest, Kipling oversimplifies and melodramatises. A comparison with the later and more successful "Mrs Bathurst" illuminates this failure clearly. The plotlines of the two stories are similar, and the subject (passion) is the same. "Mrs Bathurst" suppresses more, but hints at more,[8] and is frightening and convincing. In the early story Kipling tries to tie down his subject by use of a complex frame, and by a link with the undestructive passion of Mulvaney and Dinah, which is of the same degree. But the contrast only highlights the complex and unacceptable melodrama of the one in opposition to the simple and credible melodrama of a more fluently and naturally melodramatic figure.

The most successful of all the later soldier tales is indubitably "On Greenhow Hill." In many ways it is unique in the series, and attempts new objects. Nevertheless, one can see it as a natural extension of the *Soldiers Three* frame, a completely happy development which in some ways highlights the limitations which Kipling has left behind, and explains why "The Courting of Dinah Shadd" and "Love o' Women" are disappointing. The stories in *Soldiers Three* were equations of a human and a social condition, one finding its expression through the other. In spite of their technical expertise, those two later stories make it clear that this is no longer so. The frame no longer comments with any intensity, and the central stories break out on their own.

___

[8] Kipling seems to attempt a similar submerged narrative in "Love o' Women," but when Mulvaney says "I've tould ut as I came acrost ut – here an' there in little pieces," one doesn't feel that much has been omitted.

This division is caused by the Indian context becoming too cramped for Kipling's central themes. Even in the last of the Railway Library series this was apparent: in "The Man who would be King," which is strictly an Indian plot, the application of the story demands a wider frame of reference, which Kipling supplies by a brilliant use of the newspaper office and European news as a containing context. In "On Greenhow Hill" the approach is reversed. The story is an English one, the application extended by the Indian frame, used with extraordinary economy. It is a beautifully complex structure, with a subtle and poetic effect equal to anything Kipling ever wrote.

It follows the pattern of "The Courting of Dinah Shadd" and "Love o' Women" in that the central story is more than usually capable of standing alone. (In *Soldiers Three* it was only the lighter stories of which this might truly be said.) It differs from them in the fact that Kipling seems to have recognised the shift in weight and cut down the detail of his frame accordingly. Most strikingly, it differs from them and from the majority of the soldier stories in having Learoyd as narrator.

This last difference alters the whole tone of the central narrative, as may be seen in a comparison of scenes in "The Courting of Dinah Shadd" and "On Greenhow Hill."

"I ran out into the dhark, my head in a stew an' my heart sick, but I had sinse enough to see that I'd brought ut all on mesilf. 'It's this to pass the time av day to a panjandhrum av hell-cats,' sez I. 'What I've said, an' what I've not said do not matther. Judy an' her dam will hould me for a promust man, an' Dinah will give me the go, an' I desarve ut. I will go an' get dhrunk,' sez I, 'an' forget about ut, for 'tis plain I'm not a marrin' man.' "

"Six candles we had, and we crawled and climbed all that day while they lasted, and I said to mysen', ''Liza Roantree hasn't six months to live.' And when we came into th' daylight again we were like dead men to look at, an' Blast come behind us without so much as waggin' his tail. When I saw 'Liza again she looked at me a minute and says, 'Who's telled tha? For I see tha knows.' And she tried to smile as she kissed me, and I fair broke down."

KMA R

These two extracts reveal that in selection of words or detail there is little difference in the voices. The second (Learoyd) passage is the more highly written, with the detail of the candles, and the way in which their number echoes the number of months left to 'Liza. The crawling and climbing seem like an enactment of the slow dying to come. But this is the rhetorical peak of Learoyd's voice, and effective because each flat detail adds to the hopelessness and despair required. The rhythm is what gives Kipling's approximation to dialect speech, and conveys the overall tone of the tale. Flat, with a falling cadence, and heavy ends to the sentences, this voice gives the narrative an air of understated emotion, of dryness and brusqueness, and this tone, together with a brilliant use of evocative and moving detail, gives the story much of its intensity. Mulvaney's voice, on the other hand, is a much lighter one. The colloquial understatements are still there, but his Irish rhythms run naturally into rhetorical patterns. It is indeed a more naturally dramatic, fluent, and flexible voice, but in the context of "On Greenhow Hill" Learoyd's, with its capacity for stark simplicity, is a more moving instrument.

The story Learoyd tells is a fairly commonplace one of an unhappy love affair, but it is told with superb economy, and the understatement implied in the rhythm of the voice is echoed in the approach to the narrative itself. The story is one of isolation rather than of passion, and the love is conveyed through details relevant to this theme. Immediately Learoyd begins to speak, accent and physical detail convey a full sense of the particular society in which the tale is set, and as the narrative continues the complications of chapel people as a group become clear. Learoyd's semi-acceptance by them is fully felt through the single detail of the fiddle which Jesse Roantree makes him promise to learn, as an *entrée* into the musical circle of chapel-goers. Learoyd's essential unfitness for the group is seen in his inability to keep that promise, and in his retention of his dog, Blast. The dog, here, as his name suggests, represents the unregenerate side of humanity and of Learoyd in particular.[9] His inclusion as a chapel-member – "So th' pair on us became reg'lar chapel-members" – is no more incongruous than Learoyd's own. His isolation from them is

[9] Cp. "Rip" in "Private Learoyd's Story."

emphasised by the digression on their attitude to the Army, and by his own summary of the situation:

"Yo' see, I was not o' much account wi' 'em all exceptin' to 'Liza Roantree. . . ."

The emotional temperature of the story is raised not only by Learoyd's relationship with 'Liza herself, but by his strange love-hate relationship with the preacher, his rival, which conveys a peculiar sort of masculine delicacy very much in keeping with Learoyd's character. The central episode of the narrative is the scene in the mines where this relationship is seen at its clearest. The preacher is all that Learoyd cannot be, and yet they are part-ners rather than opposites, equal as men and as independent individuals, both outside the chapel society. But the preacher is completely independent, and Learoyd is dependent on 'Liza (as in a different way Mulvaney is dependent on Dinah Shadd). The scene in the mines is brilliantly written, showing Learoyd strip-ped of civilisation and left face to face with his passion:

"The talk was 'at they were to be wed when she got better, an' I couldn't get her to say yes or nay to it. He began to sing a hymn in his thin voice, and I came out wi' a chorus that was all cussin' an' swearin' at my horses, an' I began to know how I hated him."

In spite of its violence and intensity, this episode does not over-balance the story or move the centre of narrative interest. The physical climax – Learoyd's attempt on the preacher's life – is passed over lightly, and the final emotional impact reserved for the effect on Learoyd of the news of 'Liza's decline, and the purga-tion of feeling achieved when the two enact 'Liza's dying for themselves in their exploration of the caverns.

The major part of the tale is over with 'Liza's departure for Bradford, and Learoyd's final isolation:

"And I were left alone on Greenhow Hill."

He is rejected by the chapel-goers, and on following 'Liza and her father to Bradford he is rejected again by Jesse in words which are both amusing and touching, holding as they do the understatement and concrete suggestion in which the whole narrative is rich:

> " 'Is it thee?' he says; 'but you're not to see her. I'll none have her wakened for a nowt like thee. She's goin' fast, and she mun go in peace. Thou'lt never be good for naught i' th' world, and as long as thou lives thou'll never play the big fiddle. Get away, lad, get away!' "

Learoyd accepts this rejection himself by joining the army – the ultimate degradation in the eyes of chapel folk. But the warmth of love is shown in the way 'Liza transcends this barrier as she transcended the less obvious ones earlier, and accentuates this warmth with the warmth of belonging:

> " 'Nay, father, yo' mayn't say th' devil's colours. Them ribbons is pretty.' An' she held out her hands for th' hat, an' she put all straight as a woman will wi' ribbons. 'Nay, but what they're pretty,' she says. 'Eh, but I'd ha' liked to see thee i' thy red coat, John, for thou was allus my own lad – my very own lad, and none else.'
>
> She lifted up her arms, and they come round my neck i' a gentle grip, and they slacked away, and she seemed fainting. 'Now yo' mun get away, lad,' says Jesse, and I picked up my hat and I came downstairs.
>
> Th' recruiting sergeant were waitin' for me at th' corner public-house. 'Yo've seen your sweetheart?' says he. 'Yes, I've seen her,' says I. 'Well, we'll have a quart now, and you'll do your best to forget her,' says he, bein' one o' them smart bustlin' chaps. 'Ay, sergeant,' says I. 'Forget her.' And I've been forgettin' her ever since."

This story, it is clear, could stand on its own. Yet the frame itself adds immensely to the total effect, and shows how Kipling has increased his scope. Every piece of the story works in some way upon another part, and this gives an intensity and an excitement to the whole which is rare in any writer. Though the story is Learoyd's, all three are deeply involved because of their place in the frame narrative. This begins with the details of a native deserter who disturbs the peace of the camp. The violence and sense of loyalties in collision are quickly conveyed. Ortheris lusts for his blood, and he and Mulvaney go out the next day to lay an ambush. Learoyd joins them later, in a slightly disturbed state, since he has been narrowly missed by a trigger-happy fellow rifleman. This shock, and the landscape already described with a touch of lyricism, move him to think of the Yorkshire landscape of his youth, and make him willing to talk. At this point lyricism and violence sit disturbingly and effectively side by side:

> They were talking in whispers, for the stillness of the wood and the desire of slaughter lay heavy upon them.

Thus the *motifs* of the group and group loyalties are introduced, while the fact of death (the purpose of the ambush) underlines the basic isolation of each man.

Learoyd equates their potential victim with themselves by suggesting that his motive for deserting may have been the same as most men's motive for enlisting: "Happen there was a lass tewed up wi' it. Men do more than more for th' sake of a lass." To pass the time Mulvaney persuades him to talk, and Learoyd echoes the lyric description of the Indian hills in his own of the Yorkshire hills where he used to live. The only colour so far used in description has been the white of the violets growing by where they lie in wait. Now the description takes on full colour – Greenhow Hill has grey houses, a white road, the people red cheeks and noses, blue eyes. The transition is easy and fluent, and the story seems to grow from the landscape, with the violets forming a recurrent *motif* throughout the telling of the tale. These violets, which Learoyd plucks as he speaks, remind one of the landscape of the frame, but also by their colour and associations they recall the lyric innocence at the heart of the love story – an innocence otherwise unstressed. They have been introduced, in strange contrast to the situation, before Learoyd himself appeared.[10]

> He [Ortheris] buried his nose in a clump of scentless white violets. No one had come to tell the flowers that the season of their strength was long past, and they had bloomed merrily in the twilight of the pines.

[10] Hence the pathetic fallacy in the following quotation does not obtrude itself, and it is only in retrospect that we perceive the implied comparison between the violets and 'Liza Roantree.

"This is something like," he said luxuriously. "Wot a 'evinly clear drop for a bullet acrost. How much d' you make it, Mulvaney?"

The flowers are first grasped by Learoyd when he makes contrast between his youth and his present state – a gesture at once dramatic and evocative. They emphasise the violence of the moment in the mines when Learoyd decides to kill the preacher, mingling the two feelings of destruction and goodness in a way which fits the central theme exactly and passionately. His theoretical rejection of memory is marked by his throwing them away, at the end of his story: " 'And I've been forgettin' her ever since.' He threw away the wilted clump of white violets as he spoke." This last also effects the transition into an ending where the frame narrative and an interruption of a kind that has recurred throughout the tale exert their potential suddenly and violently.

This kind of interruption is provided by the dialogue of Mulvaney and Ortheris. Both heckled as Learoyd began his tale, but as the story progresses, Mulvaney and Learoyd are linked firmly together, leaving Ortheris as an outsider. Mulvaney shows sympathy in talking of the folly of youth, and in speaking of being nursed by a woman. Ortheris sneers at the first, and is left isolated through lack of experience of the second. Also, Ortheris is incapable of appreciating Learoyd's religious impulse, and therefore the move to idealism which the story shows. In spite of his later wish to be kind, he is not able to understand in the way Mulvaney does:

"And he would put his poor old claw on my shoulder, sayin' 'Doesn't tha feel it, tha great lump? Doesn't tha feel it?' An' sometimes I thought I did, and then again I thought I didn't, an' how was that?"

"The iverlastin' nature av mankind," said Mulvaney.

The resulting religious discussion bores Ortheris:

"Wot's the use o' worrittin' 'bout these things? . . . 'Ere's my chaplain," he said, and made the venomous black-headed bullet bow like a marionette. " 'E's goin' to teach a man all about which is which, an' wot's true, after all, before sundown."

So, when Learoyd throws away the violets, Ortheris is distracted from his emotion by the task in hand. He sees what he has been waiting for all along, and what the others have apparently forgotten, the approach of the native deserter. With Ortheris's shot, the violence and beauty and sadness of the tale all combine, as with a vivid and reminiscent flash of colour the deserter dies:

> A speck of white crawled up the water course. "See that beggar? . . . Got 'im." Seven hundred yards away, and a full two hundred down the hillside, the deserter of the Aurangabadis pitched forward, rolled down a red rock, and lay very still, with his face in a clump of blue gentians, while a big raven flapped out of the pine wood to make investigation.

The description hastens the transfer from Yorkshire to India in the mind, but in its echo of the original colour range reminds one at the same time of the beginning of Learoyd's tale, so that the stories of the two deaths are indissolubly welded together.

Each soldier responds in his own fashion. Mulvaney appreciates the shot as a necessary job of work: " 'That's a clean shot, little man.' " Learoyd, still involved in his own memories, identifies himself with the dead man: " 'Happen there was a lass tewed up wi' him, too,' said he." But they are not implicated in the shooting. They have both transcended their personal isolations in their appreciation of someone else's life. Ortheris, who has finished what they set out to do, and is cut off from their experience, is the one who in his heartlessness best expresses the feeling of calm bewilderment and detached sadness in the tale.

> Ortheris did not reply. He was staring across the valley, with the smile of the artist who looks on the completed work.[11]

[11] [One might ask whether this conclusion does not involve a more radical "placing" of military exploits than is usual in Kipling. Ortheris, the "bloodthirsty little mosquito," seems to epitomise the *murderous* impulses involved in soldiering, and our sympathies are progressively detached from him. There is the closest connexion between his failure to sympathise with Learoyd's tale and his readiness to kill at its conclusion. Kipling's equation of the two deaths breaks down our habitual depersonalising of "the enemy": it enables Learoyd to see the deserter as a man like himself, and to feel for him. Mulvaney shares this perception, while retaining a sense of present military realities, and his comment shows a neat balancing of professionalism with humanity. He admires the "clean shot" as a necessary job well done, but the

Kipling has here overcome the fact that his Indian military frame has become more limited than his ambition. He has transformed it so that the tale has an unusually wide application, moving through three societies (native, military, chapel) to a point beyond social function. He will not be able to repeat the success for some time. The difficulties of a society which to him seems amorphous (since he cannot readily accept simple class distinctions) are not surmounted, except in isolated cases, until his art has become infinitely more complex. Yet his later stories lack that simplicity which India and his soldiers three supply, and they therefore lack also some of the appeal of these first achievements of his developing genius.

phrase "little man" carries more than its customary weight here: instead of referring only to Ortheris' diminutive stature, it suggests also his smallness as a human being. The work of art *he* contemplates with such satisfaction is one of simple destruction; the creative work Kipling has just completed is one of profound sympathy and insight: and the greatness of the one defines perfectly the inadequacy of the other. ED.]

it is surely unwise to interpret his art by evidence much of which must be fragmentary and conjectural, and which is anyway mostly available only in the artistic treatment Kipling gave to it. External reference can be misleading, even where the basis of the fiction is certainly autobiographical, since it may make us overlook interpretations of the story in question which do not happen to fit in with the imaginary biography we have in mind.

A case in point is the early story "Baa, Baa, Black Sheep," which has been so much quarried by biographical critics. Now certainly the young Rudyard Kipling *had* sojourned in the House of Desolation; he *was* Black Sheep. But what psychological critics tend to overlook is that someone so warped and morally incapacitated by his childhood traumas as Kipling is said to have been could never have written the story. For our very natural pity and indignation at the treatment of Punch – who could feel anything else? – must not allow us to ignore the element of *diagnosis* which is so important in the tale. Punch came from India an attractive little boy, but already with the potentiality of arrogance towards lesser breeds, and his reaction when treated as a pariah and thrust among them is to despise them more and identify them, in self-defence, with his persecutors. Now it is true that the author feels "sympathy and understanding" for the victim, but we must emphasise "understanding"; he knows more than the boy does about what has happened; the return of the beloved mother seems to make everything "all right" for the boy, but we know, and Kipling knows, that it does not and cannot make everything "all right." The story might be compared with Sartre's "Enfance d'un chef." Kipling has imaginatively created the genesis of the state of mind which leads to fascism; he has done it from within, but we feel the constant co-presence of a mind more adult than Black Sheep's; sentimentality is not absent from Kipling's work, but it does not appear in this story. Critics have used the story to "explain" the alleged cruelty of Kipling and his tendency, springing from fear, to take the side of the bully. It would be just as easy to use it to account for Kipling's horror of religious bigotry, which appears everywhere in his work. We recall the wretched Mulcahy's terror of death in "The Mutiny of the Mavericks" (*Life's Handicap*): "He remembered certain things that priests had said in his infancy, and his mother . . . starting from

KIPLING'S LATER STORIES 257

her sleep with shrieks to pray for a husband's soul in torment."
The narrator in the futuristic fantasy "With the Night Mail"
(*Actions and Reactions*) speaks compassionately of "the men of the
old days, each one of them taught (*that* is the horror of it!) that
after death he would very possibly go for ever to unspeakable
torment." Religious tolerance is the lesson of Kabir in "The
Prayer" (from *Kim*): "His God is as his Fates assign, | His prayer is
all the world's – and mine." And young readers may have got
from *Kim* their first understanding of the simple fact that people
in other lands can believe just as sincerely in their very different
religions as Christians do in theirs. It cannot be denied that Kipling's work illustrates his interest in cruelty, and this preoccupation may well have been due to his early sufferings; but what the
literary results seem to show is, not that it made him cruel, but
that it gave him a deeper insight into cruelty, and strengthened
his conviction of the need for compassion.

A slighter instance of the dangers of the biographical approach
is the use of the Balestier episode in Vermont to explain the anti-
American phase of Kipling's writings. The most pungent of
these stories is "An Error in the Fourth Dimension." But this
story was first published in 1894, before the Balestier episode;
and the only safe inference is that this episode may have confirmed
Kipling's already existing distrust of American lawlessness. Indeed, if the author in question had been someone other than
Kipling, critics might have credited him with an intention not so
much motivated by topical or personal considerations, but the
typical *artist's* intention to show "the other side" of a theme
which interested him, the American hustle and irreverence for
stagnant traditions which he makes so attractive in *Captains
Courageous*. Again, in the later story "As Easy as ABC"[1] (1912),
another futuristic fantasy about the Aerial Board of Control, it
is easy to point out, as critics have done, that the Utopia of the
story reflects Kipling's hatred of democracy because it encourages
crowds and "invades privacy." What they frequently fail to
notice is that the story is a *tour de force* of sustained irony, in which
the narrator, a typical product of this Wellsian future in which
"Transport is Civilisation," unwittingly reveals the spiritual
emptiness of a world which has banished struggle and suffering

[1] *A Diversity of Creatures.*

from life. The Archangel of the English, in the very late story "Uncovenanted Mercies"[2] (1932), says of his people: "I am giving them each full advantages for self-expression and realisation. These will include impeccable surroundings, wealth, culture, health, felicity (unhappy people can't make other people happy, can they?) and – everything commensurate with the greatness of the destiny for which I – er – destine them." But it is plain that neither the Archangel's immediate audience, nor Kipling himself, share this attitude.

Of course it is undeniable that public and private events left their mark on Kipling's work. It was not for nothing that he began his writing career as a journalist, and his political preoccupations are everywhere obvious; the protrusion of opinions can spoil a story which otherwise might have been a self-contained whole, as, for example, at the end of the South African story "The Comprehension of Private Copper." What I am maintaining is rather that we should be careful not to apply too ready-made an image of the private or the public Kipling to the interpretation of his art: in particular, to the pattern of its evolution.

For one of the peculiarities of Kipling's art in his short stories is that, while showing obvious variety and range, it does not in any obvious sense show *development*. Of no author is it more true than for him "in my end is my beginning." This can readily be illustrated from what every reader of Kipling must have noticed, the characteristic unevenness of his work; unevenness, that is, not within a particular story, but in any of his collections of stories considered as a whole. It is not only that the stories are not all equally good; in a prolific author that might well be expected. The case is odder than that. Masterpieces as assured as anything he ever wrote can be found, at any period of his work, side by side with very inferior things; and yet on these inferior things the same minuteness of care and skill seems to have been expended. So in his work of the eighteen-eighties we find the poignant and noble tale of "The Man who would be King" inhabiting the same collection as "The Strange Ride of Morrowbie Jukes"; and at the very end of his career, in the collection called *Limits and Renewals*, which contains work as subtle and complex

[2] *Limits and Renewals.*

as he ever wrote, such as "Dayspring Mishandled," we find so
unpleasant and negligible a piece as "The Tie." In any book of
Kipling's stories ostensibly written for adults we must be prepared to find the ethos of *Stalky & Co.* cropping up in places
where it is inappropriate. Beetle represents a self that he never
outgrew.

But of course the statement that Kipling did not develop needs
both qualification and explanation. Like most writers, he made
some false starts before he found his real bent. And, as in most
writers, a certain balance of loss and gain can be seen in com-
paring his later with his earlier work. The fresh vividness of the
early work, registering the impact of India on a boy journalist of
genius, he never perhaps quite recovered. On the other hand,
some irritating immaturities, typified by the recurrent "But that
is another story" of *Plain Tales*, vanished from his style; his technical ingenuity increased; his skill took more complex and in-
tellectualised forms; and he brought to its strange perfection that
narrative manner of implication, abstention, and obliquity of
which the first considerable example is "Mrs Bathurst" (1904).
He turned to new subject-matter, the Sussex countryside, the
historic past of England, the Navy, and, in his last phase, the
work of mental and spiritual healing of war-sufferers. But all
this seems extension rather than growth; what insights Kipling
had, he seems to have had from the beginning; we do not get
from his later work the sense of a profound and radical change of
outlook, the discovery of a new spiritual dimension, issuing from
the author's changing response to his changing experience: the
sort of change we can detect in the life-work of a Melville or a
Dostoevsky. Quite apart from any question of relative value,
Kipling does not seem to be that *kind* of artist at all. Even his
best work shows this curious undeveloping poise: a formal self-
sufficiency which suggests a fixity. We may contrast Joyce's
Dubliners: in reading these stories we feel that the author could
and must broaden his form and develop his insights by going on
to something quite different. But in reading Kipling's stories in
chronological succession, we come to feel that our knowledge of
the sense of life transmitted by this writer is only being quanti-
tatively increased; there is no perceptible modification of its
quality. He seems to have worked out his distinctive technical

formulas, themselves reflecting a narrow range of fixed sympathies and antipathies and set attitudes, and applied them to a
variety of subject-matter which, while giving the stories their
sensationally contrasting surfaces and colourings, leaves these
formulas essentially unchanged.

This art, however, produced remarkable triumphs; there are
compensations for the reader in Kipling's invariable realisation
of his particular intention, even if at times we mistrust the intention and dislike what is done. The unceasing craftsmanship, the
rigorous subduing of the matter in hand to an artistic discipline.
itself becomes a moral quality and an important, if always implicit,
part of the author's "message." Henry James, as is well known,
complained that the pursuit of this particular kind of perfection
necessitated a descent "from the less simple in subject to the more
simple – from the Anglo-Indians to the natives, from the natives
to the Tommies, from the Tommies to the quadrupeds, from
the quadrupeds to the fish, from the fish to the engines and
screws."[3] This of course is not an accurate description of the
progress of Kipling's work; the bent which produced such *tours
de force* as "The Ship that Found Herself" and "The Maltese Cat"
and ".007," or the various kinds of beast-fable ranging from
Just So Stories and *The Jungle Books*, where didactic allegory can be
far or near as the author chooses, to such relentless fables as "The
Mother Hive" or "A Walking Delegate" or "Below the Mill
Dam," where the message is continuous and insistent – this bent
was not just a middle-period preoccupation of Kipling's, but was
something he reverted to at every stage of his literary career.
Nor can James's account be extended to Kipling's later work,
which was yet to come, and which cannot be said to be "simple"
in subject-matter. Nevertheless, James's remark points at something fundamentally true about the frequent results of Kipling's
intent desire to have the completest possible *control* of his form
and his medium. This desire can lead to impressive achievements
in the realm of allegory, satiric fantasy, and fable – sometimes to
the attainment of the higher reaches of symbol and myth. But it
can also lead to a simplification and distortion of human character
and human behaviour which, in an author with so recurrent and
emphatic a didactic purpose as Kipling, can become irritatingly

[3] See above, p. 50.

tendentious. The danger of a strongly symbolic art, when it deals directly with human beings, is that it makes the reader feel he is being illicitly "got at"; he is receiving, in the place of the really seen and the strongly imagined, nothing but the author's theory of life. Kipling's supreme achievements in prose fiction seem to be those in which his genius as a fabulist and myth-maker is felt to be shaping the story without detriment to the author's true and sensitive perceptions of actual human beings, "They" and "Mrs Bathurst" and "The Wish House," "Mary Postgate" and "The Gardener" exemplify this power of the short story to suggest the *distillation* of a human life, the rendering of its essence as latent within a momentary situation, or an anecdote, or an episode. Without the artistic economy, in which every detail is significant, these stories would not have their power; but the power of this selectiveness depends upon our conviction that behind the selection there is a latent reserve of fuller knowledge. They have what Kipling calls in "The Bull that Thought" (*Debits and Credits*) "a breadth of technique that comes of reasoned art, and, above all, the passion that arrives after experience."

This "reasoned art," the conscious craftsmanship of Kipling, is the most obvious and distinctive feature of everything he wrote, and it is the only aspect of his work about which he permitted himself to depart from his usual reticence. His emphasis in these remarks – strange as it must seem to those who still equate Kipling with the Jelly-bellied Flag-Flapper – is less on a "message" or a "self" to be expressed, than on a medium to be manipulated.

> I made my own experiments in the weights, colours, perfumes, and attributes of words in relation to other words, either as read aloud so that they may hold the ear, or, scattered over the page, draw the eye. There is no line of my verse which has not been mouthed till the tongue has made all smooth, and memory, after many recitals, has mechanically slipped the grosser superfluities.[4]

And, in speaking of the *Puck* books, he says: "I worked the material in three or four overlaid tints and textures, which might or might not reveal themselves according to the shifting light of sex, youth and experience."[5] The drawbacks, as well as the

[4] *Something of Myself*, Chapter Three.   [5] *Op. cit.*, Chapter Seven.

pleasures for writer and reader, of this passion for manipulation
are clear. There is the danger, to which Kipling too often succumbed, of over-writing. "My gold," says the narrator in "Their
Lawful Occasions,"[6] with a tinge of regret, "I have lacquered
down to dull bronze, my purples overlaid with sepia of the sea,
and for hell-hearted ruby and blinding diamond I have substituted
pale amethyst and mere jargoon." There is the excess of detail
which is apt to occur in a writer so microscopically concerned
with the texture of his writing; George Moore said of a description of evening in *Kim* that "Mr Kipling seems to have followed
it about like a detective employed in a divorce case." Sometimes,
of course, this detail can be very charming, as in the illuminated
manuscripts of the Middle Ages:

> The Sub-Cantor looked over his shoulder at the pinned-
> down sheet where the first words of the Magnificat were built
> up in gold washed with red-lac for a background to the
> Virgin's hardly yet fired halo. She was shown, hands joined
> in wonder, at a lattice of infinitely intricate arabesque, round
> the edge of which sprays of orange-bloom seemed to lead the
> blue hot air that carried back over the minute parched land-
> scape in the middle distance.
> "You've made her all Jewess," said the Sub-Cantor, study-
> ing the olive-flushed cheek and the eyes charged with fore-
> knowledge.[7]

But sometimes, as all readers of Kipling know, it can be a tiresome
mannerism; and the defect inherent in this manner of writing, its
extreme self-consciousness, may be suggested by these lines from
the prefatory poem to "The Captive" (*Traffics and Discoveries*):

> And the words of his mouth were as slaves spreading carpets of
>   glory
> Embroidered with names of the Djinns – a miraculous weaving –
> But the cool and perspicuous eye overbore unbelieving.

There can be a bad sense to the word "manipulation," and even
in Kipling's best work we may be reminded of the assertion, in
"The Village that Voted the Earth was Flat," that " 'Advertisin'
is the most delicate of all the sciences.' "

---

[6] *Traffics and Discoveries.*   [7] "The Eye of Allah," *Debits and Credits.*

But this long practice in word-painting reaped its true artistic reward in those stories where it is used with tact and restraint; the sudden, vivid descriptive touch can be unforgettable, Manallace drawing on his black gloves at the end of "Dayspring Mishandled," Helen Turrell of "The Gardener" in the army graveyard:

> She climbed a few wooden-faced earthen steps and then met the entire crowded level of the thing in one held breath. She did not know that Hagenzeele Third counted twenty one thousand dead already. All she saw was a merciless sea of black crosses, bearing little strips of stamped tin at all angles across their faces. She could distinguish no order or arrangement in their mass; nothing but a waist-high wilderness of weeds stricken dead, rushing at her. She went forward, moving to the left and the right hopelessly, wondering by what guidance she should ever come to her own. A great distance away there was a line of whiteness. It proved to be a block of some two or three hundred graves whose headstone had already been set, whose flowers were planted out, and whose new-sown grass showed green.

Less charged and intense, but even more typical of Kipling's mature style, is the opening of "Friendly Brook" in *A Diversity of Creatures*:

> The valley was so choked with fog that one could scarcely see a cow's length across a field. Every blade, twig, bracken-frond and hoof-print carried water, and the air was filled with the noise of rushing ditches and field-drains, all delivering to the brook below. A week's November rain on water-logged land had gorged her to full flood, and she proclaimed it aloud.
>
> Two men in sackcloth aprons were considering an untrimmed hedge that ran down the hillside and disappeared into mist beside those roarings. They stood back and took stock of the neglected growth, tapped an elbow of hedge-oak here, a mossed beech-stub there, swayed a stooled ash back and forth, and looked at each other.
>
> "I reckon she's about two rod thick," said Jabez the younger, "an' she hasn't felt iron since – when has she, Jesse?"

"Call it twenty five year, Jabez, an' you won't be far out."

"Umm!" Jabez rubbed his wet handbill on his wetter coat sleeve. "She ain't a hedge. She's all manner o' trees. We'll just about have to–". He paused, as professional etiquette required.

"Just about have to side her up an' see what she'll bear. But hadn't we best–?" Jesse paused in his turn, both men being artists and equals.

"Get some kind o' line to go by." Jabez ranged up and down till he found a thinner place, and with clean snicks of the handbill revealed the original face of the fence. Jesse took over the dripping stuff as it fell forward, and, with a grasp and a kick, made it to lie orderly on the bank till it should be faggotted.

By noon a length of unclean jungle had turned itself into a cattle-proof barrier, tufted here and there with little plumes of the sacred holly which no woodman touches without orders.

It would be easy to find openings of stories, like the famous first paragraph of "Love o' Women," that proclaim Kipling's authorship more flamboyantly than this, but none more essentially typical of him. Here, unmistakably, is this personal style, which, without ostentatious economy, establishes at once the brook itself, the animistic "hero" of the tale; the November weather; the two hedgers, with their pride in their ancient craft, their knowledgeableness, their ceremonious etiquette of "artists and equals"; the real if modest triumph of human endeavour ("By noon a length of unclean jungle had turned itself into a cattle-proof barrier"), and the final touch, that hint of "inside" knowledge which in its blatant manifestations can be so tiresome in Kipling's stories, but is here perfectly right in its tone of respectful approval (". . . little plumes of the sacred holly which no woodman touches without orders.") Kipling had implicitly criticised much in his own early work when he complained, in "Wressley of the Foreign Office," that "one of the many curses of our life in India is the want of atmosphere in the painter's sense. There are no half-tints worth noticing. Men stand out all crude and raw, with nothing to tone them down, and nothing to scale them against." This chastened later style is the opposite of "crude and raw"; it is full of "half-tints"; and much in these later stories which the reader vaguely recognises as "background" and "atmosphere" is there precisely to "tone down" and to "scale against."

One of the first stories in the distinctively "late" manner is "They"[8] (1904), and it is convenient to open discussion of the later Kipling with a work so totally different from the conventional account of him. Even that account allows Kipling an interest in the eerie and the occult (in one mode "Wireless" or "The Finest Story in the World," in another "The Mark of the Beast" or "At the End of the Passage"). But the first thing to be noticed about "They" is that the part played by the ghostly children and the blind childless woman whose love draws them to the beautiful house she has made for them, has nothing to do with a ghost-story strumming on the nerves. The mode of the tale is nearer to "Burnt Norton" than to "The Turn of the Screw." The appeal of the fantasy is to poetic feeling and imagination. Not that we are to take the ghosts as simply the projection of the blind woman's longing or the narrator's bereavement (he, it is finally made known to us, has lost a child, whom he is to find again, once, at the end of the tale.) They exist for other people in the tale, the butler, his wife, and the village mother. But their "reality" is equivocal:

> When I paused in my work I listened, but the wood was so full of the noises of summer (though the birds had mated) that I could not at first distinguish these from the tread of small cautious feet stealing across the dead leaves.

One effect of this potently evocative use of the sound of the children's footsteps, whispering, and laughter is to assimilate the narrator's and our perception of them to the blind woman's; an effect echoed in the final fading-out of the story, after the blind woman has told the narrator he must never come again:

> She left me to sit a little longer by the screen, and I heard the sound of her feet die out along the gallery above.

The reason for the equivocal status of the earth-bound spirits is plain when the significance of the story as a parable is taken; the

[8] *Traffics and Discoveries.*

fancied glimpse of the world of the dead is there to confirm that it *is* another world, and the living must go back to the world of the living.

All this is part of the manifest meaning of the tale. But there is another theme in "They" interwoven with the theme of the children, and its presence has puzzled some readers, who may not have been conscious of its distinct existence, but who have noticed certain elements in "They" which do not seem relevant. What, for instance, is the point of the incident of the dishonest tenant-farmer (who is terrified by the ghosts) at the end? We may approach this more hidden theme by asking another question: why is there so much about the narrator's motor-car? This car is one of those somewhat comic early models which frequently appear in Kipling's work, usually (as in "They") breaking down at some point in the story. It introduces a note of stridency into the dreamland of the beautiful house with its lawn and yew trees: "It was sacrilege to wake that dreaming house-front with the clatter of machinery." The narrator's references to it tend to have a *gaucherie* and a blatancy which contrast with his generally quiet and sympathetic tone: "In two minutes I was blowing all the horns of Jericho in front of the House Beautiful, and Madden, from the pantry, rose to the crisis like a butler and a man." This sentence by itself could be used to exemplify Kipling's bad style. But in the context this manner of referring to the car seems to be part of a social or sociological observation. The narrator is very conscious of not being one of what the fat village woman calls "carriage folk." This comes out in what he says to the blind woman, who *is* one: "If you had done your duty as a pillar of the State and a landed proprietress you ought to have summoned me for trespass when I barged through your woods the other day." And it is twice repeated in the story, with significant emphasis, that he comes "from the other side of the county." Of course this last touch refers also to the mystical theme. But this way of contrasting the old England and the new, the motor-car and modern people with the House Beautiful and the villagers, "deep-rooted trees of that soil," runs right through the story. The imaginative bias of the writing is *against* the modern world; the least sympathetic character is the dishonest tenant-farmer, who is represented as a characteristically modern product. And the narrator feels it "sacrilege" to "wake that dreaming house-front with the clatter of machinery." On the other hand, it is the car which takes the narrator to the House Beautiful – the second time he feels that "my car took the road of her own volition." And it is thanks to the car that the sick child is saved. "Useful things, cars," says Madden the butler. "If I'd had one when mine took sick she wouldn't have died . . . Croup. No one knew what to do . . . I drove eight miles in a tax-cart for the doctor. She was choked when we came back. This car'd ha' saved her. She'd have been close on ten now." One function of this incident of the sick child is to safeguard against idealisation of the past.

We may wonder whether Kipling showed artistic tact in interweaving these two themes. Other stories in which the motor car plays a prominent role can show him in a more defiantly philistine mood; and hostility to the "county" undoubtedly occurs in stories like "The Village that Voted" and "Beauty Spots," in such a way as to suggest that the author is working off some personal resentment. But in "They" the narrator, with his sensitive humanity and quiet grief, is an entirely sympathetic figure, and, with his poise between wistfulness and renunciation, the best possible spokesman for the present in relation to a past which it knows is irrecoverable. The two themes join delicately in the symbolic moment early in the tale, which foreshadows the end: "Here, then, I stayed; a horseman's green spear laid at my breast; held by the exceeding beauty of that jewel in that setting."

This wrenching-apart of the thematic materials of "They" must give a false impression of the tale itself, where the fabric is continuous and delicate. But for close working and subtlety of means it is far surpassed by the later story "The Wish House"[9] (1924), which has claims to be regarded as the most remarkable story Kipling ever wrote. Certainly it is difficult to think of any other short story in the language which is richer in content, and yet gives no suggestion of overcrowding. When it is brought together with "They" we see at once a parallel, in the skill with which in both tales the element of the supernatural (or non-

[9] *Debits and Credits.* For a particularly interesting examination of this and other late Kipling stories, see Miss J. M. S. Tompkins' admirable study *The Art of Rudyard Kipling.*

natural) is introduced into the tale without disturbing the reader's
sense of the human centrality of the story; and another in the
importance in both of the mysterious powers of a woman. But
"The Wish House" represents a far rarer order of achievement.
The setting and atmosphere of "They," with its beautiful old
house set in an idealised English countryside, gives a licence for a
daydream indulgence of fancy; in "The Wish House" we are
never for a moment allowed to forget the hard realism of the poor
suburban villa, the two aging women in the little room shaken by
charabancs, one of them going blind, the other dying of cancer.
The story cannot be summarised; everything is done by means of
touches, implications, details. Through the ordinary, realistic
talk of the old countrywomen (this is one of the tales in which
the suggestion of dialect is not overdone, as it sometimes is in
Kipling, and is essential to the effect) there emerges the wholly
credible picture of their two interconnected lives; by way of the
secondary story of Liz Fettley, in response to her confidence and
her sympathetic questions, we learn from Grace Ashcroft the
story of the Wish House, which for her represents the sacrifice
of her health and life she believes herself to have made for the
man she loves. The story of the Wish House, reduced to the
bare bones of anecdote, is fantastic. A Sussex cook, Grace
Ashcroft, goes to a little empty house in a back street of London
to speak through a letter-box to "the Token," whom she asks to
let her "take everythin' bad that's in store for my man, 'Arry
Mockler, for love's sake." This decision has to be taken over and
over again, until it becomes part of the irrevocable pattern of her
life. Everything that happens to Harry, who has left her and does
not requite her love, she thereafter attributes to her pledge to
make him, without knowing it, "take his good from her." At the
end of the story she is facing death, but still pleadingly insistent
that "the pain *do* count to keep 'Arry – where I want him. Say it
can't be wasted, like." The tale closes with the arrival of the
District Nurse; Mrs Ashcroft becomes "the self-contained
domestic once more," and Mrs Fettley, before she leaves,

> . . . leaned over, and kissed Mrs. Ashcroft on the waxy
> yellow forehead, and again on the faded grey eyes.
> "It *do* count, don't it – de pain?" The lips that still kept trace

of their original moulding hardly more than breathed the words.

Mrs. Fettley kissed them and moved towards the door.

Even this outline may suggest something of the moving and compassionate quality of the tale. But judgment of its human significance must partly depend on how we are to regard Grace Ashcroft's sacrifice. Clearly the business of the Token is literally incredible, and Grace is a superstitious woman. The distinction of the story is that she is none the less convincingly established for us as a tragic figure. The Wish House comes to stand for those forces in human life which are not under the control of man, but which the stoic confronts and accepts. That we do not find Grace's behaviour incredible, or a neurotic vagary, is due to the completeness with which we are made to believe in her as an ordinary person – ordinary in so far as we admit that we ourselves are ordinary people. She is seen as real and immediate, with her early amorous waywardness (so well brought out in the account of her relationship with her husband), and her later proud resignation and pathos, all conveyed amid the crisp brevities of her speech. But she is also a figure of history; for through the tale, as in "They," but quite differently and more subtly, there runs the sense of the changing English life, both local and national, which changes her individual life and the lives of her friends; the moves from country to town, and from town to country, the displacement of horse-drawn traffic by motor-buses and everything that that implies – all are brought in, not as mere background, but as a means to establishing her reality as a living reminiscence of older ways and older habits of thinking and feeling. In front of us is the little house in the modern village, a heavy tea laid out (Grace was a cook who never "owed me belly much"), and geraniums on the window-sill; in the nearer distance is London, with that other horrible little house of the walled garden and the basement kitchen; further back still the Sussex countryside of the women's youth. The richness of this treatment might lead us to suppose that the story required development at fuller length; but on reflexion we see that something correspond-ing to the laconic stoicism of Grace Ashcroft is artistically appro-priate; without this economy there could not be that sense, at once sympathetic and ironic, of the distillation of a whole life, of the universal tragedy of possessive love, in one bizarre encounter with the powers of darkness.

There is much in "The Wish House" that would repay analysis; T. S. Eliot, while praising it, has called it "hard and obscure," and in a fuller treatment of the story due consideration should certainly be given to the use of the symbolism of cancer which recurs, some would say obsessively, in Kipling's later work; we notice its association, though perhaps this is non-significant in "The Wish House," with blindness, another recurring symbol. (We remember the terrible image of "a blind face that cries and can't wipe its eyes" in "At the End of the Passage.") No doubt these symbols meant something intensely personal to Kipling. But in our impulse to psychological investigation of the author we should not forget the actual force these symbols have in the stories, and the insight (as shown in "The Wish House") which leads us, not back to the author, but to ourselves and the world. (And if Kipling *was* obsessed with cancer, is it not the characteristic obsession of modern man?)

These questions about the degree of insight and the general human significance of Kipling's more "unusual" stories are posed in a sharper form by "Mrs Bathurst,"[10] which has always been one of the *cruces* in the criticism of his work. Here the obsession of the sailor Vickery with the kind and pleasant and motherly Mrs Bathurst is powerfully done – her "blindish look" as she walks forward in the news-reel picture (the "biograph") is unforgettable, as is the grotesque business of "Click" Vickery's four false teeth, by which he is identified as a charred corpse at the baffling end of the story. But what exactly happened, and what is the significance of what happened, many readers have puzzled over. Some have thought that Kipling in this story has overdone his passion for "cutting." "Mrs Bathurst" (1904) is one of the earliest of Kipling's experiments in indirect or suppressed narrative, and its experimental character might make that explanation plausible. But it may well be that the point of the story lies in this obscurity. Pyecroft, the observer of the story, does not claim to understand Vickery and his doings. He knows, and his friends can confirm, the power of love (" 'it takes 'em at all ages' "), and its destruc-

[10] *Traffics and Discoveries.*

tiveness. This is what the story is "about." "The Wish House" also testifies to this destructiveness in love. But there the effect is totally different, because we have heard Grace Ashcroft's own story, seen the pattern of her life as she sees it, and seen her "close to" through the eyes of Liz Fettley. In "Mrs Bathurst" we see only glimpses of a stranger through the eyes of a boon-companion who, despite his assurance to the contrary, has very little essential idea of "what transpired." The emotion generated in us, as in Pyecroft and his friends, is a sort of impersonal awe or terror. We feel no incongruity when the incongruous Vickery can say "The rest is silence." Any one of us, in his relationship with his mother, may have lived through the experience of a childish Hamlet; and the rest – indeed, most – of Vickery's story *can* be silence. That the woman whom Vickery is found dead with in the teak-forest is never identified in the story is psychologically right; the sense of a pattern of life (and death) from which certain things have been dropped or repressed is essential to its human significance. Kipling makes a shell-shocked soldier say in "Epitaphs of the War":

> My name, my speech, my self I had forgot.
> My wife and children came – I knew them not.
> I died. My Mother followed. At her call
> And on her bosom I remembered all.

Vickery, as we hear of him, was in something like that condition of shock.

"Mrs Bathurst," with its cryptic quality, might be dismissed as a mere oddity. When we turn to "Mary Postgate," however, the challenge to our human and moral judgment cannot be evaded. Here nothing is hidden; we are looking at Mary Postgate from beginning to end of the story, and everything relevant to understanding and judging her is supplied. "Mary Postgate" has been more attacked than anything else Kipling wrote. No one denies that his full powers are engaged in this story, and some have regarded this as clinching their condemnation of him as a cruel writer who is here vicariously indulging a morbid passion of hatred and revenge. Now undeniably Kipling's writings during the First World War do show bitterness. There were poignant personal reasons for that. And he did not make the critical de-

fence of "Mary Postgate" easier by appending to it a poem
about how "the English began to hate," nor by including in
the same volume, *A Diversity of Creatures*, the queer fantasy called
"Swept and Garnished," a sort of parody of "They" in a Berlin
setting, which does show some signs of a desire for reprisal. But
I believe that "Mary Postgate," horrible as it is, can be shown to
have the intelligence and insight which those who hate it wish to
deny. It is certainly a tale of horror. The middle-aged English
spinster gloating over the dying German airman – it is not a
tableau that the reader will want to revert to very often. No one
will deny that, in the circumstances of the story, Mary Postgate's
indulgence is understandable, if still terrible. What is at issue is
the author's attitude towards it.

From the outset we must be conscious that Mary Postgate is
"placed." We are shown her limitations, and her unimaginative-
ness:

> Mary was not young, and though her speech was as colour-
> less as her eyes or her hair, she was never shocked [*i.e.*, by her
> elderly woman employer's *risqué* stories]. She listened un-
> flinchingly to every one; said at the end, "How interesting!" or
> "How shocking!" as their case might be, and never again
> referred to it, for she prided herself on a trained mind, which
> "did not dwell on these things."

Her inarticulate devotion to her employer's nephew, the "un-
lovely orphan of eleven" who

> . . . repaid her in his holidays by calling her "Gatepost,"
> "Postey," or "Packthread," by thumping her between her
> narrow shoulders, or by chasing her bleating round the garden,
> her large mouth open, her large nose high in air, at a stiff-
> necked shamble very like a camel's.

Later on, we are told, "he filled the house with clamour, argument and harangues as to his personal needs, likes and dislikes,
and the limitations of 'you women', reducing Mary to tears of
physical fatigue, or, when he chose to be humorous, of helpless
laughter."

The presentation of young Wynn is consistent; as a young man
he remains painfully callow. He joins the Flying Corps and is

killed during a trial flight: the effect of his death on Mary is cataclysmic, but with her usual inarticulateness she cannot express it; her immediate reaction to the news is to say " 'It's a great pity he didn't die in action after he had killed somebody'." Later, she is burning his belongings in the incinerator – the interminable catalogue of Wynn's possessions is dwelt on with all Kipling's relentless detail – when she hears the dying German airman groan in the shrubbery. To herself she justifies her own cruel behaviour – she refuses to help the man, brings a revolver, hums to herself ("Mary never had a voice"), shouts, finally "drinks in" the sounds of his dying agony – by remembering the child who has just been killed in the village, and whose body she has seen; a bomb has been dropped, perhaps by the airman who is dying in front of her. She speaks to him, as she has been thinking, in Wynn's idiom:

> "Stop that!" said Mary, and stamped her foot. "Stop that, you bloody pagan!"
> The words came quite smoothly and naturally. They were Wynn's own words, and Wynn was a gentleman who for no consideration on earth would have torn little Edna into those vividly coloured strips and strings. But this thing hunched under the oak-tree had done that thing.

The crowning horror is in the last sentence of the story, where we see the plain dull spinster satisfied and fulfilled as a woman, "taking a luxurious hot bath before tea, and . . . looking, as Miss Fowler said when she saw her lying all relaxed on the other sofa, 'quite handsome!' "

It will be clear that the diagnosis of Mary Postgate's contradictory state of mind, due to her emotional upheaval, is fully given; we have only to reflect on the contrast between her words on hearing of Wynn's death, and her self-justification for hating the German airman. What those who condemn Kipling would say is that the author is quite aware of the moral incoherence of Mary, but exploits her as a vent for the release of emotions which a sahib himself cannot admit that he feels; women, as contradictory and inferior beings, can be allowed the indulgence which the author himself desires. But this amounts to attributing to Kipling – the Kipling of this story – the outlook of young Wynn. It ignores the careful art of the story in avoiding any sentimentalisation of Mary or Wynn or the relationship between them. Above all, it ignores the essential identity – symbolic, of course, not literal – between the dying airman and Wynn. (He too, like Wynn, has fallen from his aeroplane.) The tale perhaps could not have been written by someone who had not experienced the agony of the bereaved civilian in war-time. But what it gives us is not a self-indulgence, but art: the imaginative understanding of what has happened to a Mary Postgate, and the moral intelligence to direct our horror to what *is* horrible, the stripping of a human soul, war and the cruelty of war.

It is natural to contrast the compassion of the later tale, "The Gardener,"[11] with the cruelty of "Mary Postgate." But this contrast need not be used to emphasise a change of heart in Kipling. No doubt the dates are significant; "Mary Postgate" belongs to 1915, "The Gardener" to 1926. But the dramatic self-sufficiency of each tale is complete. "The Gardener" is a piece of grave irony; the ironic tone is sustained to the very end. What is remarkable is that this irony does not preclude – indeed, is the medium for – compassion. "Everyone in the village knew" that Lieutenant Michael Turrell was not Helen Turrell's nephew, but her son. She has lived a lie, and we are made to feel that there was nobility in this lie, but only the truth can make free. Helen is not free; her silence cuts her off from the human response which she desires to make, after Michael is killed and she goes on a pilgrimage to the war-cemetery, to the woman whom she meets and who has confessed to a love like hers. The woman is repelled by Helen's apparent coldness and lack of sympathy. Release from the past is given by the man she takes for the gardener, when she is searching for Michael's grave:

A man knelt behind a line of headstones – evidently a gardener, for he was firming a young plant in the soft earth. She went towards him, her paper in her hand. He rose at her approach and without prelude or salutation asked: "Who are you looking for?"

"Lieutenant Michael Turrell – my nephew," said Helen slowly and word for word, as she had many thousands of times in her life.

[11] *Debits and Credits.*

The man lifted his eyes and looked at her with infinite compassion before he turned from the fresh-sown grass towards the naked black crosses.

"Come with me," he said, "and I will show you where your son lies."

Even after this cathartic moment, the irony does not cease; the story ends with Helen turning away, still "supposing him to be the gardener." The reader will pick up the reference to the Gospel, but Helen can be left to assume that the gardener was mistaken. Thus the symbolic force, for the reader, of Helen's alleviation can be conveyed without the explicit assurance that for her it was a religious experience. This deliberate ambiguity is not there because of Kipling's own equivocal attitude towards Christianity. It is the imaginative delicacy of art: the art that we find in the best of Kipling's later stories.

But it may be said that, though "The Gardener" is one of Kipling's best stories, it is hardly typical of him. And, indeed, it may well be that Kipling's best stories are not his most representative. We do not find, in the stories I have discussed, the typical Kipling "world-picture," the emphasis on the tribal and the arcane, the passion for being an initiate, "one of the brotherhood," in the know, and above all, the overriding insistence on the Law. Certainly this "world-picture" never disappears from Kipling's work, and it is one of the things that makes it hard to describe his art as showing development. To bring out the essential line of continuity in Kipling's work we may look finally at one of his latest stories, "Dayspring Mishandled" (1928).[12] This tale is so sombre and bitter in feeling, as well as so complex and elliptical in style, that it is not at first easy to recognise the closeness of its relationship to one of Kipling's most characteristic and frequently exploited *genres*: the story of a hoax. The place of these stories in Kipling's work, and his sense of the ludicrous in general, is not always understood. Often the *ethos* of his comedies seems to contradict what we all tend to regard as the most fundamental of Kipling's beliefs – the necessity of obedience to the Law. It need not be stressed how often this is reiterated, in different keys, all over Kipling's work. It is the message of the *Jungle Books*.

---

[12] *Limits and Renewals.*

Purun Bhagat, in his withdrawal to the contemplative life, is "looking for a law of his own." St Paul in another story tells the neurotic sea-captain to serve Caesar: then, at least, he will be following some sort of law. Yet, in the farces, law and order is constantly being flouted with the author's evident approval. This comes out oddly in *Stalky & Co.* The message of the book is ostensibly the breaking-in of the young colts by the benevolent Chirons. But most of the action in fact consists of a series of rags and practical jokes in which the school authorities are constantly being disobeyed and outwitted. How is this contradiction reconciled in Kipling's world-picture?

The answer seems to be that Kipling's emotional interest in hoaxes is closely connected with his feeling about imaginative creation. All his practical jokers are artists, but artists in the manipulation of men and circumstances rather than the usual media of art. There is no mistaking the creative joy of the impresario Bat Masquerier in his organising of the vast hoax of "The Village that Voted." It may be, as indeed is indicated in the story, morally irresponsible. But by itself it represents a triumph of imagination, as much as the scheme of conquest in "The Man who would be King." In imaginative creation man seems to be a free agent, no longer the powerless victim of circumstances and forces outside his control. So Kipling's delight in the farcical hoax is not really in contradiction with that sense of the impotence of the lonely individual which makes him insist so strongly on the necessity of subordination to the law or the tribe. The hoax, as work of art, supplies an emotional holiday, in allowing man the illusion of freedom.

What is remarkable about "Dayspring Mishandled" is that, uniquely in Kipling, it is both the story of a hoax and a tragedy. And the tragedy resides precisely in the eventual demonstration, in the story, that human freedom *is* an illusion and that man is powerless. "Dayspring Mishandled" is a tale of revenge; or rather, of a plan for revenge to which a man devotes his whole life without ever carrying it out. The scheme of revenge thus remains a pure imaginative creation, but one in the elaboration of which the essence of a man's life has been drained away. Manallace, a middle-aged writer of popular historical fiction, conceives a subtle scheme of revenge on an unpleasant highbrow man of letters, Castorley, who has wronged (in some way which is left rather obscure) the woman Manallace loved. Castorley has made himself an international authority on Chaucer, and it is at this reputation that Manallace resolves to strike. His scheme requires the forging and "planting" of a medieval manuscript containing a hitherto unknown fragment of a tale by Chaucer. Castorley is to "discover" it, become famous, get a knighthood, and then be shattered, by the irrefutable proof of the forgery which Manallace has cunningly worked into the "discovery." The account of the forgery and "planting" is done with all Kipling's beloved technical expertise and know-how. The scheme succeeds up to a point; Castorley duly makes the "discovery" and is elevated to the pinnacle of renown from which Manallace plans to topple him. But now Manallace incomprehensibly delays his revenge. He finds all sorts of excuses and ways of delaying (he has by now become the close collaborator in Castorley's learned labours). Meanwhile Castorley is ailing of a mysterious disease, obscurely connected – as disease often is in Kipling – with his sense of guilt about the wrong he has done. Manallace in the outcome never carries out his revenge. The ostensible reason is that he feels that Castorley's wife, aided and abetted by another sinister character, Castorley's doctor, has in some way found out his secret intention to destroy her husband, and is using him to further her own plan to get rid of Castorley. The tale ends with Manallace at Castorley's funeral, pulling on his black gloves; he is left with the *raison d'être* of his life gone, accepting the role of good friend and loyal collaborator of Castorley that he has so long pretended to be. Lady Castorley and the doctor are left in possession of the field.

Many readers have found "Dayspring Mishandled" difficult. In its elliptical mode of narrative, significant turns and developments are played down. The point at which Manallace's "real life-work" began is indicated cryptically. It is never quite clear just what Castorley's original offence was – the offence that has poisoned two lives. And the business of Lady Castorley and the doctor, Gleeag, remains somewhat obscure. But these obscurities are appropriate in a tale which deals so much in the hidden springs of action. Manallace himself cannot have been clear about the motive which led him first to delay and then to abandon the con-

ABIGAIL E. WEEKS MEMORIAL LIBRARY
UNION COLLEGE
BARBOURVILLE, KENTUCKY